The Scheme is managed by the Association for Business Sponsorship of the Arts (ABSA).

THE MARC FITCH FUND,
Oxford

THE JAMIESON LIBRARY OF
WOMEN'S HISTORY, Newmill

Benefactors

A Edwin Bryant + Associates,
   Chartered Quantity Surveyors,
   Penzance

Mrs Simon Bolitho,
   Trustee, Newlyn Art Gallery

The Cornishman
   (Cornish Weekly Newspapers Ltd)

Patricia Garner,
   Arragon Conservation Studio,
   Twickenham

Judith & Charles Hancock, Falmouth

Hayle Dental Practice, Hayle

National Westminster Bank (UK) PLC

Trelawney Fish Company, Newlyn

& the generous subscribers listed
in Chapter 12

DIARY OF A GALLERY

Melissa Hardie
Editor

Patten Press

in association with
Newlyn Art Gallery

1995

Text © Melissa Hardie
Extracts © Copyright holders
© Images & photographs as identified in text.
Published by The Patten Press, in association with the Newlyn Art Gallery,
at The Old Post Office, Newmill, Penzance, Cornwall TR20 4XN, England

A CIP catalogue record for this book is available from the British Library

Casebound edition ISBN 1 872229 17 4
Softback edition ISBN 1 872229 22 0

Printed in Great Britain by
The St Ives Printing Company, St Ives, Cornwall

CONTENTS

Acknowledgements

Michael Canney, Keith Gardiner, Eileen Hunt, Mrs George ('Dach') Lambourn, Rhoda Littler (neé Harvey), Pat Pickles, Phoebe (neé Nance) Procter, Jane and Ken Symonds, Alexander Mackenzie, John Miller, and John Halkes have all contributed time and 'enlightenment' to the authentication process. Correspondence with Jeremy Le Grice, currently on a painting fellowship in Worpswede, Germany, has been invaluable in understanding some of the underlying currents of the nineteen-fifties and -sixties.

Necessarily some of our 'family' of artists and supporters no longer live in West Cornwall or even in the United Kingdom. Hence, all have not been aware of our search for documentation, nor, perhaps, of our centenary. Inevitably a great number of our would-be informants are dead, and cannot be questioned except through additional studies of their lives and letters and sometimes in interview with their families and descendents.

Wilhelmina Barns Graham, Janet Bennette, Mary Beresford Williams, Hazel Berriman, Max Chapman, Bernard Evans, Catherine and Paul Feiler, Gay Sagar Fenton, Peter Garnier, Anthony Harvey, Philip Hogben, Jonathan Holmes, Mervyn Levy, Peter Laws, Margo Maeckelberghe, Ian Nalder, Sheelagh O'Donnell, Margaret Perry, Maryella Piggott, Allan Shears, Mary Stork, Professor Charles Thomas, John Foster Tonkin, Vaughan Tregenza, David & Tina Wilkinson of the Book Gallery, St Ives, Polly Walker and Marion Whybrow have provided additional information and photographs unavailable in our archival mass. Special acknowledgement for the personal attention given to our requests for help is made to Georg Jensen, Silversmiths of Bond Street, London, and Copenhagen; to the Sir Alfred Munnings Art Museum, Dedham Essex; Linda Gill (Editor) & The University of Auckland Press for permission to extract relevant pieces from *The Letters of Frances Hodgkins*. Also to the Cornwall County Records Office, Truro, the Cornish Studies Library, Redruth, Frank Ruhrmund, *The Cornishman*, and the *Western Morning News* for permissions to reprint liberally from their published articles. Thanks are given also to all the authors and publishers listed in the bibliography of sources. Their previous research has been invaluable, and I am grateful to them for shared interests.

Emily Ash, Cairney Down, and Blair Todd, current staff of the Gallery, have generously spared time in their hectic schedules to provide up-to-date information.

The Editor's personal thanks are given to Dr Katherine Russell Tait and Ryya Sanders for the great care they gave in building up the informative lists in Chapter 12 about the 'honoured friends' of the Gallery. This involved long hours of interpreting handwritten Minute Books, cross-referencing, and re-checking seemingly interminable lists. Hilary Shrapnel and Ann Bellingham were invaluable assistants at the final stages of indexing and proof-reading. I must also give special thanks to my husband, Philip Budden, who has patiently and quietly encouraged my additional 'marriage' to Newlyn over the past eighteen months. In the later stages he has also helped with design features and proof-reading, a true partner in the work.

To the subscribers, both named and anonymous, and to the generous corporate sponsors -- we give sincere thanks for your good wishes in our birthday year. May we share many more creative years together in the appreciation of the arts!

Melissa Hardie, Chairman
Council of Management, Newlyn Art Gallery, 1995.

FOREWORD

A *bona-fide* Bucca, born and bred in Newlyn, I grew up in the village during the "Hungry Thirties".

It was a time when my horizons, like the cobbled streets of my birthplace, were very narrow indeed. A time when, despite the building of the Harbour Road which linked Newlyn Town and Street-an-Nowan, where I lived, the two places were still distinct and separate and I went "up the Slip" to where the Newlyn Towners lived only when I had to. A time when, with my mother, I journeyed to Penzance once a year only for its Christmas Market, and to Mousehole not at all -- "Funny people around the Point!"

The boundaries of my tiny boy's world were Mrs Mitchell's house and garden at the top of the Fradgan, and the communal water tap at its bottom. A water tap which I still associate with my growing and gradual awareness of another bigger world elsewhere, for it was there by the water tap that the artists came and set up their easels -- there was always an artist on our corner. When it was my turn to fetch water for the house I would stop "to have a geek" at what the artist of the day was doing, and more often than not got my boots wet while watching.

It is likely that he or she would have been a student at Stanhope Forbes's 'School of Painting', or it might even have been the great man, "Daddy Forbes", himself, who, although having painted the best of his pictures by then, was still very much alive and active. Whether or not anyone famous ever sat by the Fradgan water tap, I don't know for certain. It didn't matter at the time, nor until many years later, when I began to realise that Newlyn, "my town, my yesterday town, of salt and ice, of ropes and tar", as well as being of importance to me and, of course, to fishing, also occupied a position of some importance in the world of art.

Looking at Newlyn today it is, perhaps, difficult to appreciate the delight artists once found in the village. There have been so many changes that the Newlyn of 1995 is a far cry from "the cluster of grey-roofed houses" which Forbes found it to be in 1884 when he first "came along that dusty road by which Newlyn is approached from Penzance". Since then, and particularly in the late 1930's, it has been so plundered and abused by authority, by developers and so-called planners, that little of its former glory remains. Yet, if one looks closely enough -- digs deeply enough -- one might even excavate an actual Newlyner, and find sufficient forgotten corners to remind one of the attractiveness that was Newlyn's.

It was exactly a century ago that the doors of Newlyn Art Gallery were first opened, an event sandwiched, chronologically, between the opening of the North Pier, when "young folk of the village danced like Hacky and Marky until they could dance no more", in 1894, and the 1896 Newlyn Riots. One of the many public buildings to owe its foundation to John Passmore Edwards, it was known variously as the Opie Memorial, The Passmore Edwards Art Gallery and Newlyn Art Gallery but, for native Newlyners like myself, it was always, and still is, simply "the art gallery".

A special place for me -- apart from the chapel and school I attended -- for some time, it was the biggest building I had ever seen. Yet it was to be in situ for half a century and more before I crossed its threshold. After all, one had to pay to go in there and in those "Hungry Thirties" pennies were precious. I much preferred moving pictures to painted ones, and I could go three times to "the fleapit", the Regal Cinema in Penzance, for what it cost to go once to the art gallery.

Unlike some others with elephantine memories, I can neither remember when I first went into the Gallery nor what I saw there. It was sometime in the late nineteen-forties, not long after I had been issued with my "demob suit". The flames of modern art were beginning to burn brightly, fanned by outbursts from opponents like the President of the Royal Academy and former Newlyner, Sir Alfred Munnings and the St Ives painter, poster designer, caricaturist and former contributor to *Punch*, Harry Rountree. The latter, stated at the opening of the Newlyn Society of Artists' 1948 Winter Exhibition, that "I will not agree that any blotch on canvas, as long as it looks like nothing on earth, must be a masterpiece!"

In those, my salad days, such warring words, plus the approaching fire of modern art which appeared to distress certain artists, dressed the gallery with allure for me. I wanted to know what all the fuss was about. I had no idea that my appetite for sensation would lead to such a long association with the art gallery, a period of more years than I care to count spent writing about its exhibitions and events. If nothing else, this period has brought home to me that it is the people passing through its portals, not as long-lived as its granite and slate, that have made, are making and will make the art gallery the place it is.

I deem myself lucky in being old enough to have known many of those people: its secretaries, curators, directors, call them what you will. The retiring, somewhat shadowy Mr and Mrs Wallace B Nichols who, during the Second World War, provided a place in Newlyn where "more than one Serviceman or Servicewoman expressed themselves as grateful for the spiritual oasis they found there." The gentle Eileen Hunt who not only created a pleasant atmosphere in the gallery but also increased its sales. Then, of course, the dynamic trio of Michael Canney, Alister J McLeod and John Halkes, each of whom in his different way performed near miracles in the place. The artists themselves -- I have been privileged to be around at time when it was commonplace to rub shoulders in the art gallery with such living links with its past as Dod Procter, Alethea Garstin, Charles Simpson and Mary Jewels, as well as the bright hopes of its present and future.

Without sounding too much like Father Time, I must add that I have seen a number of alterations to the interior fabric of the building, seen two staircases come and go, and entrances and doorways 'flit' about. It is still the people that really matter. There was the hilarious evening when we were to be presented with the key to modern poetry by W S (Sydney) Graham, and he demonstrated once and for all that, as good a poet as he was, he was no lecturer. The black and white, and often seemingly endless, film nights and lectures, the wild parties and their guaranteed hangovers -- and the exhibition opening when the irascible Roger Hilton provided a spirited touch to the start of the Society's Spring show by removing one of his paintings from the wall, and set about performing a public execution upon it.

All of this is part and parcel, as the cliche has it, of the rich tapestry of art and life in general, and of the art gallery in particular. Its threads, many of them golden, others not quite so valuable, are countless and have been strewn in disarray for far too long, here, there and everywhere. There must be many, who, like myself, have wondered if the historical records had been destroyed or forgotten, were beyond rescue or repair? Could the art gallery's tapestry be restored, its history told?

Even if it was possible, then who on earth would have the courage, enterprise and energy -- or be crazy enough -- to consider, let alone undertake, such a herculean task? In the event, as we now know, the hour came and so, happily, did the woman.

The people of Newlyn have already erected public plaques in honour of its celebrated sons, William Lovett and the crews of the "Mystery" and the "Rosebud". They should now seriously consider erecting another in honour of its adopted daughter, the industrious, indefatigable and inspired, Melissa Hardie, for producing this splendid "100th birthday book" which, like the art gallery itself, is unique.

FRANK RUHRMUND

I

A CENTURY OF ART-FULL CHANGE: 1895 - 1995

N*ewlyn.--It is dim work groping after the genesis of things--even recent things--there is such a tangle of prehistoric causes shaping themselves out of the formless void...*

Norman Garstin

Introduction

Attempting to present the background of the Newlyn Copper Industry in 1896, Norman Garstin presaged, in more romanticised form, the feelings of the current editor when faced with the 'archives' of the Newlyn Art Gallery. Where and how does one start with over sixty cartons of material: one hundred years of minute books, financial records, correspondence, newspaper cuttings, exhibition programmes, personnel files and lists of names together with the waste-paper of many arts-related committees far and wide-- all filled with the future plans and intentions of individuals and groups? It took some weeks to arrive at a rough guide of what we did *not* have, and then months more locating most of the missing information, another story in itself.

The 'actors' in the drama of an institution are seen through the eyes of the recorders at the time, whether that record-keeper is a journalist, a more removed and heavily-biased critic, or a minute-taker at a meeting. The actors are variously identified, sometimes by surname, often by initial, and occasionally by a familiar first name, all of which may be different! Equally, the best laid plans and good intentions of the players often remain unrealised and unrealisable; an idea is subsequently dropped, or never mentioned again. One comes to realise this latter type of 'making do', or agreed compromise, only after reading through subsequent decades of written records. Suddenly, there is a gap or an enigmatic silence as to the meat of the subject under debate. What happened then? It is like a long-running detective story. The researcher is piecing together the time-tables and the events, and then putting the perpetrators into the resulting framework -- all of these in *any* order.

Then add to this mass of written material the hearsay evidence or 'popular' characterisations of the principal actors , alive or dead, in the life of the Gallery. These individuals march through the papers-of-the-house like cats' paws leaving a few muddy prints, perhaps only a signature. Some are artists, some children of artists, some patrons and supporters, others passionate collectors of works of art and artistic memorabilia. Of these people's lives and arts, films and books are made. Without these people the bricks and mortar, stairs and railings, rooms and windows make only a building. With these tireless 'volunteers' to the service of art, an active, creative force continues.

The Creative Force

John Passmore Edwards commissioned the building of an Art Gallery in 1895 for a known set of artists, the Newlyn 'school' or 'Newlyners', and much was made of this unique inheritance. A Cornish-born journalist who progressed to the proprietorship of newspapers and journals, his wife was the daughter of an artist. This generous public benefactor had already underwritten the costs of the South London Art Gallery, Camberwell in 1893, and in 1900 Passmore Edwards went on to commission the building of the Whitechapel Picture Gallery.

The land given for the purposes of the Cornish art colony was located on the sea front at Tolcarne in Newlyn, and generously offered by Charles D N LeGrice. From that day to this, the LeGrice family have remained interested supporters of the arts, and Trustees of the Gallery. It is of interest to note, despite the initial infringement of planning regulations, that the construction period encompassed a period of just six months.

The building had a social and architectural purpose from the outset:'a show place for the artists','for the public good'. The artists, with the impetus of the new building in view, formed themselves into a fraternal arts organisation which from 1895 was called The Newlyn Society of Artists (NSA). Originally, the institution was to have been combined with a reading room, as the most typical interest of Passmore Edwards was public education and public health in the widest sense of the term. Of the twenty or so public institutions established by him in Cornwall, seven were libraries, and others were technical schools incorporating libraries. But, rather mysteriously, the 'reading room' at Newlyn vanished from the final plans. The locals at Newlyn suspected the high-handed artists of not caring about their needs after satisfying their own for 'an artists' club'. This we know due to their complaining letters to *The Cornishman*.

Most likely, the reasons were more financial than artistic. Passmore Edwards' bequests were always made as a capital expenditure. A principle of his was that he was willing to give, but others should show their interest and thanks by supporting the gift with their own. Therefore, it was solely the concern of the chosen Trustees and the artists as to how they would maintain the building and underwrite the expenses of the exhibitions they would hold. Purchasing books and magazines was not first priority, when the Morrab (Subscription) Library was already in existence. Of primary importance were setting the level of subscription that the artists could afford to pay, seeking outside support in the way of interested 'Fellows' and deciding the entrance fees to the public.

'Scheme for Financing: *The artists have taken the initial step of raising amongst themselves a guarantee fund, which has been called in, but feeling that used in the way herein indicated the Gallery will be quite as much an affair of public interest as for their own private benefit, they venture to appeal for support in maintaining it. This can be given in one of two ways which we will now indicate --*
First. *By becoming a Donor of a sum not less than Ten Guineas; this will entitle the giver to two annual season tickets, admitting to all Exhibitions held in the Gallery, and also to all Private Views.*
Second. *By becoming a Fellow, the qualification for which shall be a subscription of One Guinea annually, payable in advance. Fellows will be entitled to two annual season tickets, admitting to all Exhibitions and Private Views. On ceasing to pay the annual subscription, the Fellowship lapses.'*

Any student of the Gallery archives will find that the organisation has been bedevilled at every stage by lack of financial security. The initial hope expressed in the document prepared to launch the scheme in 1895 was never realised: 'The subscriptions of Fellows and the interest on capital will go towards defraying the annual expenses, and at the end of each year, should there be any profit in favour of the Gallery from this or any other source, the amount will be added to the capital already held by the Trustees, in the hope that by this means before long the Gallery may be handsomely endowed.' The lack of endowment funds remains a problem to the present day.

Percy Craft, in particular, put a great deal of personal effort into setting up the artistic regime, acting as Honorary Secretary, pro tem. He, in turn, acknowledged the hard work of his fellow artist, Stanhope Forbes, and the provisional committee. In his inaugural address, Forbes pointed, also, to the help and advice of Howard Buller, an American artist, in setting up the arrangements for funding and working the exhibition programme.

The sculptured panel of Forbes, on the lower front facade of the Newlyn Art Gallery attests to the importance of his pre-eminent role as the 'Father' of the Gallery. It was sculpted by the Reverend Allan Wyon, and unveiled by Sir Alfred Munnings, RA, in 1948. No other person has been so honoured, with the exception of the founder patron, Passmore Edwards, whose name is engraved in stone in the central panel, as one of the terms of benefaction. Edwards' original tribute of the Gallery in the name of John Opie, another illustrious Cornishman -- hence the early mention of the Opie Memorial Gallery -- was rarely used after the nineteen- thirties. The engraved foundation stone on the facade of the building notices this initial dedication.

Despite the dominance of its 'prime mover', Stanhope Forbes, in the early half of the history of the Gallery, there are many others whose energies were given to the Gallery with great generosity -- and sometimes to the point of sheer exhaustion. The Honorary Secretaries, later the Secretary-Curators and now the Directors, have been, without doubt, of critical importance at every stage. Henry Rheam (who died in post as Hon Sec) and Reginald Dick who carried on from him, both artists themselves, gave much more time than they had bargained for, and periodically raised serious questions about whether or not they could stay in their posts any longer...too much work, too little time...honorariums needed...and above all, assistance required.

Mr Charles DN LeGrice, one of the much diminished band of remaining Trustees by 1921, suggested that wider support for the Art Gallery, *might* be secured by widening the base of The Committee. Tentative in his approach and not wishing to offend the artists, rather to aid them, he thought that non-artists or 'lay members' (subscribers) might be co-opted onto The Committee. The artists reacted nervously, thinking that one day it might prove that lay members would be able to outvote the artists, and this had not been the intention of Passmore Edwards. The power of co-option was, nevertheless, granted by the Trustees to the Artists forthwith.

In 1921 Miss Churchill-Tayler arrived and with a willing assistant, Miss M A Hall (also an exhibiting artist) as custodian, they rescued Reginald Dick from the organisational mire. The latter continued to act as Hon Sec until well into the 1930s and they assisted him. Women had played roles previously in the life of the arts in Newlyn: as artists themselves, like Elizabeth Armstrong Forbes and Laura Knight (later Dame); partners in the functioning art schools which tutored pupils; and, as consorts on ceremonial occasions. They also served as the members of the arrangements committees for teas and conversaziones. Miss Churchill-Tayler and Miss Hall, however, were the first of their gender to be of more than passing importance to the organisation of the Gallery, and their coming signalled some changes. For the first time indoor bathing and plumbing facilities were installed. Miss Churchill-Tayler was the first to convert from an Assistant Secretary (an employee) to a member of the Joint Committee (voluntary), and then to become an Honorary Fellow for life.

Possibly the success of these two women as residential assistants to Reginald Dick set a new precedent. When the post was advertised again, in 1934, the candidate of interest was also a woman, Mrs Wallace Nichols (Renee), who was asked to explain whether she would be coming on her own or bringing her husband along to assist her? They both came, Wallace Nichols acting as note-taker at some meetings, and otherwise as general factotum, making repairs and acting as custodian. From all accounts they were much loved and respected, annually thanked for going much beyond the call of duty in their services to the Gallery, and, like many of the gentleman-artists and their families of the time, living on some form of private income.

One of the touching Minutes of a meeting soon after the Second World War, was the comment that it was now time to restore the commission-on-sales to the Curator, regularly a part of the stipend, as she had forgone it throughout the war to assist the Gallery. Wallace Nichols, a writer and poet, wrote periodic articles in *The Cornishman*. One was a particularly clear account of the contemporary workings of the Gallery, and this is reprinted in Chapter VII. Renee Nichols died in post as Residential Curator/Secretary in 1952, and her husband took over for a few months while her replacement was chosen.

This was Eileen Hunt who began her tenure that same year. Thankfully she remains with us, striding around Penzance with her white cane, immediately welcoming and interested when one stops and addresses her. She lived, with her young children, in the basement rooms of the Gallery as her predecessors had, and began to aid a lively, revival programme in the post-war years. Eileen Hunt brought a fresh and artistically unfettered approach to her role as curator and constantly encouraged new, young artists as did her successor, Michael Canney.

Another 'high-point' for the Gallery was arriving as Peter Lanyon, Alexander Mackenzie, Jack Pender, Ithell Colquhoun, John Tunnard, and John Armstrong exhibited. The nineteen-fifties can be characterised generally as the period in which the Gallery gradually moved away from being so much of a 'gentleman-artists club' based on the great days of its origins. It was moving toward a period of more open and flexible ideas about what qualified as art. As late as 1948, when unveiling the Newlyn Gallery Memorial plaque to Forbes, Alfred Munnings had used the occasion to rail against 'the moderns'. A decade later, Peter Lanyon, argued that since all art is likely to be considered passe in time, that all the artists, old-fashioned and new-fashioned, should be allowed to submit and hang their work.

During his eight-year curatorship beginning in 1956, Michael Canney, a teacher, writer and professional artist, generated great enthusiasm amongst artists and supporters, instituted a Film Society, and curated a number of external and travelling exhibitions at home and abroad. The increase in the activities of the Gallery was sufficient to persuade the Arts Council to give Newlyn an annual grant of five hundred pounds. There are advantages and disadvantages in having a practising artist as curator-director; in Canney's case his ability with words and his knowledge of art combined to produce an organiser and critic with flair. He wrote occasional pieces for magazines and newspapers, and produced excellent introductions to the increasingly elaborate programme notes for exhibitions, as well as contributions to books. The open-air sculpture exhibition which he organised in Penlee Park, together with Barbara Hepworth, was typical of the forward-thinking ideas which he promoted.

The lack of sufficient financial backing for the Gallery's activities, however, continued to be a source of stress and political friction. Though the flat in the Gallery was given to the curator rent-free together with a small salary and commissions on sales, by the nineteen-sixties the meagre wages were insufficient for a family who had to live on earned income, a feature of life which 'crept up' on the world of art post-war. The talented husband and wife team, Michael and Madeleine Canney, like the Nichols before them, generously had given the services of two for the price of one curator. In 1964, retiring from the Newlyn fray, Michael first instituted the Porthleven (Summer) School of Painting. Madeleine assisted John Miller, the artist and architect, in his offices at Sancreed House. Canney then spent a year in California directing the Santa Barbara University Museum and teaching art, before returning to join Paul Feiler and Hassel Smith at the West of England College of Art, Bristol.

Two curators followed in short succession, David Coad and David Smith, and there were periods when there was no-one, meaning that the artists did whatever was done themselves. Committees carried on, as did the hardworking chairmen like Charles Breaker, John Miller, and Ken Symonds, but with only the back-up of volunteers and fee-for-job technical assistants. In 1967 Alister McLeod or 'Mac', as he was affectionately known, was employed as resident curator. Despite hard work on his part, and his well-documented attempts to interest the Trustees in the declining state and fortunes of the Gallery, the financial situation became increasingly parlous.

Together with John Miller, then the Chairman of The Committee, Mac approached the Arts Council for desperately needed funds to redesign and improve the internal fabric of the building. At this stage his curator's flat was diminished so that more exhibition space could be used. The renovations were an enormous success, and an important event in 1969 was the visit of the Minister of State for Education, Jennie Lee, to re-launch the Gallery with a flourish. Nonetheless, the chronic lack of cash prevailed, and finally Mac's resignation was sparked by his feeling that the Gallery could no longer afford to have a curator. Simultaneously, the Arts Council was querying the public status of galleries and museums which were operating as private and profit-making institutions, and asking whether grants to them from the national or regional purses could be justified?

In 1974, a new phase in the life of the Passmore Edwards Art Gallery was to begin. The 'sea-change' taking place was the management of the Gallery by professional directors, not necessarily artists themselves, but at least experienced in the running of institutions and the organising of exhibitions.

The Fabric of the Gallery

The 'state' of the Gallery building, within and without, has exercised the minds of The Committee and Council throughout the century. Prime matters of record are the details of concerns about damage, dilapidation, and decorative order -- in both the exhibition rooms and the residential accommodation. To mention every re-paint and re-jig of space would be to bore the reader, so commentaries on these are only occasionally extracted from voluminous notes within Minutes. A resume of architectural changes is best presented visually, and is included on the following pages.

The original architect, James Hicks of Redruth, also designed the Redruth Free Library in 1895, at the commission of Passmore Edwards, and in the following year, he also effected the same benefactor's gift of the Liskeard Public Library. It is important to realise, as Sheelagh O'Donnell explains in her paper on 'The Four Copper Plaques' [see Chapter II] the contribution of the artists' ideas to the final design and appearance of the building. The original plan by Hicks, shown as Figure 1, was modified in several ways

THE·PASSMORE·EDWARDS·ART·GALLERY·NEWLYN·CORNWALL·JAS·HICKS·ARCH^T

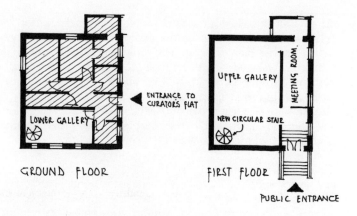

GROUND FLOOR   FIRST FLOOR

ENTRANCE TO CURATOR'S FLAT

LOWER GALLERY

UPPER GALLERY MEETING ROOM.

NEW CIRCULAR STAIR

PUBLIC ENTRANCE

ALTERATIONS DURING MICHAEL CANNEY'S CURATORSHIP

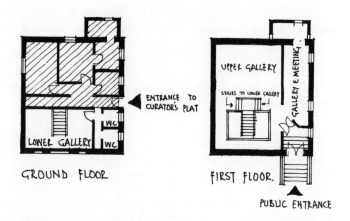

GROUND FLOOR   FIRST FLOOR.

ENTRANCE TO CURATOR'S FLAT

LOWER GALLERY WC WC

UPPER GALLERY

STAIRS TO LOWER GALLERY

GALLERY & MEETING

PUBLIC ENTRANCE

ALTERATIONS DURING ALISTAIR McLEOD'S CURATORSHIP

CURATOR'S FLAT HATCHED ON ABOVE GROUND FLOOR PLANS

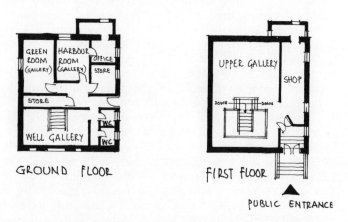

GROUND FLOOR   FIRST FLOOR

GREEN ROOM (GALLERY) HARBOUR ROOM (GALLERY) OFFICE STORE

STORE

WELL GALLERY WC WC

UPPER GALLERY SHOP

DOWN DOWN

PUBLIC ENTRANCE

ALTERATIONS DURING JOHN HALKES'S DIRECTORSHIP

N.B THE ABOVE PLANS ARE DIAGRAMMATIC AND NOT TO SCALE J·M

before completion and is much out of proportion to the human figures depicted. On the right-hand face of the building, one pitched gable was ultimately substituted for the two shown on the plan. The window arrangement was altered, and the doorway was completely changed in style. Internally, the reading room was not fitted. The builders in 1895 were Symon & Son of Newlyn, and they continued to be called upon to make repairs, within tight financial limits, well into the twentieth century. G Sherwood Hunter, both an artist and an architect/builder was relied on in the nineteen-twenties and -thirties to advise and oversee repairs, and was also appointed as a Trustee in the first intake after the Great War.

Except for essential repairs, the addition of electric lights, indoor plumbing, various devices for spot heating (always inadequate), and periodic re-decoration, no major structural changes were made until the early nineteen-sixties. The voluntary services of Trustee and architect Geoffrey Drewitt, were called upon infrequently, from the late nineteen-forties, taking over from Sherwood Hunter as the expert to inspect suspected fissures, cracks and subsidence.

Michael Canney, with the architectural help of John Miller introduced the use of a second-hand spiral staircase , purchased from the Penzance Library in the mid-sixties. This enabled the lower gallery to be employed as an exhibiting space, rather than the occasional meeting room and studio area it had been previously. Internal walls in the upper gallery were removed and re-placed in an attractive new format and the entrances altered. These decorations were considered a triumph of modernity within the pepper-corn budget allowed for the project.

John Miller, artist, architect and, by then, experienced Chairman of The Committee and the NSA, was again asked to help by Mac McLeod. The spiral staircase was sold on, and a central staircase effected, leading to the lower gallery and the visitors' toilet facilities below. The building work was undertaken by Jack James of H James & Son, Builders, of Newlyn. Wider vistas and perspectives opened up, and a feeling of space and airiness was achieved. Photographs of the exhibition halls used throughout the book will illustrate these changes, and bring back a flood of memories to many readers.

New lower galleries were made available when residential accommodation was withdrawn in 1973-74. Mac McLeod was the last curator to live in the Gallery flat, and after his departure, the hard physical labour of John and Ella Halkes and their team, cleared these rooms to become the 'Harbour Room', and the 'Green Room' respectively. The latter was colloquially known as 'the squeaky room' with a floor responding vociferously to the lightest of footfalls. Architectural plans were drawn up in the late nineteen-seventies for a large extension, which finally could not reach fruition, despite hopes well into the -eighties, due to the unavailability of major funding.

The renovations of 1994-95 have come about through the combined planning efforts of members of the Council of Management together with the curators of the past five years. Gerald Deslandes and Emily Ash, and their teams, built constructively on long-standing contacts with arts advisers, and introduced some new sponsors and foundations to the on-going work of the Gallery. It is a tribute to the work of a great number of people -- artists, arts administrators, grant-giving bodies, and not least, Council members such as Vice-Chairman Graham Dark, and the Building Sub-committee working with the quantity surveyor, Edwin Bryant, and architect, Robert Evans -- that a fresh start for the Passmore Edwards Art Gallery is promised for the second century.

Exhibiting in the Gallery

It was with certain disappointment that this Editor discovered a major deficit in the records of the Gallery. This is the lack of a complete list of exhibitors, together with the titles of their exhibits, over the century. Admittedly, such a register would include several thousands of names, each sitting at the head of a sheet of submissions. Even if ultimately successful, an indexing project would start with the disadvantage of an incomplete collection of exhibition catalogues and exhibitors' lists. Through generous loans , five exhibition programmes prior to 1950 have been located: Winter 1911, Summer 1928, the Cornish Loan Exhibition of 1936, Autumn 1937 and Spring 1941. Should any reader be able to supply a programme from any exhibition -- a copy is sufficient, rather than the original -- it will be added to the collection toward a definitive catalogue, which the Editor is now attempting.

The supporting records which are extant, though incomplete, are sales books kept by the secretary/curators for the Newlyn Society of Artists; herein, the works of art do not consistently bear a name -- though always a number which could be correlated with a catalogue. The other major source for the names of exhibitors and occasionally the titles of their exhibits is the series of scrapbooks which form a valuable part of the Newlyn archives. Quite extensive and particular coverage of exhibitions occurred in the newspapers throughout the early history of the Gallery, making long though incomplete lists of exhibiting artists available to the researcher (but little additional information).

An interesting and important adjunct to the life of the Gallery -- perhaps inaccessible in detail through the lack of written record -- has been the continuous existence of the artists' schools. Many artists are also teachers of art even now -- witness the faculty status of such present-day Newlyn Society artists as Philip Hogben, Carole Page, Michael Chalwin, and Robert Jones, amongst some twenty others, who currently teach at the Falmouth College of Art, and have been regular exhibitors at the Newlyn Art Gallery. Several long-time exhibitors at the Gallery are former principals and lecturers at Falmouth: Michael Finn, Tom Cross, Ray Atkins, Francis Hewlett being notable names. The current academic dean, Charles Hancock, is an active, serving member of the Council of Management, as Alan Livingston, current Principal, was before him.

The artists' schools, however, were and still are, indigenous to the West Cornwall art scene, and operate separately from the established organisations such as the St Ives School of Painting (Roy Ray, Principal) and the Penzance School of Art (currently part of Penwith College, Penzance). Nevertheless, the existence of the Newlyn Art Gallery has always acted as an extra spur to the efforts of pupils studying in the private tutorial 'schools' such as those of Stanhope & Elizabeth Forbes, Norman Garstin, Julius Olsson, Louis Grier, Algernon Talmage, Harold Harvey & Ernest Procter, and Charles & Ruth Simpson , situated on both sides of the peninsula. All of these offered tuition in painting well into the nineteen-twenties and attracted pupils from far and near.

Selection by the hanging committee at the Gallery could not, of course, be guaranteed to pupils, but nevertheless many entered their work which was hung. The early letters of Frances Hodgkins from Newlyn make clear her delight in 'having their own gallery', though she had come to study the work of Newlyn artists and was not a member of the NSA. Geoffrey S Garnier (etchings, aquatints) and Jill Garnier (paintings, needlecraft) are outstanding examples of two who came to study at the Forbes School,

and remained to become not only loyal members of the NSA exhibiting throughout their lives, but an integral part of the Newlyn community.

Later artists have also taken recourse to this additional method for supporting themselves and gaining further inspiration for their own work. Notable amongst these were the artists Charles Breaker and Eric Hiller, who with their friend Marjorie Mort, ran their 'Holiday Sketching Groups' from the nineteen-forties, based at the Gernick Field Studio, complete with prospectus printed by Guido Morris. After leaving the Newlyn Art Gallery in 1964, Michael Canney's first stop was in instituting the Porthleven School of Painting. From the nineteen-sixties Lamorna Kerr gathered friends and pupils around her in the informal 'Painting Group' at the Birch family home, Flagstaff Cottage, in the Lamorna Valley. A small tuition fee was paid, and a critique of work done by pupils was offered at the end of each weekly session. A yearly exhibition of work was then organised at the Lamorna Village Hall.

The more formalised modern-day equivalent to the schools of Forbes and colleagues, is that programme of residential courses offered by Bernard and Audrey Evans in Newlyn, and that of Leonie Whitton and David Westby at their converted 'collegio' in Tuscany. The history of these 'schools' and sketching/painting groups is not the focus of this volume, as officially they are unrelated to the Gallery. Only some of the pupils could have been classified as 'professional artists' in intent and as ones who aspired to pay the hanging fees necessary to show their work at the Gallery. Nonetheless, the principal artists were themselves members of the Gallery constituency, and sometimes if not always, active in its affairs.

Present-day members of the NSA are also the backbone of the educational programme sponsored by the Gallery in its outreach to children and adults through art clubs and lectures. In the nineteen-eighties, the Gallery was fortunate to have the energies of a part-time, then full-time education officer, Diana Morris, who built up an exciting programme of activities under the umbrella title 'Artshare'. The re-allocation of some arts funding nationally, and the taking on of a 'contracting-in' policy on the part of schools, has caused a shift of emphasis in the nineteen-nineties.

The Monday and Saturday Clubs of the Art Gallery now, are led by artists such as Anthony Frost, Graham Jobbins, David Kemp, Amanda Lorens, Billy Wynter and Benjamin Gay who have also supported innovative projects in schools. Special shows are held annually in the Gallery to show the work of these 'new artists coming up', but exhibitions may also be jointly sponsored at other venues, such as the John Daniel Centre in Penzance, or in local church halls and out-door venues.

Managing the Gallery
The organisational history of the Gallery may be considered in three distinct phases, though the transition between the first and second was gradual and somewhat blurred.

Phase One: 1895 - 1950
The Gallery was jointly managed until 1953-4 by the Executive Committee or 'The Committee' as it was known, to which both the Newlyn Society of Artists (NSA) and the Trustees of the Passmore Edwards Art Gallery (PEAG) appointed members. From 1895 The Committee was constituted of six members, with two standing down each year -- though quite often those doing so were immediately re-elected. Some of the Trustees through the decades, notably the LeGrices, the Bolithos, and the Cornish brothers

served in person on The Committee; otherwise, artists or others were invited to represent them as 'Appointed Agents of the Trustees'.

In Phase One, though the money to run the Gallery had to be generated by the artistic activity within and supported by the subscriptions of members, the ultimate responsibility for the building and its maintenance resided with the Trustees. During this period the NSA attended a separate set of meetings from those of The Committee, and came together for the Annual General Meeting with all three 'bodies' represented (PEAG, NSA, Trustees). Nevertheless, the Minutes and the subjects discussed were often the same and interlaced (filed within the same books of Minutes), and those attending the meetings were also the same individuals. At times the membership fell to disastrously low figures -- eg, fifteen artists and twelve local supporters after the Great War -- and then concerted effort and activity would be put in to resurrect the Gallery. In 1924 Stanhope Forbes suggested that the first postcards depicting the works of Newlyn artists should be produced, at the cost of the artists themselves, and sold in the Gallery for the profit of both 'partners'. There is no record of who might have taken up this suggestion.

The works of art produced by the early artists and craftsmen for exhibition in the Newlyn Art Gallery have long ago dispersed into treasured collections of local, national and international importance. Until the nineteen-sixties there was no concerted move to inaugurate a permanent or museum collection to reside at Newlyn, though historical shows had been mounted with great success. Once the Permanent Collection began to grow after 1974, and with the encouragement of the Arts Council, a plan for the Gallery's extension was approved. This would include housing for a standing historical exhibition with emphasis on the work of the early Newlyn School. Economies have waxed and waned in the meantime, and the proposed development has not occurred. The record of the second century of the Newlyn Art Gallery may have another story to tell.

The main sources of information about this period, apart from the Minutes kept for meetings of The Committee, the NSA and the Trustees, are newspaper cuttings meticulously kept by the first and temporary Secretary of the Gallery, Percy Craft. Following on in his father's footsteps, H N Craft presented the *'Percy Craft Scrapbook'* to the Newlyn archives in the nineteen-fifties. A second scrapbook, presumably kept by the various curators in the early years provides extracts from newspapers and journals after 1900, by which time Percy Craft had departed Newlyn. This was carried on, with the occasional gap of a decade, until the nineteen-seventies.

A third source of information, about Elizabeth and Stanhope Forbes in particular, is provided by a scrapbook made up of newspaper cuttings taken on their behalf by 'cuttings services' in the eighteen-eighties and -nineties. The latter is of especial interest, due to the widespread and international notoriety accorded to the life and works of the gentlemen elected to the Royal Academy of Art. In one sense, the Royal Academicians and other noted artists, achieved the status of the 'pop stars', sports personalities and film idols of today.

The so-called 'second-wave' Newlyn Gallery artists -- who centred as much in Lamorna and further afield as in Newlyn itself -- were first encountered by the current editor in researches undertaken to place into appropriate context the memoirs of Elizabeth Lamorna Kerr. Her father, Samuel John Lamorna Birch, can be said to be the second great sustaining figure in the life of the Gallery, after Stanhope Forbes.

"Unlike many of his fellow academicians, Birch showed a keen interest in avant-garde painting, in particular that of the younger generation of painters in St Ives and Newlyn, who held him in respect. Lanyon often referred to Birch's sympathetic attitude to his work. Birch maintained that the technique and colour of his own painting owed much to the artists of his youth, to Sisley, Monet and Pisarro..." (*Newlyn Notebook*, M Canney). Now in 1995, the first major biography of S J Lamorna Birch, by author and former journalist, Austin Wormleighton, is to be launched in the Newlyn Art Gallery during the centenary year celebrations.

Phase Two: 1950 - 1973

In another resurrective flush of post-war activity, The Committee felt the need to expand, to bring in 'new blood' and to spread the responsibilities of managing the exhibition programme. A new 'licensing' arrangment was mooted between the artists (NSA) & the Trustees, at the suggestion of Charles LeGrice (the third of this name). In 1953-4, The Committee was expanded to a maximum of twelve members, including officers, with the power of co-option (which had been in effect previously). In 1957, the Trustees decided to consider the now enlarged NSA committee as 'licensees' or tenants, thereby making the artists wholly responsible for the Gallery maintenance and management. After many discussions, delays and some resistance, this was finally effected by written agreement in 1959.

The Chairman of the NSA became *ipso facto* the Chairman of the Gallery Committee, which assumed responsibility for the building and its management. Thereafter, the Trustees appointed one liaison person to represent them on the NSA Gallery organisation. From a position of co-operative partnership in the running of the affairs and a permissive ownership of the building's fabric, the Trustees stepped back to become interested landlords. The provisions of the Trust deed remained -- that as long as the artists continued to employ the Gallery for artistic and educative functions related to art promotion, and stayed within a manageable financial position in doing so, then they would stay in possession of the place itself.

This second phase was quite trying for the artists, but also energising. Without the dedication of the curator/secretaries, the whole burden of trying to support, maintain and run the Gallery was on the shoulders of the management committee, most of whom were also trying to earn their living as professional artists and teachers of the arts. Nonetheless, this was also the period of three much respected and loved Curator-Secretaries in the persons of Eileen Hunt and Michael Canney followed later by 'Mac' McLeod.

In this quarter of the century, roughly from 1950-74, the Chairmen did much more than chair the meetings. Being Chairman was not so much a honorary post as one of unremunerated leadership and service. E Bouverie Hoyton, Lamorna Kerr, Denys Law, Charles Breaker, John Miller, Jack Pender, Peter Lanyon, and Ken Symonds, put tireless energies into the Gallery and its activities, as did the officers and members of the NSA. Wives like Inez Hoyton, Madeleine Canney and Jane Symonds, as those of many of the original Committee -- the two Mesdames Forbes, Mrs Gotch and Mrs Garstin -- gave numerous hours in support of the Gallery.

There was no particular recompense except for the joy of 'putting on a good show', though naturally it was in their own interests to preserve the showcase. Much more was also asked of the committees, even as far as physically decorating and cleaning the Gallery, invigilating for exhibitions, creating handmade posters, and making arrangements for tea. 'In the mid-fifties, the picture-hanging at Newlyn was done by hired workmen. For an institution with so little money this seemed ridiculous and unrealistic. It was then agreed that members and the curator would carry out this task in future. The days of the gentleman-artist were over!' [*Newlyn Notebook*, M Canney].

Extracts from the 'Newlyn Notebook' of Michael Canney, the books and letters of John Miller, the books and letters of Peter Lanyon, the explanatory narratives of Alexander MacKenzie, Mrs M E ('Dach') Lambourn, Ken Symonds, Margo Maeckelberghe, Mervyn Levy, Sheelagh O'Donnell and Eileen Hunt, and the written comments of Wilhelmina Barns Graham and Jeremy Le Grice do much to bring this period alive. Now in the nineteen-nineties, the opening of the Tate Gallery St Ives [the so-called 'Tate of the West'] provides a standing and changing exhibition of the work of some of the West Cornwall artists working in those post-war years.

14   Michael Canney writes of his one regret that 'Hepworth, Nicholson and one or two of the other moderns did not show at Newlyn; but most of the others did. In fact nearly all the artists who showed in St Ives, also showed at Newlyn at one time or another'. As Alexander MacKenzie explains now, Newlyn in the nineteen-fifties and -sixties was a haven for the rebels against the hanging rules prevailing in St Ives, which were strongly informed by Barbara Hepworth and Ben Nicholson. The rules categorised the artists into three sections: Group A Traditional/figurative; Group B Modern/abstract and Group C Craftsmen. The jousting, based on the divisions, seemed to preclude the showing of representational work, and drove away some who held a more holistic view of art. These 'wars' are referred to obliquely in Lanyon's correspondence in his mention of 'tachist' and 'tachisme'. [Art pieces made up of spots, blotches, or blobs fashionable at one time.] Just as colourful is Jeremy Le Grice's memoir of the time, reprinted in Chapter VIII.

The exhibiting regulations at Newlyn were straightforward, and the atmosphere often was said to be 'friendly' and open. Commonly, there were three exhibitions a year -- in spring, summer, and at Christmas. This routine could be disrupted by wars, strikes, riots or floods but usually proceeded unperturbed. 'Members of the Society elected a Committee by ballot and this Committee in turn elected the members of the Society, the membership being for life. Members had the right to have at least two pictures shown in each exhibition, or a maximum of four; this meant that members who should never have been elected in the first place, or those whose work had deteriorated, could still claim a place on the gallery walls, a perennial problem for all art societies. Lanyon always contended that since all members might one day become unfashionable or decrepit, the committee was obliged to show generosity to *all* members when selecting work! This was in contrast to the practise in 'another place', namely, the Penwith Society.' [Canney, *op cit*]

One of the features of the Gallery introduced during this period, was the organised letting of gallery spaces for one-man shows, in the small downstairs room. Though not entirely new -- Stanhope Forbes, Elizabeth Armstrong Forbes, single memorial exhibitions for dead artists, had occurred previously -- the tradition at Newlyn, due to the policy of the Society and its hanging rules, had been to stage large mixed shows. The one-man shows were and still are of great educational interest in allowing the professionals and the public a view of the artist's development. The 'artist's lecture' is the modern equivalent of the 'conversazione' of the early years, though the original conversazione might often include music and theatricals as well.

In the nineteen-fifties the 'one-mans' (be it he or she) were held at a steady rate of six per year, and were in great demand. In conversation, Ken Symonds recalled his own first one-man which was offered to him by Michael Canney in 1960. Still actively painting and showing today, Ken Symonds looks back upon that exhibition as the inauguration of his life in Cornwall.

Phase Three: 1974 - present

The extracts from John Miller's pictoral autobiography (see Chapters VIII - X) express in a most amicable and straightforward fashion, the way that Newlyn Orion Galleries Limited came into existence. Rather than re-tell the story -- which naturally was complicated with negotiation and detail -- the editor prefers 'to let the records show...' In briefest of summaries: 1974 was the year of the amalgamation between two operating galleries, The Newlyn Art Gallery in Newlyn, and The Orion Gallery, a relatively young gallery run by Ella and John Halkes, in Penzance, which showed the work of contemporary artists. The outcome was the formation of a new limited company under the name of Newlyn Orion, with John Halkes as the Director operating on both sites. For some months prior to the new arrangement, John O'Dell, the artist, had been acting as Honorary Treasurer then as temporary Curator-Secretary to the Gallery and the NSA. With the amalgamation, he remained as Administrator, and like the Curators before him, dedicated huge chunks of his life to the Gallery for the following five years.

For the first time in 1974, the management of the Gallery, was incorporated as a limited company, The Newlyn Orion Galleries Ltd, headed by a Director (John Halkes) and backed up by a team of professional staff. With some variation in title and function, the pattern of employing three full-time and two part-time staff, with specified job definitions has continued to the present day. Dating from this time are the subtle changes in employment and conditions, which inform the current managerial climate in the arts and other fields.

Becoming a limited company was a prelude to applying to become a charitable trust, a topic which had exercised the Trustees and The Committee for more than twenty years (with tax and rate concessions in mind). This did not occur until 1977, but in the interim period from 1974 several changes and considerable organisational progress was effected. Due to the economic recession of the time, it had proved inadvisable to keep open the Orion Gallery in Penzance. This was a major disappointment because the idea had been to be an in-town marketing 'flag' for the Newlyn Gallery. Hence the Galleries became one Gallery on the Newlyn site in 1975.

An elected Council of Management of fifteen people, inclusive of officers, was formed and Jack Pender, the artist, became the first Chairman of the new company. Peter A S Pool, the Hon Solicitor and well-known Cornish historian, formulated a constitution, and representatives were sent from constituent organisations as specified therein: Cornwall County Council, Penwith District Council, South West Arts, and not least, the Newlyn Society of Artists. With this energetic team, the Halkes built a new and vigorous company and forged links far and wide, making the Newlyn Orion an exciting venue and the westerly gallery of prestige in the United Kingdom. Major retrospectives of the early painters, accompanying publications of note, and a full range of contemporary art exhibitions were established, grant aid acquired, and a modern renaissance entered.

The membership continued to be made up of supporters to the Gallery who paid an annual subscription, and the artist-subscribers, part of whose subscriptions to the Newlyn Society of Artists, was paid into the Gallery funds. The Council of Management, replacing the old Committee, is composed of artists and non-artists in virtually equal numbers though this is not specified by statute. Even those who would not describe themselves as 'professional artists' may, nonetheless, have pretensions!

From 1974, the NSA was able to re-constitute and re-invigorate itself, growing both in size and in outreach as a Society, separate from the Gallery, but working in conjunction with it. The financial stability gained, through being relieved of the Gallery management and maintenance, was important and encouraging, though the trade-off was the loss of exclusive control over the use of the building and the activities within. Inevitably a 'certain something', a loss of the NSA family atmosphere was felt to have gone, and was mourned. Nevertheless, the exhibition hours devoted to the NSA shows have not diminished, encompassed as they are within the Newlyn year. Rather, the rest of the programme has expanded, and the Gallery is open throughout the year, with only minor closures for the purposes of re-hanging.

Traditionally, one part of the curator/secretary's wage was paid through commission on sales, and another part through the provision of living accommodation. After Mac McLeod departed, the live-in arrangement ceased and the whole of the building became available as exhibition and office spaces. With the arrival of a professional 'team' rather than a single focal person as curator-secretary, it was deemed complex and unsuitable to make commissions on sales a part of the wages paid to staff.

The implications of these subtle changes in compensation are both wide and important. Rather than personal and often 'by gentlemen's agreement' arrangements for running the Gallery, employment legislation and 'salary scales' were to be conjured with. Selling incentives changed, office hours adhered to, and time-off calculated 'in lieu' of extra time spent. It was clearly understood that no gallery or museum could support itself, pay rates, and build its collections on the back of artists' sales to the public. Therefore, the immediate need was for reliable and steady grant-funding, legacies and donations.

The 'knock-on' dangers of requiring external funding are those of moulding an exhibition programme and other activities to 'suit' the purposes -- potentially, though not always actually -- as identified by the funding body. In other words, the arts promoter must appeal to the market and the market may not always be the local community, rather another bureaucracy with its own image to build.

In 1977, the Newlyn Orion became a registered educational charity, and a major part of its work continues to be in the community, through educational projects in schools, art clubs, and lecture series. In the past, lectures had been held, such as Bouverie Hoyton's on the 'Italian Scene', and 'Elephant Bill's' about his friends in the animal kingdom, but held in aid of the Gallery funds. Lecture series such as that given by Jane Symonds in 1980, eight lectures on the topic of design in costumes, were a new and unusual departure.

For educational work, much local sponsorship and support is given -- even though West Cornwall has traditionally been an impoverished geographical area, with little industry. As government policy has shifted away from the intent to equably spread a public subsidy, toward encouraging commercial and private sponsorship in the arts, those to suffer primarily are the areas where there are few profitable enterprises alive. For this reason, the financial involvement of the Arts Council from Canney's time, stepped up considerably from 1974 to 1982, and then devolved to South West Arts thereafter, has been crucial to the survival and capabilities of the Gallery. Those supporting the Gallery are spread widely -- on all continents -- and there is genuine gratitude for the considerable sums of outside money which has benefited West Cornwall through the arts.

The hallmark of Newlyn Orion was the emphasis it placed on art as an expression of the human spirit working in and through the community. Apart from major retro-spective exhibitions of the Early Newlyn School, an active contemporaneous programme of mixed and one-person exhibitions was mounted, many of which toured thereafter to other venues. The Newlyn Orion Company was noted for its energetic participation and co-sponsorship of locally-based activities such as the Newlyn Green Summer Art Fair, and other festivals. Its outreach was wide, and its importance as a focus for cultural activities was established.

In the mid-seventies a Permanent Collection of paintings and art objects was instituted through donations from artists, supporters and collectors. Several notable bequests were received, but storage and financial difficulties have stood in the way of continued acquisition and exhibition of the collection. In 1991 an agreement was reached whereby a major part of the Permanent Collection has been put on loan to the Penzance & District Museum and Gallery at Penlee House, Penzance.

John and Ella Halkes and their staff, are well remembered for the warmth and welcome they offered to visitor and local, professional and amateur alike. As a team to both rescue and sustain an art gallery which could have been lost in changing economies, they could not have performed more effectively. In artistic terms, they could not have been more innovative and constructive, working within quite stringent circumstances. It is perhaps indicative of John's outgoing and inspired nature, that in 1990, after sixteen years as Director of Newlyn Orion, he entered the (non-stipendiary) ministry of the Church of England while continuing as a consultant to a number of arts organisations.

Meantime, two Directors have served the Newlyn Art Gallery management team. Gerald Deslandes, an experienced exhibition organiser, was in post for some eighteen months, and then succeeded by the present Director, Emily Ash in 1993. In an introductory article by author and critic, Frank Ruhrmund (in *The Cornishman*), the 'firsts' brought to Newlyn were underlined: 'The appointment of Surrey-born Emily Ash as its director notches up a double first for Newlyn Orion Galleries Company -- she is its first woman director and the first practising artist to hold the position. At 26, she is its youngest director yet, if not one of the youngest gallery directors in the country. A graduate of Goldsmith's College, University of London, where she obtained a 'First' in Fine Art and Textile Art, it was while she was studying there that her interest in Cornwall began with the writing of a thesis upon Barbara Hepworth...'

It is for Emily Ash and her successors to manage yet another 'sea-change', and altogether in a different cultural climate of conflicting opinions about the direction for the arts and their subsidy, both public and private. The immediate cultural environment has also changed, with the addition of the impressive Tate Gallery in St Ives, a museum showcase of the twentieth-century modern and abstract arts. The major renovation and expansion plans for the Penzance & District Museum at Penlee House may also make it now the natural repository for the historical collections of West Cornwall, including that of the early Newlyn School of painters. It then remains for the Newlyn Art Gallery, as it was originally established to do, to serve as 'a show place for the contemporary artists' 'for the public good'. And, this is quite in line with the wishes of Passmore Edwards, even though the arts and artists have changed meanwhile, leading to much guessing as to what is 'good' and what is 'bad'.

The people who support the arts locally and engage themselves in the activities of the Gallery today, are naturally a talented and public-spirited 'lot'. They enjoy a good wrangle -- as of old -- and want a good show; they can argue for balance in exhibiting our past achievements and contemporary artistic practice, quite vociferously and intelligently. They give to the Newlyn Art Gallery a great deal of time, care and expertise without recompense, and little honour! They are not the close-knit community of artists and their admirers of a century ago, which effected the opening of the Gallery in order to show their own work, 'a show place for the artists'. Neither are the artists themselves a 'school' who share one way of working, 'en plein air' or otherwise, or one kind of fine art such as painting.

The Council of Management of today is, nevertheless, aware of its public responsibilities and the need for public 'ownership' of a wide range of visual arts. Therefore, Newlyn Art Gallery today is more politically engaged with the second part of the equation, 'for the public good'. The dual concerns of Passmore Edwards, for the artists and for public education in the arts, still stand, as does the building. The changing faces are those of community, society and environment.

Being 'in the Chair'

From the beginning to 1952 the chairmanship of The Committee moved from meeting to meeting according to availability of a person to be 'in the Chair'. Because of their interest and prominence in the national and international art world, some of the artists travelled extensively. New artists arrived, and the original set moved away. The Great War also took its toll. During their lifetimes, Stanhope Forbes and Thomas Cooper Gotch were most frequently Chairmen, as were the Reverend Allan Wyon and Samuel John 'Lamorna' Birch in theirs. As early as 1911, it was suggested that Forbes should become President to make room for some new face on The Committee, but the idea was not pursued at that time, and seemingly not mentioned again. In 1952, three years prior to his death, Lamorna Birch did achieve that status, one which was decided, not so much to make room for another, but to bring honour to the recipient and the Gallery.

In the archives there are no records of elections to the position of Chairman until 1952 and the subsequent expansion of The Committee. A regular rotation of members to The Committee occurred from before the turn of the century, thereby also rotating the people available to chair. Chairmanship was simply for chairing the meetings. Nevertheless, the same reliable few rotated with regularity.

One woman, Mrs Norman Garstin, sat 'in the Chair' for one meeting in 1897, and upon this occasion she put into parentheses the title 'Chair-woman' with a certain flourish. Though women were sent as Appointed Agents of the Trustees, ie Miss Julyan, or co-opted to 'tea and arranging committees', The Committee was firmly a male preserve until the 1930s. In that decade Mrs Eleanor Hughes, RI, Alethea Garstin and Mrs Ella Naper, beside the active supporter and Assistant Secretary, Miss Churchill-Tayler, took part in the work of The Committee, and Mrs Hughes sat 'in the Chair' upon two occasions in 1935.

With the successful appointment of Mrs Wallace Nichols in 1933 to take over with her husband as Curator/Secretary (Residential) & Custodian respectively, the place of women in the management of the Gallery was finally established. The advent of the Second World War ensured that The Committee was essentially female for the duration and for sometime thereafter. Nevertheless, throughout this period the person chairing the meetings was virtually always the Rev Allan Wyon, a stalwart of The Committee for some 20 years.

It was not until 1953 that the first woman chairman of the NSA was elected. Elizabeth Lamorna Kerr remains the only woman to have become President, an office to which she was elected for one year following the death of her father in 1955. Though it has been mooted from time to time that the Newlyn Art Gallery should have a President of some standing -- Presidency was offered to Dame Barbara Hepworth, but declined -- this office has not been filled since.

19

Though The Committee was the all-important focus of the Gallery itself, a sub-committee of influence was appointed by them to supervise the selection and hanging of exhibitions. Inevitably, this was called the 'Hanging Committee' and places on this selection panel were highly valued. Sometimes these were appointed positions and sometimes elected, either for a year or specifically for each exhibition. It would be of interest to correlate the membership of the Hanging Committees with the resulting selections contained in the major exhibitions (usually three a year). Controversies have always arisen about exhibition and hanging policies. The on-going debate, between exponents of traditional and representational art, and the more abstract and expressionist forms, threads its way through the history of the Gallery. This type of analysis, however, is not the purpose of the current book.

One reiterated theme which the reader will follow throughout this procession of extracts is that of financial difficulty, and the need for repairs and decorations. The Gallery has always been supported by the subscriptions of the artists and those of the 'Fellows' (the original name for the non-artist subscriber, or a supporter who had not applied for or not yet been elected to the Newlyn Society of Artists). Since the nineteen-thirties and -forties, however, subscriptions and commissions on sales could not meet the costs of maintaining, repairing and staffing the institution.

Grants have been sought since grants were 'invented' and the Arts Council, Southwestern Arts, and its successor, South West Arts, have all in their turn been instrumental in times of change, supporting the Gallery with funds and advice. Nevertheless, some voices have been raised against this type of external, governmental intervention, with the argument of 'the one who pays the piper calls the tune'. Latterly, a much wider range of commercial, non-governmental and charitable sponsorship of the arts has been forthcoming and the Newlyn Art Gallery has been supported in numerous ways by a host of generous benefactors. In 1994, major alterations and renovations of the internal fabric and roof of the building, were undertaken with substantial grant aid from the Foundation for the Sports and the Arts, the Henry Moore Foundation, and several others, matched by funds from the European Union.

Fundraising activities of all kinds, musicals, theatricals, lectures, poetry readings, tea parties, cocktail parties, bring-and-buy sales, auctions, dances, even raffles have been tried over a long number of years. These activities were in addition, of course, to the contributions of the artists through the payment of agreed commissions on sales made in the Gallery, and through the Gallery's introduction. Some of the more inventive ideas for 'keeping afloat' emerge from Minutes and news-cuttings, and should help us all to understand 'that there is little that is *new*!'

Michael Canney, in his 'Newlyn Notebook' records, 'There was some committee resistance (or resentment) after I had gone to all the trouble of getting the grant [Arts Council Grant]. There had always been a resentment about the Trustees, by the artists, although the Trustees were merely a rubber stamp, but the Society's fear of the Arts Council was that they would influence the Society in some way and over-ride the original intentions of Passmore Edwards and the old Society. Bouverie Hoyton was particularly concerned about modern cliques and a Hepworth/Nicholson infiltration, via the Arts Council'. The sums of money required to maintain a contemporary Gallery today are quite different, but there is little new, even amongst the attitudes of some.

By choosing to take on this job in mid-1994, of editing and publishing the history of the Newlyn Art Gallery, my feeling is that I have joined the long line of people from the time of Percy Craft, who have taken on more than each thought initially, and more than any one could accomplish alone. Thankfully -- and despite what Norman Garstin said in his *Studio* article of 1897, about the granite picture-gallery flung down amongst us bringing 'committee meetings' to rend the artists friend from friend -- there is not 'the one' who carries it all, but the many who contribute some and willingly. Personally, I have gained immensely in learning 'little-known facts' about exhibitors at Newlyn long-forgotten locally but of enormous interest to the art world at large. In corroboration, I must cite the discovery of Georg Jensen, the Danish silversmith, much admired by my grandmother and mother in Texas, therefore well-known by name to me. Prior to this knowledge of his three or more years of exhibition at Newlyn in the late nineteen-twenties, I visited his Copenhagen showrooms eighteen months ago. A long-time aficionado of silver, I was also delighted with the 'find' that Omar Ramsden, the fine metal-designer, exhibited at Newlyn from its first craft exhibition in 1924 until approximately a year before his death in 1939. Also that he was elected a member of the Newlyn Society of Artists in 1935. The fact that Anne Sefton, known as 'Fish' and 'Eve of the Tatler' was not only an exhibitor but also a member of The Committee, for me was simply a bonus. There are many more -- regiments of wonderful artists and craftsmen -- who deserve more than our interest, rather our gratitude for having coloured our lives.

Where further information and correction to this record is forthcoming, we will welcome it, add it to our archive, and perhaps in due course, issue an addendum. As Editor, I am aware of gaps in documenting in detail certain identifiable trends in the development of twentieth-century artistic institutions and of art itself. Surprisingly perhaps, there are few of the artists who stopped to put their reputedly strong views on record. Perhaps they were too busy working! But it is interesting to find throughout the century that there were but a handful of artists who wrote or spoke about art and its developments; these 'commentators' have been Norman Garstin, Stanhope Forbes, Elizabeth Stanhope Forbes, A J Munnings, Peter Lanyon, Michael Canney and latterly, Jeremy Le Grice. In one sense, this book is their 'Happy Birthday ' card to the Gallery at Newlyn.

The trends are there, encompassing concepts with which we are all familiar -- such as increasing secularisation, creeping managerialism, growing democracy and sometimes overwhelming bureaucracy. The multiplicity of art forms giving rise to the haunting modern question: 'but is it art?', and the popular marketing or commercialisation of art through lavish promotional material, advertisement, and gallery shops, are all themes which also thread through the history of the Passmore Edwards Art Gallery in Newlyn. What one finds in the everyday negotiations of local people-in-committee is mirrored in the rest of the art world. It is for the reader to recognise the landmarks, and the researcher to come and look more deeply. We have fertile ground.

Exterior perspective of Newlyn Art Gallery, 1994. Drawing by Robert Evans, & reprinted in *The Cornishman*

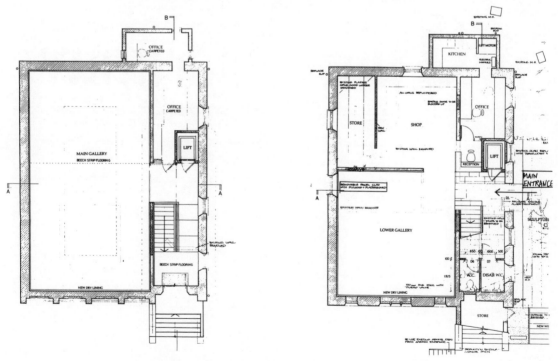

Floor plans, Newlyn Art Gallery, 1994. Drawings by Robert Evans, Architect

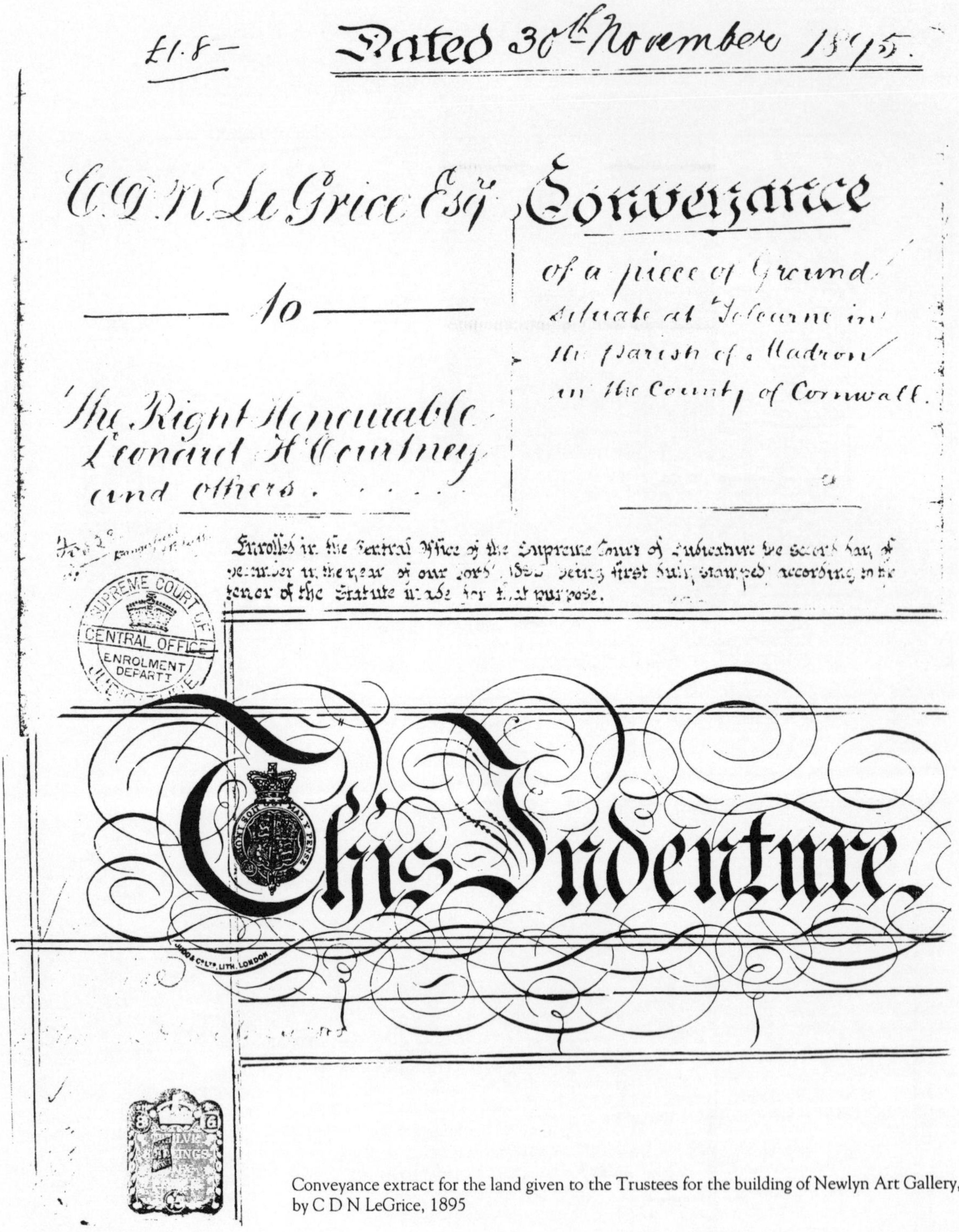

£1.8—   Dated 30th November 1895

C D N LeGrice Esq

— to —

The Right Honourable
Leonard H Courtney
and others . . . . .

Conveyance

of a piece of Ground
situate at Tolcarne in
the parish of Madron
in the County of Cornwall

Enrolled in the Central Office of the Supreme Court of Judicature the second day of
December in the year of our Lord 1895 being first duly stamped according to the
tenor of the Statute made for that purpose.

This Indenture

Conveyance extract for the land given to the Trustees for the building of Newlyn Art Gallery,
by C D N LeGrice, 1895

II: 1895 - 1904

John Passmore Edwards

from *Passmore Edwards Institutions,* by J J MacDonald

...On the day that Mr Passmore Edwards opened the Free Library at Redruth, a deputation of artists from the Newlyn Art Colony consisting of Mr Stanhope Forbes, ARA, Mr Frank Bramley, Mr Gotch and Mr Walter Langley, waited on him in reference to providing an Art Gallery at Newlyn. The result was that Mr Edwards undertook to provide the gallery, that Mr C N LeGrice gave the site, and Mr James Hicks, of Redruth, was selected as architect.

from *The Cornishman,* April, 1895

PROSECUTION OF MR PASSMORE EDWARDS

Building at Newlyn Stopped

At the West Penwith Petty Sessions at Penzance, yesterday, before Messrs C C Ross (in the chair), G P Bazeley, A Chennalls, H Laity, E L Millett, J R Branwell and Major Ross, J Passmore Edwards, of London and John and Frank Symons, Builders, Blackwater, were summoned at the instance of Madron Urban District Council for a breach of the by-laws in that before commencing to erect an art gallery at Tolcarne, they did not give notice in writing of their intention, and did not deliver complete plans and sections...Mr G L Bodilly appeared for Madron Local Board, Mr J B Cornish for Mr Passmore Edwards...

Mr Cornish said Mr Passmore Edwards was well known to all of them as one of the most generous of men of whom they were all proud, and he understood the Board would be satisfied with an explanation and an expression of regret.

The whole of the building arrangements were in the hands of Mr Edwards' architect, Mr James Hicks, who was first under the impression that the site was in the district of the Paul Urban council. Discovering his mistake, he on April 3rd sent the plans to the Madron Council but at that time the building had been technically commenced because the foundations had been got out and a concrete bed laid in. Mr Edwards was quite unaware that plans had not been sent, and now wished to express his regret that he should have been the innocent cause of a breach of the by-laws. Mr Edwards had decided at that moment to discontinue building operations...

Mr Cornish hoped Mr Edwards might reconsider his decision, because it would be very unfortunate if a mistake of that kind should deprive the neighbourhood of such a building...

from *The Times*, May 23, 1895

Mr J Passmore Edwards visited Penzance yesterday for the purpose of laying the memorial-stone of a new art gallery which he is building for the Newlyn artists. Mr Stanhope Forbes, ARA, Mr F Bramley, RA, Mr Walter Langley, Mr Norman Garstin, Mr Percy Craft, Mr Lionel Birch and Mr C T Garland of the Newlyn School, were present and took part in the ceremony. Mr Passmore Edwards, in replying to a vote of thanks, said that he had decided to build that institution because of his admiration of art and of the Newlyn School of Art, and because he wished the world at large to appreciate the beauty of Cornwall.

24

from *Passmore Edwards Institutions*
by J J MacDonald, London, 1900

...In due time and form the foundation stone of the building was laid by Mr Edwards, with Mr Stanhope Forbes as chairman. The trowel used on the occasion was not of the ordinary silver type, but one of artistic design in beaten metal--a mixture of tin and copper--an example of *repousse* work* produced in the Colony.

Mr Passmore Edwards, in response to the usual vote of thanks to foundation stone layers, said the artists residing and working in Newlyn had secured distinction by their unique craftsmanship and companionability. They had formed themselves into a school or colony, or both, and were known and criticised beyond the borders of Cornwall or the boundaries of the British Empire. In ancient times not only did individual artists compete with each other, but cities like Athens and Corinth rivalled each other in art culture and art production; and many centuries afterwards Florence, Genoa, Bologna and other Italian cities imitated the example of classic times and formed themselves into rival schools of painting and so became named. In Newlyn a number of artists had not only entitled themselves to be called a "school," but they also called themselves "colonists."

Art and colonisation did not always accompany each other, but they were, all the same, two distinguishing elements of human activity; and it so happened that whilst artists were forming a colony of their own in Cornwall, Cornishmen, in greater proportion to the inhabitants of any English portion to the inhabitants of any English county, were peopling the new colonies of the world. One of his motives in complying with the request made to him to build an Art Gallery in Newlyn was to assist to root these artistic colonists in that locality. Being there he should like to keep them there. He was, naturally, interested in anything appertaining to the good of Cornwall; and as the mines of Cornwall were drying up, under the soil, he was desirous that the world at large should know more of the scenic wealth of Cornwall on the soil, and which was scattered in rich abundance around their rugged rock-bound coasts. The Newlyn School and Colony of Artists were illustrating and interpreting that wealth in line and colour on canvas and thereby benefiting themselves, Cornwall and the world.

*It was due to the interest in this unique trowel that J D MacKenzie and his Industrial Class were commissioned by Mr Edwards to produce the four plaques for the front of the Art Gallery. For greater detail, see Berriman, *Arts and Crafts in Newlyn, 1890-1930*.

from *Arts and Crafts in Newlyn, 1890-1930*, by Hazel Berriman

The Art Gallery Plaques

The most lasting and public tribute to the work of Mackenzie and the Industrial Class are the four superb decorative plaques representing the Elements, on the facade of the Newlyn Art Gallery...

Norman Garstin observed '*On the end facing the road there are four spaces to be filled with repousse copper-work beaten by the Newlyn Industrial Class, from designs by Messrs Mackenzie and Gotch...and these panels representing 'Earth', 'Air', 'Fire' and 'Water', will, it is pretty certain, be a most interesting feature of the facade*'.

The following year he devoted a whole article in the Studio magazine to the work of the Industrial Class and the production of the plaques, which are illustrated by photographs. He states, '*These plaques were beaten on lead, by Mr Hodder, according to the system pursued by Pearson. They are exceedingly effective now, and we expect that when the weather covers them with a tone of green they will be even more pleasant.*'

25

PASSMORE EDWARDS ART GALLERY,

NEWLYN, PENZANCE.

Inaugural Exhibition.

THE

OPENING CEREMONY

WILL TAKE PLACE

On TUESDAY, 22nd October,

At 11.30 a.m., when THE RIGHT HON.

LEONARD H. COURTNEY, M.P.,

SUPPORTED BY

Right Hon. LORD St. LEVAN,   T. B. BOLITHO, Esq., M.P.

General PEEL YATES, C.B.   DAVID HOWELL, Esq., J.P.
Rev. Prebendary HEDGELAND   EDWARD HAIN, Esq., J.P.
QUILLER COUCH, Esq.   Dr. MONTGOMERY, J.P.

And others will declare the Gallery Open.   Doors open at 11 a.m. to 5 p.m.

ADMISSION to the OPENING CEREMONY, and FIRST VIEW of PICTURES, **1/-**

A PUBLIC LUNCHEON

Will be held at the "QUEEN'S" HOTEL, PENZANCE, after the Ceremony.

T. B. BOLITHO, Esq., M.P., in the Chair.

Tickets **4/-** Each, can be obtained at the Hotel, or of the Hon. Sec., Mr. PERCY R. CRAFT.

IN THE EVENING,

A CONVERSAZIONE will be held in the Gallery,

At which several Ladies and Gentlemen have kindly consented to assist.

MUSIC, DRAMATIC SKETCHES, &c.   Doors open at 8.30 p.m.   Music, &c., at 9.30 p.m.
Refreshments.   Carriages at 11.30 p.m.   Evening Dress.

Tickets for the Conversazione, price **5/-** including admission to the Opening Ceremony, can be obtained of Messrs. Beare & Son, or of the Hon. Sec.

Gallery Open on ensuing days from 10 a.m. till dusk.   ADMISSION **6**d.

F. RODDA, STEAM PRINTER, PENZANCE.

Copper plaques executed by Philip Hodder, under the supervision of John D MacKenzie,
for the facade of the Gallery, representing the elements, Earth, Air, Water, and Fire in that
order, L to R facing.

from Sheelagh O'Donnell, 'The Four Copper Plaques'

...The plaques were designed by two of the Newlyn Colony of Artists: J D Mackenzie,
who worked mainly as an illustrator and designer close to the style of the Arts and Crafts
movement, and T C Gotch, the painter, who at this time was very influenced by the
symbolic and decorative style of the Pre-Raphaelite Brotherhood. Philip Hodder was the
craftsman who made the plaques; he had been taught the art of repousse copper beating
at the Industrial Class by John Pearson.

...looking at the architect's plan and drawing for the Gallery [see Fig I], Hicks
obviously had intended that the facade should be decorated by carved frieze work, giving
his clients a choice between plaques depicting great inventions of the past or a reproduction frieze of the Elgin Marbles. It seems feasible that the Newlyn artists wanted their
gallery to be decorated by work more relevant to Newlyn and its Art Colony, and
therefore engineered Passmore Edward's introduction to the work of the Industrial
Class. When laying the foundation stone for the gallery in May 1895, he used a copper
trowel manufactured by the metal workshops there ... and afterwards was given a tour
of the Classes.

...The collaboration of the Newlyn artists and designers of the plaques with the
architect, had a definite impact on the final design of the Gallery, for the facade of the
finished building changed considerably in style from the architect's original drawing...the
final four copper plaques are very simple and bold in appeal becoming far more prominent
on the much plainer, lighter gallery facade. The angle of the roof gable end has been
altered lowering the building and changing its proportions, the windows on the ground
floor have been reduced and simplified and the heavy side buttresses have been removed.
The plaques are now larger and the profile of the corbels framing them has been changed,
shifting the curved emphasis from their base to the top. The columns either side of the
entrance door have been removed and the new gothic style doors are surrounded by a
simple stone arch. All these alterations work together to produce a definite change in
style for the building which now shows clearly the influence of the Arts and Crafts
movement in architectural design...a movement that had grown out of the philosophy
of Ruskin and Morris -- in reaction against the art establishment. Their new aesthetic
encouraged working directly from nature using subjects closely linked to England's own
heritage...calling attention back to the rural traditions with their emphasis on "Art made
by the people and for the people, a joy to the maker and the user." [William Morris, 'The
Beauty of Life']

...John Pearson spent six years in Newlyn and had been working with the Industrial Class for three years when they accepted the commission to make the copper plaques...The subject chosen for the plaques was the four elements -- earth, air, fire and water -- a relatively abstract and Biblical subject that must have appealed to both artists [J Mackenzie, T C Gotch]. They chose to treat the subject in both a figurative and symbolic manner with a combined approach that reflects very clearly their two different styles of work at this time. [Fig a, b, c, d]...

...Mackenzie produced most of the designs and transfers for the work of the metalwork classes, working straight from nature and often depicting such local subjects as fish, seabirds, shells, seaweed and flowers. All of his designs were simple and direct in approach without too much attention to fine detail.

...By 1895 Gotch had established his own style frequently called 'romantic symbolism' which explored childhood and womanhood, often within a religious medieval setting...He painted with a dreamlike quality using meticulous realism and decorative detail.

...Pearson had a more elaborate and ornate approach to design than Mackenzie and his influence clearly can be seen in the copper working of the plaques...He had developed the practice of beating the copper onto a lead rather than pitch base; it was the soft yet resilient nature of lead that made such depths of style possible. He had also introduced a direct, almost engraved, approach into his work which enabled him to include much delicate detailing into his designs.

...Although the plaques were beaten by Philip Hodder, one of the students at the Industrial Class, Pearson must have overseen their production with great care, and the use of his clearly marked tooling technique is much in evidence in the finished work.

The Newlyn copper plaques were conceived within the confines of a craft-based workshop, yet they displayed many of the fine art qualities of a painting or piece of sculpture. It is in this way that they brought together two of the nineteenth centuries strongest movements in art and design. The Pre-Raphaelites and the Arts and Crafts movements had developed alongside each other sharing the same roots -- in the philosophy and work of Ruskin and Morris -- and it was this equality in the foundation of their beliefs that enabled them to fuse together so successfully in one unique piece of work.

from *The Cornishman*, Saturday, October 19, 1895

OPENING THE NEWLYN ART GALLERY

Interview with Mr Stanhope Forbes, ARA

"Then you have no fear that the Newlyn artists will desert the locality made famous by their works?" I said to Mr Stanhope A Forbes, ARA. The new art gallery erected by Mr Passmore Edwards seems solid and durable enough, built as it is mainly of Cornish granite, but some people have wondered how a large number of artists could long be expected to find fresh subjects for their brushes in such a limited area, and some members of the colony have certainly proved themselves to be birds of passage.

"I never thought" replied Mr Forbes, "that there was much chance of the Newlyn colony dwindling. As long as the beauty of the county lasts it will always attract painters...Even if modern builders, imbued with excusably utilitarian ideas, succeed in thoroughly defacing the village, they can hardly rob the moorlands, Mount's Bay and the fisherfolk of their distinctive and picturesque characteristics...I hope it will attract many really good men who will try to keep it up on the lines of its founders."

"And those lines are...?"

"Well, we wish the people of Penzance and neighbourhood to understand that the gallery is a public institution, not an artists' club, and it is only with the intention that the public shall participate in the advantages of having such a gallery in the locality that we have accepted the public-spirited offer of Mr Passmore Edwards, and are zealously co-operating to make it attractive to visitors...

"It will be thrown open to the public," said he, "and the charge for admission on most days will be 6d, but on special occasions, such as private-view days, the charge will be 1s...To make the public feel they have a real interest in its success we invite support on several lines. Anyone who wishes to become a life-member with the title of Donor can do so by giving a donation of not less than ten pounds. These donors will be entitled to two season-tickets and two tickets to a conversazione to be given each year. Or the same privileges can be obtained by payment of an annual subscription of one guinea...We also hope to derive an income from letting the gallery for entertainments, dances, etc and we are going to charge a commission on the sale of pictures, so there will be a three-fold source of revenue to meet the cost of maintenance...

"...an occasional break will be necessary if the quality is to be maintained at a high level. We shall endeavour to hold the exhibitions as frequently as possible on Cornish lines, and we shall have a very representative collection. We have not found it necessary to break our rule even in order to secure works by the president of the Academy, for Sir Frederic Leighton spent some time at Kynance and the Lizard a year or so ago...

Stanhope Forbes, painted by Elizabeth Stanhope Forbes, 1889

CORNISH TELEGRAPH
Thursday, October 24, 1895

PASSMORE-EDWARDS ART GALLERY

The Opening Ceremony

Speeches by Lord St Levan, Mr Court-ney, MP, and Mr Bolitho, MP

The gallery presented by Mr Passmore Edwards to the Newlyn Art Colony and built on land given by Mr C D N Legrice, was formally opened on Tuesday in the presence of a numerous company of ladies and gentlemen. A temporary platform had been erected at one end of the gallery to accommodate the speakers and others. Lord St Levan presided, and was supported on the platform by Lady St Levan, Mr Bolitho MP and Mrs Bolitho, the Rev Prebendary Hedgeland, the Hon John St Aubyn, the Right Hon Leonard Courtney, MP and Mrs Courtney, General and Mrs Peel Yates...&c

...[The Chairman] acknowledged the debt which, in his opinion, they in Corn-wall owed to the members of the Newlyn Art Colony. In the first place they con-tributed to the education and formation of the tastes of the people of the neighbour-hood, and in the second place they con-ferred celebrity on the locality. Newlyn, if he might say so without offence, was not a particularly celebrated place before their advent; it was known as a fishing centre and history recorded the fact that it was burnt by the Spaniards in the sixteenth century, but otherwise it was not famous. Now, however, it was the home of a school of artists, and that was a great distinction.

They had heard of the schools of Bo-logna, of Venice, of Milan, and in later years of Dusseldorf and Munich, but he was not aware that any place in the United Kingdom had previously given a distinctive name to a separate school of art. They were also, he considered, the means of bestow-ing practical benefits on many people in the neighbourhood...

...The Right Hon Leonard Courtney, MP, said it appeared that a Member of Parliament was supposed to be able to talk about anything; to open a chapel, a school, a bazaar, or an art exhibition was all the same...He had heard elsewhere that when Mr Passmore Edwards selected an object for his generosity some little embarrass-ment was occasionally produced. There were persons who doubted the utility and expedience of everything...he did not know whether any feelings of that kind ever arose about this art gallery. But, if there were pessimists in relation to this institution their pessimism must disappear if they came there and saw what they saw that day. There were pessimists about everything; there were people who would abstain from all action because it might not turn out so productive of good as one could desire, but if these people could have their way the world would come to an end....the value of it [the gallery] would depend upon the things which were put in it. He might say to them, with some assur-ance, "If you want to discover the value of the Passmore-Edwards gallery look around you; if you want a monument here it is on the walls."...He then formally declared the Gallery open. (Applause)

...Mr. Stanhope Forbes, ARA, gave some particulars of the circumstances which had led up to the erection of the gallery and the establishment of the scheme for working in it... While the build-ing was being erected, the problem of its maintenance seemed no nearer solution until at last they hit upon a plan which they had carried out. It was not their own in-vention, it had been carried out with great success in New York, where a large institu-tion was similarly managed; and he here expressed their indebtedness to Mr Ho-ward Buller, an American artist, who had given them a vast amount of useful infor-mation and advice. They decided on asking for the support of the people of the county and neighbourhood, and the response had been most generous...(applause)

29

from *The Cornishman*, October 24, 1895

OPENING THE NEWLYN ART GALLERY

The Luncheon

Mr T B Bolitho, MP presided at the luncheon at the Queen's Hotel, Penzance, which was well attended. The usual loyal toasts were proposed from the chair, with a reference to the artistic tastes of some members of the Royal family who wield the chisel and brush...

...Mr JOHN B CORNISH proposed the health of the guests and spoke of the fame of the school. People have been asking "What is this school?" and have readily been told "It is a large college near Penzance." (Laughter) Amongst those who have done most to bring Cornwall into notice in the literary world is the man who has erected Troy Town upon Dead Man's Rock. (Laughter)

Mr A T QUILLER-COUCH, in response, said he took it the welcome they had given the guests might be compared with the cheers that salute the vanguard of an army.

He took it they are the vanguard of a host of visitors who are going to follow the course of empire westward to the Newlyn Art Gallery. The feelings of the guests were that they had come down to witness a testimony in solid stone and mortar to a brief experiment in the history of Art. Some say that it is more than an experiment. Undoubtedly it has left its mark already upon the history of art for this century. He thought Mr Forbes and his art friends would be the first to smile at him if he were to pretend to complacently say Newlyn had said the last word about art. If that were the case the building would indeed be a monument but a sepulchral monument. (Hear hear)

For in art finality means death. Art lives by experiment and the pursuit of an idea. They were there that day to commemorate a colony which had come there after an idea and had thrust that idea upon a nation not too tolerant of ideas. They had chosen carefully and were happy in their choice of Cornwall and cornwall was proud of their choice (hear hear) because they have given Cornish people to see their own county with new eyes, and yet to see it as it is. There are "carpet baggers" in art as well as in politics. He had known people quite capable to coming to Newlyn shore and painting there a Highland lassie with a pet lamb in a snow-storm. (Loud laughter) But these gentlemen of Newlyn have studied Cornwall patiently and given us much and why this memorial now stands at Newlyn. (Applause) But if they asked what the visitors are to do to show their gratitude the question staggered him. He had looked around on the present company and had seen many whose features were at once typically Cornish and well worthy of preserving for the contemplation of posterity. (Laughter) They might begin with the members of parliament, but they had already begun with the Mayor of Penzance. He had read the speeches made the previous night at the presentation dinner to the Mayor and thought for obvious reasons the Mayor of Market-jew would make a bad sitter, (laughter)

Arthur Quiller-Couch, age approximately 32 in 1895, when he spoke to the inaugural luncheon.
Photo courtesy of Cornwall County Records Office

but hoped soon to catch the train to Truro, where he should meet many mayors and he should have the opportunity during 26 speeches (laughter) of studying the municipal features of the chief Cornish boroughs, and will be able no doubt, if necessary, to prepare a report for the Newlyn school. He thanked them for their toast, as a Cornishman, and as a humble practitioner of an art which, in some respects, is allied to the art they had come there to celebrate that day. (Applause)

Mr FORBES proposed the health of Mr Bolitho which was drunk with musical honours.

Mr BOLITHO said it was one of the most agreeable and pleasant afternoons he had ever spent.

The Opening Exhibition
[List compiled from *The Cornishman*, October 24, 1895 and the sales record book of PEAG]
Exhibitors
Mr Lionel Birch
Mr Ireland Blackburne
Mr Frank Bramley
Mr Charles E Brittan
Mr A J W Browne
Mr Arnesby Brown
Mr Chevallier Tayler
Mr S H Carr
Mr R H Carter
Mr W Casley
Mr George Clausen
Mr Percy R Craft
Mr J DaCosta
Mr Lowell Dyer
Mr F M Evans
Mr C A Evo
Mr Folliott Stokes
Mrs Elizabeth Armstrong Forbes
Mr Stanhope Forbes
Mr W Fortescue
Mr C T Garland
Mr Norman Garstin
Mrs Caroline Gotch

Mr T C Gotch
Mr Harold Harvey
Mr Charles Napier Hemy
Miss R Holmes
Mr G Sherwood Hunter
Mr George W Jevons
Mr Walter Langley
Sir Frederick Leighton
Mr Leonard Lewis
Mr GBPS Lillingston
Mr H Martin (the original 'Newlynite')
Mr Arthur Meade
Mr J O Nash
Mr H L Norris
Mr Julius Olsson
Mr H M Rheam
Mr H H Robinson
Mrs Robinson
Mr Algernon Talmage
Mr Arthur J Tanner
Mr R C Todd
Mr H S Tozer
Mr J C Uren
Miss Wing

Opening Exhibition
22 October - 14 November, 1895
Sales £323/-/-
Commission to Gallery £32/6/6
23 paintings sold at exhibition, 4 by arrangement after
At least 141 paintings exhibited, perhaps a few more.*
Sales made by Lionel Birch, Frank Bramley, Charles E Brittan, W Casley, P R Craft (2 sold), F M Evans (3), Elizabeth Forbes (3), C T Garland, Norman Garstin (2), Caroline Gotch, T C Gotch, Miss R Holmes, G Sherwood Hunter (2), Walter Langley, GBPS Lillingston, H L Norris, Henry M Rheam (3), and H S Tozer.

Purchasers included John Jones, Esq of Falmouth (11 paintings), T R Bolitho, MP (4 paintings), Richard Bolitho (3 paintings) and Mrs Stanhope Forbes who paid ten guineas for Frank Bramley's painting (title not given, but sketch reserved). T A Dagg, Esq purchased Charles E Brittan's 'Near Princetown, Dartmoor' for the Royal Cornwall Infirmary, Truro.

*[Editor's note: In the sales book, each painting sold is given an identification number and an artist, though not always a title. The number of exhibited paintings can only be estimated by the highest identification number listed as sold. There may have been more paintings exhibited which did not sell.]

from the Minutes of General Meeting held at the Gallery, Nov 14, 1895

Present: Messrs Langley, Rheam, Gotch, Craft, Garland, Hall, Blackburne, Todd, Evans, Forbes, Crooke, Mrs Forbes, Miss Gotch, Mrs Lionel Birch

Mr Gotch was voted into the Chair.

...the Hon Secretary's position had to be filled owing to the resignation of Mr P R Craft but at the same time stated that a scheme was being considered to obtain a deputy secretary and that therefore the point might be left to the decision of the Committee.

Mr Langley proposed that a circular be sent round to the Guarantors suggesting that they allow their guarantee to take the form of an annual subscription of one guinea...

Sketch Exhibition
December 19, 1895 - 6 January, 1896
Sales £99/15/-
22 sketches sold at exhibition

At least 117 sketches exhibited, perhaps more. Sales made by Mrs Lionel Birch, Frank Bramley (2), Elizabeth Forbes (3), Stanhope Forbes, Norman Garstin, Miss K Goode, Miss Holmes (3), J D MacKenzie, H L Norris, H M Rheam (7), A J Tanner.

Purchasers included Mrs T R Bolitho (3), Dr Evershed (3), Percy R Craft (2), Stanhope Forbes (2), and J D MacKenzie who paid six guineas for Frank Bramley's 'Magnolia'.

from the Minutes of General Meeting held on January 4, 1896

Present: Langley, Gotch (Chair), Garland, Birch, Evans, Rheam

...Proposed and seconded, that the Executive Committee consist of six with power to appoint an Hon Sec either from their own number or from the guarantors with power to fill vacancies in the committee caused by absence. Following elected to the committee: Messrs Forbes, Gotch, Garstin, (Lionel) Birch, Rheam and Hall, for 1896.

...Proposed Garstin, seconded Forbes, that commission shall be paid on any picture negotiated for during the exhibitions. Carried, three dissenting...

...Mr Foster would assist the secretary in his duties.

Signature: Percy R Craft

from *The Studio,* April 15th, 1896

NEWLYN -- In former years it was the custom for the painters to collect their pictures into a group of studios overlooking the grey roofs of Newlyn and Mounts Bay, and to send out invitations to all the world to come and see-- and all the world came and saw. But now the Art Gallery seems the natural place for this function, and accordingly, not without some regrets over the changing of the old order and the commercial basis of the new, it was settled to show our spring goods in the Gallery.

A Parisian wit once remarked of the omnibuses that ply between the Odeon and Clichy that they were an utter failure, and might as well be suppressed, because they were always so full that one could never get into them. Something of this kind of failure was the fate of the Art Gallery venture; it was so full that no one could see the pictures -- though, for that matter, the same thing was said for years of the exhibitions in the studios.

Fifth Exhibition*
July - October, 1896, with re-arrangement in October
Sales £220/6/-
Commission to Gallery £22/17/-
After rearrangement: Sales £17/17/-
Commission to Gallery £1/16/-
Sales made by: F W Baker, Frank Bateson, Lionel Birch (2), Mrs Lionel Birch, A J W Browne, Percy R Craft, Elizabeth Forbes, E G Fuller, Walter Langley, Alfred Mitchell, H M Rheam (2), G B Spooner, and after re-arrangement by C T Garland, Norman Garstin, and S Lillingston.

Purchasers included John Jones, Esq (5) who has since moved from Falmouth to Wolverhampton, and who on this occasion paid record prices for Mrs Forbes "The Sage of the Wood" (£80) and for H M Rheam's "Gathering of the Mistletoe" (£60) which accounts for almost two-thirds of the sales from the exhibition.

*[Editor's note: The Exhibition book continues in similar fashion until the 51st Exhibition, which was held in August of 1913 or 1914 (undated), soon after which the Gallery was closed for the duration of the Great War.]

Some famous names & when their first sale at the Gallery was recorded, in the first sales record

Fred Hall -- November, 1896
H S Tuke -- November, 1896
Julius Olsson -- March, 1897
S J Lamorna Birch -- September, 1897
Leghe Suthers -- December, 1897
Harold Harvey -- October, 1899
Frances Hodgkins -- April, 1902
Frank G Heath -- May, 1902
Benjamin E Leader -- May, 1904
A Chevallier Tayler -- July, 1904
Ernest Procter -- July, 1904
G Wolseley -- July, 1908
Charles W Simpson -- July, 1909
C S Mottram -- June, 1910
Harold Knight -- September, 1910
Robert Morson Hughes -- 51st Exhibition

from the Minutes of the Guarantors Meeting, 1896 (undated)

Present: Messrs Lewis, Birch, Mrs [Lionel] Birch, MacKenzie, Evans, Craft, Rheam, Foster

...The Society read Mr John Cornish' letter of thanks for the Album...*

It was decided to send a cheque for five guineas to the Secretary of the Cornish Miners Relief Fund, Camborne.

Thanks were accorded to Mr MacKenzie for Copper Plaques.

Tea was arranged for in the Gallery for future at approx 6d per head...

*[A large leatherbound volume of prints, drawings and engravings by the artists of the Newlyn school, was presented to John Cornish, in gratitude for all the legal work he had done toward the establishment of the Passmore Edwards Art Gallery, throughout its planning and building phases. He was to continue to serve the Gallery for more than thirty years, as Trustee, Hon Solicitor, and Hon Treasurer. This album, presented back to the Art Gallery in 1927, at John Cornish's death, forms part of the Archives, and may be seen at Penlee House.]

from *Newlyn Copper* by John Curnow Laity, Newlyn Copper Exhibition (1986), Penwith Town Council

...John D MacKenzie stands head and shoulders above the rest as instigator, innovator, and artist craftsman of the Newlyn Copperworkers. Arts and Crafts had been very much practised by local individuals long before he came to Newlyn in the late 1880s but it was he who not only inspired and created the classes for young men, but persevered in teaching them for nearly two decades...MacKenzie came to Newlyn in his late twenties, an educated and mature young man having, during the previous decade, established himself in the London art world and gained some reputation as a painter...John MacKenzie began developing what has become the 'real' Newlyn copper before the turn of the century. He produced a host of patterns mostly associated with Newlyn, its indigenous industries and the local scene, marine and bird life. Undoubtedly fish designs became the favourite with all concerned although fruit, luggers, cormorants and galleons all appeared repeatedly on a variety of pieces...

Two paintings by Stanhope Forbes of the village industries, picturing John D MacKenzie, supervisor and teacher with his pupils

from the Minutes of the Trustees Meeting, December 5, 1896
Present: Rev T N Perkins, John Cornish, Committee: Stanhope Forbes, Lionel Birch, Evans and H M Rheam
Accounts showing balance in hand
Deposit £71/15/-
Current a/c £48/7/3
Cash £3/17/1
Total £123/19/4 Approved and passed
Executive Committee reported that Gallery had been successful and in their opinion the plan adopted would continue to work satisfactorily.
The Trustees inspected the premises and it was left to the Executive Committee to call Symons attention to the condition of the East Wall and...to obtain estimates for necessary repairs.
Signature: John B Cornish

from the Minutes of the PEAG Gallery General Meeting, September 22, 1897
Present: Mrs Garstin (Chair-Woman) Messrs Forbes, Garstin, Hunter, Craft, Garland, Evans, Birch & Rheam (Hon Sec)
...proposed and seconded that Mr [Lionel] Birch undertakes to get up some other operetta for conversazione.
...that Rheam should communicate with the Nunns about music.
...that Messrs Forbes, Gotch & Hunter be appointed to consider whether it could be possible to act a scene from Shakespeare. Carried, Craft dissenting.
...Mr Garstin proposed that the Entertainments to run two nights...
Trustees to allow the Dramatic Club to meet in Gallery.

Minutes of the Trustees Meeting, January 19, 1898 [Full transcript! Ed]
Present: J B Cornish; Committee: Hunter, Gotch, Garstin, Langley, Rheam, Foster
Accounts approved & adopted by JBC on behalf of Trustees.
The state of the Gallery was gone into & it was decided that Mr Cornish should call the attention either of Symons or Passmore Edwards to the matter.

from *Cornish Post*, March 24, 1898
We must compress our comment on the other pictures into a small compass, though many are worthy of ampler notice. In "Walls have ears" one figure, that of the eavesdropper, has been vividly painted by Mr Percy H Craft. The best of Mrs Forbes' pictures, we think, was that of "Imogen lying among the flowers that's like thy face, pale primrose" -- a notable work.

from the Minutes of The Committee Meeting, November 24, 1898
Mr Garland's application for Gallery, Dec 5 & 6 readily granted...allowing him same free of charge, provided he announces the close of Gallery for the time...
Mrs Forbes Private View to be held Dec 20.
Proposed and seconded 'That in future it is the duty of The Committee to consider the selection of a new artist subscriber on the recommendation of any artist subscriber.' Carried.
Two dozen additional chairs to be obtained to be left in the hands of the Hon Sec.
Mr Gotch was permitted the use of the Gallery on Feb 3 & 10th for the lecture he proposes to give in aid of the Newlyn Nursing Fund.

from *Cornish Post*, Spring, 1899 (undated)

The Newlyn Artists

A Peep at their pictures for the Royal Academy.

One of the charms of the annual show-day at Newlyn is that we renew our acquaintance with the works of celebrities who have made Newlyn famous. New comers are not without interest, but those who have for eight or ten years regularly seen the masterpieces of the Newlyn colony naturally know something of the leaders, their style and their usual sources of inspiration, and wonder how they have fared in the last twelve months. It is pleasant to conjure up many notable productions of former days and compare them with the canvases on the walls of the Passmore Edwards Art Gallery; and it is not pleasant to remember that many talented and familiar painters of other years are no longer represented at Newlyn. For instance we recall F Bramley's black eyes and see him putting a few finishing touches to "The Golden Wedding". We recall the cheery and well-beloved Bateman who died in California; John Da Costa, Ralph Todd, Leghe Suthers, John Crooke, Frank Richards, E R Ireland Blackburne, and Chevallier Tayler, who have either temporarily or permanently cut themselves adrift from Newlyn, leaving us all the poorer.

And as if that were not bad enough we this year have no picture from Mr Stanhope Forbes, ARA, because the remarkable cartoon of the Great Fire of London which Mr Forbes painted for the Royal Exchange, London, was his great work for the year. We miss the work of Mrs Forbes and Mrs Gotch; we look in vain for one of the masterpieces of Mr Fred Hall; and in conversation we get another shock -- Mr T C Gotch and Mr Percy Craft are on the brink of deserting Newlyn in favour of somewhere nearer the metropolis. Let us hope that for the sake of old times they will continue to send pictures to Newlyn and so remain members of the colony, though separated from it by many a league.

36

from an unattributed cutting, spring, 1899, referring to the same exhibition as above

ACADEMY PICTURES AT NEWLYN

...Apart from this noteworthy absence [of Mr & Mrs Stanhope Forbes], the pictures exhibited well maintained the standard of excellence of previous years. One feature of the exhibition was that it was essentially a cheerful one: there was entire absence of the weird and the sad which have sometimes been seen at similar exhibitions in the Art Gallery...

from the Minutes of the General Meeting, January 10, 1900
Elected to The Committee -- Forbes, Garstin, Birch, Hunter, Langley, Rheam
...It was proposed to approach the Trustees with the object of obtaining increased support to the Institution.

from the Minutes of The Committee, July 1, 1900
To get estimates from Peak for decoration of Gallery.

from the Letters of Frances Hodgkins, Linda Gill [Editor]
'FH went to England equipped with some useful information. She had probably made up her mind before leaving New Zealand to study at the artists' colony at Newlyn, the fishing village on the south coast of Cornwall near Penzance. Two Newlyn artists, Norman Garstin (1847 - 1926) and Stanhope Forbes (1857 - 1948), had exhibited in the 1889-90 New Zealand and South Seas Exhibition in Dunedin, and the latter's "Preparations for the Market, Quimperle, Brittany" had been bought for the Dunedin Art Gallery in 1890 when William Mathew Hodgkins was active in gallery affairs...'

to Rachel Hodgkins [Mother of FH, in New Zealand] from Grand Hotel, Oneglia Italy, February 8, 1902

> *...We are looking forward to going down to Penzance & meeting the artists there. We have mapped out a rough sort of plan for the year -- we though we should go abroad again in July either with the Garstins or Mr Stanhope Forbes, this time to Brittany, and then about Sept make our way slowly South to Venice & paint there for a month or two...& then return to England...*

to Isabel Field [Sister] from 1 Wellington Terrace, Penzance

> *...We are housed two doors from the Garstins* with a friend of theirs, a Miss Parks, a kind old thing who treats us very well...we are paying 30/- this week but after that by foregoing late dinner & having tea instead she is taking us for 25/-. Of course we could do it cheaper than this by boarding ourselves but neither of us feel equal to it just at present...*

*[Linda Gill (Editor) writes, 'In Norman Garstin she found an excellent mentor. An articulate, well-informed Irishman of great personal charm, he had painted in Belgium, Paris, and Morocco, admired Manet, tolerated the French impressionists, who never completely appealed to English taste, and loved Japanese art. Unlike many English painters he had only a very small private income and had to rely on selling paintings, teaching and writing to support his family.']

to her sister, [Penzance] March 27, 1902

We have been here now three weeks & it has blown & rained & drizzled & fogged in what the Cornish people try to make us believe is an unprecedented manner but we know better -- we have had two or three fine days and everyone seemed so inordinately proud of them & swaggered so much that we saw at once how unused they are to good weather. Penzance is not beautiful tho' they try to make you believe it is -- but Newlyn a mile away along a muddy road is charming -- it is a fishing village (but your nose tells you that long before you reach it) -- & the queer uneven streets & the forests of trawlers in the harbor make it a much more interesting place than Penzance...

The next day was our show -- that is Newlyn. We have a gallery of our own & are very proud of it. It was a brave show & the Stanhope Forbes' work raised it to a much higher level. Her work was magnificent -- much better than her husband's -- they were mostly Shakespearian, mediaeval things -- but they simply sang with color & light & brilliancy -- no one could touch her -- she is head & shoulders above them all down here or in fact in England. I think she is pretty generally regarded as the first woman artist in England -- she together with Mrs Adrian Stokes [Marianne, nee Preindlsburger]. I had 5 things on the walls 3 for the Academy & 2 for the New English Arts Club & they all said nice things about them -- & seemed to think I painted like Arthur Melville, which is rubbish -- or if it is [true] it is quite unconscious. I went down in the morning with Mr Garstin and was introduced to Mr & Mrs Forbes -- W Langley, Rheam RI, Lamorna Birch & several others, it was all very nice & interesting. Mrs Stanhope has asked me to go & see her & I am to go this Saturday...I am at Mrs Forbes feet -- she wins one with her strength of color & design -- tho I dont want to be influenced by her -- merely seeing her work helps one.

to her mother, 13 April 1902

...I have already committed myself to a studio & feel more inclined to work indoors for a bit...This studio is at Newlyn and I am paying 10/- a month for it furnished, the artist is away till June. It is a nice little room & has as one of its properties the old table which Frank Bramley put in his famous "Hopeless Dawn" & next door is the identical cottage in which he painted it...

to her mother, 29 May 1902

...We are very sad at leaving Penzance...You and I will have to come back here & live some day. They never die in these parts -- nearly everyone lives to over a 100...

from the Minutes of the General Meeting, March 23, 1904

Forbes (in the Chair)

...Proposed Garstin, seconded Mackenzie that in view of the prosperous condition of the Gallery and the services of the Secretary in providing of, that a sum of 40 pounds inclusive of salary be given to Mr Rheam for the financial year.

...that the Secretary be instructed to apply to John Cornish for the land-deed in order to make a copy of same to be kept in the Gallery.

...that John B Cornish be invited to act as Hon Treasurer...that Garstin be appointed to approach Mr J B Cornish on the subject...that the pennies received between 5 & 6pm on Show Day from the Newlyn people be handed to the Nursing Fund.

Signature: Stanhope A Forbes

Norman Garstin, painted by Elizabeth Stanhope Forbes. Published in *The Paper Chase*, 1909.

Newlyn Penzance April 15

Dear Mr Secretary

I see that the copper plaques are getting very dusty and dull.

If the Committee wish them to be kept at all bright they should be rubbed over frequently, with a cloth and some petroleum.

If Deacon* cannot get up to them by means of a ladder - I believe a long brush like those used for cleaning windows - would do sufficiently well to keep the raised parts of the designs plain and clean. I am, yours truly, John D Mackenzie

40

FRED HALL.
SKETCHED BY PHIL MAY.

from the *Fred Hall Scrapbook*, Newlyn Archives.

III: 1905-1914

illustration of wood-block by Winfred Tennyson Jesse ('Fryn') for *The Paper Chase,* Summer, 1909, a journal published Elizabeth Armstrong Forbes, of which Fryn was the Editor, her pseudonym being 'The March Hare'.

from Mrs Lionel Birch, *Stanhope A Forbes, ARA and Elizabeth Stanhope Forbes, ARWS*

...There used to be one day of the year when the meadow, and, indeed, all Newlyn, was *en fete*. This was "Show Day," when the pictures intended for the Academy were exhibited, and all the studios thrown open to the public. Then the gay crowd streamed in and out of the studios, some ramshackle, some spacious and well-built, some hidden in creepers and under trees. Greetings were exchanged and congratulations made to the artists, for whom the people of the neighbouring town have always cherished kindly feelings; and when tea was served in the sunny field, with its clumps of flowers and glorious outlook, 'Show Day' seemed like a pleasant picnic.

But these things belong to the past. The yearly show is now held in the Art Gallery -- Mr Passmore Edwards' gift to the painters of Newlyn; and a new generation has taken possession of the meadow."

Committee meeting March 1907
Present: Hunter, Rheam, Langley, Garstin, Mackenzie
...that students be allowed in [RA show] from 10am to 12noon only.
...that the Secretary be instructed to apply to Lanham for an estimate for cost of canopy for Gallery.

General Meeting, April 12, 1907
Present: Forbes (Chair), Mrs Forbes, Garstin, Langley, Dick, Heath, Lionel Birch, Lamorna Birch, Hunter, Evans, Harvey
...that the AGM shall in future be held during April.
...that the Secretary's salary of 40 pounds a year having been drawn from the last General meeting in 1904 be confirmed.
...that the salary of the Secretary shall remain at 40 pounds a year during the continuance of the prosperity of the Gallery & while the accounts show a profit on the year's working.
...that the number of members on the committee be raised to 8. Lost.
A new committee was then elected, namely: Langley, Garstin, Forbes, Hunter, Dick.
Mr Garstin announced that Mr John Cornish had accepted the position of Hon Treas.

from *A Portrait of Fryn, A Biography of F Tennyson Jesse*, by Joanna Colenbrander

...To this simple place [The school of Stanhope and Elizabeth Forbes, in The Meadow, at Newlyn] Fryn came in her nineteenth year...She and Cicely [C Jesse, her cousin, who was to meet there and marry the Norwegian painter, Cardale Luck] settled in at Myrtle Cottage, which they were to share with Mrs Shaw and her daughter Dod...'At Myrtle Cottage we had a trick of talking in double-inversion between ourselves, and we became so adept at it that we rarely fell into normal speech,' wrote Fryn. In no time at all, everyone had a new name derived in this fashion. Mrs Forbes became Forces Mibs, and indeed she was called Mibs until the day of her death and she loved the name...Myrtle Cottage was always The Myrtage...

...Dod Shaw, as Dod Procter was then, was much the cleverest of the students, not only as regards drawing and painting, where she was streets ahead of anyone else except Ernest Procter whom she eventually married, but in the management of her life. 'We used sometimes to have fancy-dress dances, known as drencies, in the studios, to which the Professor--as we always called Stanhope--and his wife came with their son Alec...(pages 43-44)

42

...Another suggestion Mibs made was that it would be a good thing if they produced a magazine, and that Fryn must be the editor. It was called *The Paper Chase,* and was printed at the little printing works in the village, which was run by amateurs. But it took such a great amount of time and energy that it was all they could do to produce one annually. 'We only had two volumes of it before it died a natural death by Mibs becoming ill. ..The first copy appeared in March 1908, on fourteen-inch hand-cut art paper. The reproductions were by Lamorna Birch, Ernest Procter and Elizabeth Stanhope Forbes and are of high quality...(page 47)

...25 March 1908 [from her 'Intermittent Diary'] Show Day, and we all went down to the Gallery. The pictures were mostly splendid, and St Ives admitted we had licked them into fits. The Professor had his big portrait; Mibs her sunny oil of three children; Mrs Knight had a beautiful small oil, "Child with Toy"; and Mr Knight had a village wedding procession that was clever, but I was disappointed in it...(page 51)

Charcoal sketch of Samuel John 'Lamorna' Birch by Elizabeth Armstrong Forbes for the first edition of *The Paper Chase* in 1908.

FOREWORD

To the Judicious Reader,

Comrades of other Seasons, who have wandered far from the fair West Country: Intelligent Sir or Madam, we venture—with a tug of the forelock—to attract your attention. We are a company of youngsters newly equipped for the road of life, pencil and note-book in hand, and knapsack on shoulder.

Like the cheap-jack with his ribbons and laces, so we with our wares. Only give us leave to open our pedlar's pack, and we will set in order before you its Contents :—

PRINTED BY

Published by Mrs. Stanhope Forbes, Meadow Studio, Newlyn.
Printed by R. T. Dick, J. D. Mackenzie, and D. Gilardoni, at the Newlyn Press, Gwavas Studios, Newlyn.
Reproductions printed by The Swan Electric Engraving Company, Ltd., London.

1

CONTENTS

THE NEWLYN PRESS.

General Meeting, April 12, 1907

Present: Forbes (Chair), Mrs Forbes, Garstin, Langley, Dick, Heath, Lionel Birch, Lamorna Birch, Hunter, Evans, Harvey

...that the AGM shall in future be held during April.

...that the Secretary's salary of 40 pounds a year having been drawn from the last General meeting in 1904 be confirmed.

...that the salary of the Secretary shall remain at 40 pounds a year during the continuance of the prosperity of the Gallery & while the accounts show a profit on the year's working.

...that the number of members on the committee be raised to 8. Lost.

A new committee was then elected, namely: Langley, Garstin, Forbes, Hunter, Dick.

Mr Garstin announced that Mr John Cornish had accepted the position of Hon Treas.

44

from *Journal of the Women's Art Slide Library*, May/June 1990 by Katy Deepwell

Dod (Doris) Shaw studied under Stanhope and Elizabeth Forbes in Newlyn in 1907-8, and for a short period at the Atelier Colarossi in Paris. Perhaps her concentration on the single woman figure and children shows the indirect influence of the work of Elizabeth Forbes, and her careful controlled use of silvery light that of Stanhope Forbes. She met her future husband Ernest Procter in Newlyn at the Forbes school in The Meadow. Their circle of friends included Harold and Laura Knight, Lamorna Birch and A J Munnings: all were to become members of the R A in the twenties and thirties...In 1912 Dod and Ernest Procter married. They had one son, Bill, born in 1913...'They talked literature, some wrote tales & poems, some did woodcuts, some painted, some did all three. They dressed in tussore, silk, browns, and art colours...'

from the Minutes of General Meeting, April 21, 1908

Present: J B Cornish, Langley, Forbes, Garstin, Dick, Hunter, Rheam, Gotch, Heath

...that the Committee be requested to address the question of the investment of the funds of the Gallery and to take action accordingly. Carried.

...that a donation of 5 pds be given to the Artists General Benevolent Fund out of the funds of the Gallery.

New committee was elected: Garstin, Langley, Hunter, Dick, Forbes.

from the Minutes of Committee Meeting, Oct 5, 1908

...with reference to the loss in cash at the Gallery mentioned by the Secretary, the Committee decided to refund the amount (10/-/-) out of the Gallery funds.

...It was then decided to spend about 30 pds improving the appearance of the Gallery and vestibule, and a committee was appointed to undertake the job.

from the Minutes of General Meeting, Oct 5, 1908

Present: Cornish, Forbes, Hunter, Langley, Dick, Rheam

Mr Cornish announced that he proposed to invest the money in Natal 3 1/2% accountable stock 1934.

...that the accounts be audited by Messrs Gotch & Mackenzie in conjunction with J Doidge.

Wesleyan
College
Apl. 13. '09.

PENZANCE.

Dear Sir.

It has occurred to me more

than once since coming to

Penzance to write to you with

reference to the Annual Ex-

hibit...

Passmore"

My girls

those of oth

appreciate

Letter from E C Hanna April 13, 1909, Penzance Wesleyan College

Dear Sir,

It has occurred to me more than once since coming to Penzance to write to you with reference to the Annual Exhibition of pictures at the Passmore Edwards Gallery.

My girls in common with those of other schools greatly appreciate these exhibitions and between 50 - 60 of us go over to Newlyn every year.

We cannot go in the morning as it interferes with classes, and in the afternoon there is always so great a crowd of visitors that one can do no more than glance at each canvas.

Do you think it would be at all feasible to have a special time for schools, when the pupils might do more than look at the pictures? It has struck me every year how great an opportunity we miss by being unable to make the annual exhibition really valuable educationally.

I have seen in connection with the Toynbee Settlement in Whitechapel, how boys and girls were taught what pictures were, through the exhibitions at S Jude's. It may be that it is quite impossible from local circumstances to allow any period longer than one day for the Exhibition. If so, of course, I at once withdraw my suggestion and can only say how glad we are even to have a short time with the pictures.

I am sure you will pardon me for troubling you on the matter. Very truly yours E C Hanna

Illustration by Ernest Procter for *The Paper Chase*

from the Minutes of Committee meeting, August 18, 1909

Present: Gotch, Langley, Rheam

...It was decided not to have a new Exhibition at present.

...The committee discussed the question of running the *conversazione* in a modified form & were of opinion that it would be desirable if it should take place early in November at the opening of a new Exhibition. Also that it should take the form of a musical entertainment without the necessity of unhanging the Gallery.

from the Minutes of Committee Meeting, October 13, 1909

Present: Cornish, Gotch, Mackenzie, Langley, Forbes

...It was decided not to have the telephone at present.

...discussed the idea of having a conversazione. Mrs Forbes was deputed to ask Mr Barnes to bring his orchestra or part of it & to have a concert.

...decided to offer three guineas for the best poster suitable for advertising the Gallery in two colours.

Signature: Norman Garstin

from Studio-Talk, *The Studio,* February 1910

...An event of note last month was the resignation of Mr Norman Shaw from membership of the Royal Academy. His action, it is stated, was prompted by the very generous wish to make room for some one else after forty years' membership. As a precedent, we are not sure that it is one that should be followed, having regard to the essential character of academic honours. The vacancy in the ranks of the members has been filled by the promotion of Mr Stanhope A Forbes, who was born in 1857 and became an Associate in 1892. Mr Forbes was the first painter of the Newlyn colony to gain admission to the Academy, and his election to full membership will prove popular not only in the colony itself -- which, largely owing to his influence and personality, is now far more numerous than when he became Associate -- but among an extensive circle of admirers elsewhere...

from the Minutes of Committee meeting, April 15, 1910

Present: Garstin, Cornish, Mackenzie, Langley, Rheam

To be brought up at the next General meeting: the committee recommends that the policy guiding the selection of pictures and their arrangement-inclusion in a new Exhibition should be in favour of those that are in the opinion of the Committee most worthy irrespective of how long such pictures may have been already on Exhibition.

The committee also recommend that at the R A Show there shall be a hanging committee with five members, three of whom shall be elected by and from the committee and two by & from those artist subscribers not in the Committee.

Further that at the other Exhibitions the Hangers should consist of two members of the Committee and one artist subscriber not on the committee to be selected by the committee.

THE HARES DISGRACED   **Drawn by Doris. M. Shaw.**

Illustration by Doris (Dod) Shaw for *The Paper Chase*

from the Minutes of General Meeting, April 19, 1910

Present: Gotch (Chair), Cornish, Lamorna Birch, R. Dick, Langley, Evans, Mackenzie, Knight, Harvey, Rheam

...Proposed Knight, seconded Dick that, when the artist gives a price for his pictures with the stipulation that the commission for the Gallery is not to be deducted from that price, whatever profit is made should go entirely to the Gallery. Passed.

Mr Dick proposed that the recommendation of the Committee with regard to the hanging of old pictures be referred back to the committee for reconsideration. Lamorna Birch seconded. Carried, The Committee dissenting.

Proposed Dick, seconded Knight that the recommendation as re hanging the pictures at the Exhibitions be accepted. Carried.

...that a donation be sent to the Artists Benevolent Institution.   New committee: Gotch, Forbes, Langley, Garstin, Mackenzie. Mr Gotch was elected auditor.

...this meeting recommends that the committee should consider whether the downstairs room can be cleared, the walls hung with pictures, and room furnished with current art publications and books of reference & be open to the fellows and artist subscribers & if found practicable shall take steps to carry this out. Carried.

47

from the Minutes of Committee Meeting, October 31, 1910

The following appointed to hang the exhibition: Rheam, Garstin, Harvey

The Committee decided that in the forthcoming Exhibition no offers for pictures should be entertained & to have a notice printed in the Catalogue to that effect.

from the Minutes of Committee Meeting, Feb. 13, 1911

Present: Garstin (Chair), Gotch, Langley, Rheam

The date of the Academy show is fixed for Friday, March 17.

Pictures must be delivered at the Gallery on Wednesday, March 15 before 6:30pm.

Committee Meeting, March 1, 1911

...the resignation of the caretakers was discussed. Mr Garstin suggested that some sort of recognition of their services should be made by the Gallery in the shape of a present...

5 pds for Deacon & 3 pds for Maggie would be a suitable present.

from the Minutes of Committee Meeting, March 23, 1911

Present: Langley (Chair) Gotch, Garstin, Mackenzie, Rheam,

G Wolseley & C W Simpson were elected subscribers to the Gallery.

...filling the caretakers' place was discussed & it was decided to pay the expenses of Vincent & wife when they came to interview for Secretary.

from the Minutes of General Meeting, March 23, 1911

Present: Forbes (Chair) Gotch, Langley, Dick, Mackenzie, Garstin, Lewis, Simpson, Hunter, Knight, Wolseley, Harvey

Mr Gotch suggested that one member of the Committee should retire by rotation every year and not be eligible for re-election...then that the meeting adjourn for a fortnight & the committee remain in office until then.

...that the Artists Benevolent donation should be given to Mrs Forbes' Fund *this year.

*From 1910 Elizabeth Armstrong Forbes had been suffering from tuberculosis, and required full-time domestic help and nursing at home. She had returned from London and Italy where she had received diagnosis and treatments. The fund was set up to help defray the costs of nursing services.

from the Minutes of Committee Meeting, April 3, 1911
 Present: Mackenzie (Chair), Garstin, Gotch, Langley, Rheam
 ...that Mr Mackenzie should interview Mr Maidment about whether he would be willing to take charge of the Gallery for a short time.
 The Secretary was asked to get an estimate for the doing up of the rooms downstairs and also for putting in sink. (Wants Pitch Pine)
 It was suggested by Mr Gotch that Mr Forbes should be elected President of the Gallery (This would make a vacancy on the Committee) (Withdrawn)
 Proposed & seconded that the committee should offer themselves for re-election and that at the end of the year that member who had been longest on the Committee should not be eligible for re-election. The others would all be eligible...Mr Langley proposed as an amendment. That at the end of each year the oldest member should retire in rotation, the rest of the committee remain.

48

from the Minutes of Committee meeting, April 7, 1911
 Present: Gotch, Mackenzie, Garstin, Langley, Rheam
 Triggs estimate for painting and papering was accepted.
 The secretary was requested to take lawyers' opinion about fence round Gallery.

General meeting, April 7, 1911 (Continuing)
 Present: Gotch (Chair), Langley, Garstin, Mackenzie, Rheam, Hunter, Harvey, Evans, Knight, Simpson
 Mr Langley proposed: That the Committee be elected and that two senior members retire in rotation every year and are not eligible for re-election for one year. Seconded Mackenzie. Carried.
 The Committee elected were: Forbes, Langley, Gotch, Knight, Harvey. Mr Mackenzie was elected auditor, Mr Gotch having resigned.

from the Minutes of Committee Meeting, April 10, 1911
 Present: Langley (Chair) Gotch, Harvey, Rheam, Knight
 It was decided subject to references being satisfactory to offer the Vincents 36 pounds a year.

from *The West Briton* April 27, 1911
 The death occurred at his London residence on Saturday of Mr. John Passmore Edwards, aged 88. There are few Cornish lads who have attained a more eminent position as reformer and philanthropist than Mr Passmore Edwards. He was born on March 24, 1823, at Blackwater, his father being a carpenter. The only education he had was at the village school...The following is a list of buildings in Cornwall which owe their existence primarily to his generosity: [twenty institutions follow, Newlyn Art Gallery being the ninth].
 ...Mr Edwards had conferred upon him the honorary freedom of Truro, Falmouth, Liskeard and West Ham, and was made a member of several City companies, in recognition of his noble efforts in the cause of higher education. He was twice offered a knighthood, but with the permission of Queen Victoria and King Edward respectively, he humbly declined the honour.

Woodcut, possibly by J D MacKenzie for the Winter Exhibition Catalogue of 1911.
Loaned by the Book Gallery, St Ives.

from the Minutes of Committee meeting, June 16, 1911

Present: Gotch (Chair) Knight, Harvey, Langley, Rheam

The hanging committee for our show was elected, namely Gotch, Rheam, Wolseley.

It was decided to forget the commission on all pictures hitherto exchanged for carpets and other commodities, but that in future transactions of this description, the commission due to the gallery as from a sale shall be paid.

from the Minutes of Committee meeting, October 27, 1911

Present: Harvey, Gotch, Rheam, Langley (Chair)

The committee authorised the Secretary to take necessary steps to repair roof.

Next exhibition sending - in day Nov 15

Hang Nov 16

Open Nov 17

The following were elected hangers: Langley, Simpson, Harvey

The Secretary was authorised to go to St Ives to collect pictures - from Gallery photographer.

from the Minutes of Committee Meeting, March 4, 1912

Present: Harvey, Langley (Chair) Gotch, Knight, Rheam

The regulation with regard to non-subscribers exhibiting at RA Show was reviewed, namely that they must produce a written invitation signed by two artist subscribers -- Date of RA Exhibition March 22. Hanging March 21, Sending in day March 20 up to 4:30pm.

The hanging committee for the RA Show: Gotch, Knight, Harvey.

Horse & cart outside Oakhill Cottages (where Laura & Harold Knight resided), in Lamorna, loaded with paintings destined for 'Show Days' and then the RA (via the Great Western Railway).

from the Minutes of Committee meeting, March 11, 1912

Present: Gotch (chair), Knight, Langley, Harvey, Rheam

Mr R M Hughes was elected an artist subscriber.

The votes were counted & the hangers for Subscribers, not on the Committee, were S J Birch & Mrs Knight. The whole committee is therefore: Gotch, Knight, Harvey, S J Birch and Mrs Knight.

from the Minutes of Committee Meeting, March 29, 1912

Present: Gotch, Langley, Knight, Rheam, Harvey, J B Cornish (on behalf of Trustees)

The secretary read the architect's report on the state of the building.... Mr Cornish asked to call the attention of the Trustees to the state of the buildings & furnish them with a copy of Mr Maddern's report.

...to ask the Trustees to consider the possibility of improving the light on the end walls of the Gallery by the insertion of two skylights in the lantern in accordance with a suggestion which the committee is prepared to make.

from the Minutes of General Meeting, April 24, 1912

Present: Gotch (Chair) Garstin, Wolseley, Simpson, Mackenzie, Evans, Langley, Rheam

The letters from Maddern & from the Trustees on the state of the building were read by the Secretary...the meeting approved of what the committee had done...

Election of two new members was proceeded with. Mr Forbes, Mr Langley retiring, Mr Garstin, Mr Simpson now elected on the Committee.

...one guinea sent to the Artists General Benevolent Institution.

It was unanimously resolved that a message of sympathy be sent to Mr Forbes from this meeting.

Elizabeth Stanhope Forbes (1859-1912) painted by Stanhope Forbes in 1889.

from the Minutes of Committee Meeting, June 4, 1912
    Present: Gotch, Simpson (Chair), Garstin, Cornish, Rheam
    The Committee commissioned the Architects' specification of work required for repairing Art Gallery...the secretary to write to Mr Maddern to solicit tenders.
    Another exhibition to be held next week.

from the Minutes of Committee Meeting, Feb 25, 1913
    Present: Rheam, Simpson
    The RA show to be held on Friday, March 14
    The Secretary to send invitation from the Committee to A J Munnings to exhibit.
    Hangers for Committee: Rheam, Garstin, Simpson...

from the Minutes of Committee Meeting, July 13, 1913
    Present: Knight (Chair), Cornish, Rheam, Harvey
    ....Secretary to see Maddern, about the tenders & to explain that the prices quoted are much too high. If Maddern can find a plan for doing it for 50 pounds.

from the Minutes of General Meeting, September 15, 1913
    Present: Langley, Leader, Heath, Rheam
    Mr Simpson undertaking to take Mr Wolseley's place.
    Mr Gotch & Mr Knight retire from Committee
    Messrs Leader & Langley were elected, the committee being Simpson, Garstin, Harvey, Leader, Langley.
    ...a letter to Mr Langley with reference to the possibility of obtaining some Chantrey Bequest pictures for an exhibition at the Gallery.
    ...Gallery should subscribe 10/6 per annum to the Imperial Arts League. Adopted.
    ...consideration should be given to best method of improving the attendance and sales at the Gallery.

Committee Meeting, October 29, 1913
    Present: Rheam, Langley, Harvey
    ...decided to sell 50 pds of India stock subject to the consent of the Trustees if necessary.
    ...Garstin & Rheam were appointed to hang the next show with Heath.
    With regard to Mr Gotch's proposal to consider the best means of increasing attendance & sales, the Committee are of the opinion that the Exhibitions can be made more interesting. That the practice of hanging the same pictures, however good, time after time in successive Exhibitions is detrimental to the best interest of the Gallery. That in future preference should be given to new work. That there has been a slackness and want of interest on the part of some members in exhibiting and that it is necessary to impress upon members the importance of sending fresh work if possible to each exhibition.

from *Elizabeth Lamorna Kerr, In Time & Place, Lamorna* (about 1913-14)
    ...The distinctly cold and matter-of-fact approach of Augustus John when he painted the portrait [of Mornie]   was stark in her mind. Describing this notorious painter, a gleam came to Mornie's eye and her finger twitched side to side, as she emulated the curt gestures he used toward her [when she was aged nine]. "He had no small talk at all," she added. Over the turn of the year from 1913 to 1914, John and his wife Dorelia had gone to stay at the Temperance Hotel where Munnings was also lodged. And between the artists quite spectacular, sometimes raucous, always diverting parties were held to include and to enjoy the visitors. John appeared to exercise himself with verve, and went away much impressed with the hospitality of Newlyn and Lamorna circle,

praising also the beauty of the young girls of the area. Dorelia, in her strange and wonderful clothes, and riding "hatless" in the carriage on Sunday, was widely remarked and criticised but this only added to the sense of grand occasion. Through the years various members of the John family have remained in contact with Mornie, and Caspar and Edmund John with some family retired to nearby Mousehole. Later generations and some in-laws of John visited and maintained a relationship with Lamorna, Mornie and Flagstaff Cottage.

from the Minutes of the General Meeting, June 5, 1914
    Present: Garstin, Gotch, Simpson, Langley, Rheam
    The accounts & balance sheet were passed.
    Mr Gotch proposed & Mr Langley seconded that the question of exceptional treatment with regard to commission on sales of pictures to dealers be referred to the committee for consideration and that the rule of 10% in all cases be suspended in respect of sales to dealers.
    Messrs Harvey & Garstin retired from Committee.
    Messrs Forbes & Mackenzie were elected.
    Committee consists of Langley, Simpson, Forbes, Mackenzie, Leader
    Signature: W Langley,
    19 February 1918*

*[The Newlyn Art Gallery was closed for the duration of the Great War.]

Engraving by Ernest Procter for the end paper of *The Paper Chase*, 1909.

IV: 1915 - 1924

Frances Hodgkins from St Ives, 6 January 1915

> ....On New Year's Day, Mr Garstin came over from Newlyn to see me. He talked very fervidly of the War & its horrors. He is writing some lectures on Disarmament & the Prospect of Peace -- but he might as well preach the Sermon on the Mount & expect people to follow it....

28 January 1915

> ....Next day, very cold & blowey to Penzance & Newlyn [with a visiting friend from Edinburgh]. We consulted a Fortune Teller who gave us rather unpleasant characters...Both of us are to live to a great and undistinguished old age; rather depressed we went & had a large & expensive lunch at the Queen's Hotel on the Parade. We afterwards visited the Art Gallery & freely criticised the pictures, bought a piece of copper work for Betha, took photos of the Newlyn streets, tea & train & home...

from *The Times*, Friday August 3, 1990

...Frances Hodgkins is odd-person-out [of the three persons exhibiting and considered in this review, in 1990: Dod Procter, Ernest Procter, and FH. See Chapter 11 for the contemporary review of the Procter show.] for very different reasons. Many of them were of her own making. She was in a sense, a late developer, and was embarrassed about how late, so she tended to fudge the evidence of her birth date, birthplace, and early life in general.

The current London exhibition at least leaves us in no doubt about where she was born, since it is part of the 'New Zealand 1990 in Britain' festivities marking the 130th anniversary of the Treaty of Waitangi, which founded modern New Zealand. It also reveals that she was born in 1869, and so, when she came to prominence among the British modernists in the Twenties, was already in her fifties.

Sometimes an artist's vagueness about origins is infuriating, since it obscures vital evidence. In FH's case, there does seem to have been a lot of sense behind it. She began painting early, as she would, being the child of a locally famous professional artist and teacher. But it took her a long time fully to become Frances Hodgkins, and if she felt it was best to draw a veil over her false starts and discarded styles, she was actually helping people to understand the later work by

Illustration by Ernest Procter
for *The Paper Chase*

which she is remembered today. This is charming and light, rather French-looking, but in the way that much British art of the Thirties paid tribute to the Gallic grace of Dufy and such.

It is sensible that she sould be classified with early John Piper, early Julian Trevelyan, and mature David Jones: it was the generation she essentially belonged to, whatever her chronological generation. Now that the world knows more of her story, it would be ironic, if, as a result, it thought less of her...

from *The Cornishman*, December, 1961

AN ARTIST RECALLS THE EARLY DAYS OF CORNISH PAINTING

Interview with Mr Charles Simpson

Memories of West Cornwall in the old days were recalled by Mr Charles Simpson, RI, when interviewed by "The Cornishman" recently...Mr Simpson first came to Cornwall in the autumn of 1905, after studying for a year in Bushey, Herts. at the school of animal painting run by Miss Lucy Kemp Welch, the well-known painter of horses. A friend told him of the colour and light in Cornwall and the facility of getting studios there. He stayed for a short time in Newlyn and then at St Ives, where he met J Noble Barlow, from whom he later had some lessons in landscape painting and Arnesby Brown, RA, whose pictures of cattle he had always admired...He left for Paris in the winter of 1910 and studied at Julian's famous academy...Back home in Cornwall, he found painting in Newlyn about to enter its most brilliant period. Among newcomers were Dame Laura Knight, RA, and Harold Knight, RA. Sir Alfred Munnings was now at work there and the Newlyn Art Gallery held some of its finest exhibitions.

And at Mr Forbes' school were many students who later became famous. Besides Dod Procter, RA and the late Ernest Procter, RA whose brilliant career was cut short by his early death, there were Mr C E Vulliamy, the writer, and the late Winifred Tennyson Jesse, also a distinguished writer. There were others who made a name as artists, especially Miss Ruth Alison whom Charles Simpson married in 1913.

They first met when Mr Vulliamy was entertaining friends at his rooms in Newlyn, and became engaged a few days later. There were also two students from Sweden, Mr Johnson and Mr Luck. From them Mr Simpson heard of the work of the great Swedish painter of birds, Bruno Liljefors, and was able to get many reproductions of his paintings...

from 'St Hilary, Cornwall' a leaflet published by the Friends of St Hilary from information compiled by Mrs E W Coward

...The church stands 190 ft above sea level, between two seas, where its lovely thirteenth century broach spire, formerly whitewashed, made a landmark for ships in St Ives and Mounts Bay. It was amongst the oldest possessions of St Michael's Mount..

Entering by the south door and turning eastwards, one comes to a picture of St Joan of Arc, painted by Annie Walke, wife of Father Bernard Walke...Moving to the chancel, the east window should be noted for its Victorian glass. The pictures on the stalls either side were painted by the Newlyn artists Harold Knight ARA, Norman Garstin, Alethea Garstin, Gladys Hynes, Ernest Procter, Dod Procter and Annie Walke...The pictures on the pulpit, the work of Ernest Procter, represent legends connected with St Neot, St Kevin and St Mawes. On the north side of the screen of the chancel are pictures painted by Joan Manning Saunders at the age of 12...[In the Lady Chapel] the reredos represents the House of Visitation and the picture of that event was painted by Ernest Procter...The large crucifix on the north wall is the work of Phyllis Yglesias*...West of this crucifix the reredos was painted by Roger Fry...In the southwest corner of the church there is the reredos, painted by Ernest Procter, of an Altar of the Dead...

[*Phyllis Yglesias, 'Pog' or 'The Golly' as she was familiarly known, was a talented sculptor and sometime exhibitor at the Newlyn Gallery. She was the daughter of the Basque landscape painter, Vincent Yglesias; her friendship with Laura Knight and the S J Lamorna Birch family is followed in E. Lamorna Kerr's book, *In Time & Place, Lamorna*.]

Vignette of St Hilary Church
(unidentified artist)

about 1914-15...Bernard Walke, Vicar of St Hilary

"Now A J Munnings is as enthusiastic over his friends as he is over a landscape or passage of literature. Having discovered the Walkes, he was eager to introduce them to his friends in Lamorna. 'Mrs Sidgwick shall give you a party, and you and Annie Walke shall be there,' he said. 'I will get them all to come and see you; and you will love every one of them; Harold and Laura Knight, wonderful people,' he continued; 'Lamorna Birch and the Hughes. You will like them, I tell you.'

Annie Walke had already met Laura Knight and several other painters from Lamorna at the Newlyn Show. She would be at home with these people, but it was difficult for me to plunge into this company of which I knew nothing....

Munnings, however, was insistent, and so it came about that we rode on our bicycles one morning in the spring of 1915 for the first time to Lamorna..."

about Laura Knight...Bernard Walke

55

"During the war, at a time when she had failed to apply for the necessary permit for painting out of doors, I went with her to the Corpus Christi Fair in Penzance and kept a look-out for the police while Laura made sketches in a note-book. After the first day Laura was known to every one on the plot. Showmen, fat women, contortionists and mountebanks were all willing to be her models and anxious to serve her..."

ACROSS THE MOORS

moorland. The greatest breadth of the Pool is rather more than a quarter of a mile. For the most part, the banks are soft and sedgy. Close to the northern rim stands a little croft, and above the croft are the two huts built by Mr. and Mrs. Naper of Lamorna and my good friends Harold and Laura Knight. That such a place should be chosen by painters for an occasional residence is not to be wondered at, for nowhere on earth are there landscapes more austerely beautiful.

PAINTERS' HUTS : DOSMARY

Two illustrations by Charles Simpson for C E Vuillamy's *Unknown Cornwall*, 1925, one near Dozmary Pool, Bodmin Moor, where the artists took painting holidays, and the other of Newlyn.

NEWLYN

West Lodge, Alverton, Penzance -- Monday
Dear Munnings

I am much obliged for a guinea received from Birch last Thursday and gather that you wish to become a subscriber to the Gallery. You don't send me the name of a proposer or seconder but I will gladly put you up at the next meeting.

I understand that you are fired with a laudable ambition to improve our Exhibitions -- In fact that you are inaugurating something in the nature of a crusade! This information was communicated to me by Harvey who was quite unaware that he was telling me anything about it!!!

But I heard something of it from Lamorna B. The same old "wheeze"!! Do come and see me about it next time you are in Penzance. Meanwhile you might try and impress upon modern Lamorna & its satellites that one of the first things necessary is to answer letters from the Secretary when he writes and asks for pictures. I'm afraid I must include yourself among the defaulters and there are some who have never yet answered a letter of mine until the second or third time of asking unless a stamped and directed envelope or postcard has been enclosed!! I gathered from Harvey that there are other people who are so upset at the idea of the Gallery being in rather low water that they are frightfully anxious to send me a guinea to save us from bankruptcy!!

But come & see me & I will give you the fruits of something over twenty years experience! Yours H M Rheam

57

Lamorna, April 17
Dear Mr Rheam

I haven't written to you because I have not dared. Your knock out of a letter has made a big crater where it landed and the shrapnel exploded at every page..

I am sorry if I haven't answered letters from you at once. I am indeed -- I haven't done so I know -- neither have some others - But I think it's because the damned post goes at such a foolish time. 2.30. One works (just at that time of year) until nearly 2 instead of one - Then into lunch and put off letter writing because there isn't time & so it goes on. We mean well but being a sad fleshed lot we fail --

About the Gallery - I'll come and see you if I may. It isn't a crusade or anything of the kind. All I said was. Why couldn't we try having a change of exhibition at the Gallery over 2 or 3 months and send work which we wish to try there in order to see how it is looking and so use it in that way as well as selling -- one day some Penzance friends were saying to me that its no use going to the Newlyn Gallery. There was never anything there only a lot of little pictures for sale and always the same lot. It was only that made me begin to think we ought to send better work and try a show now sales are hopeless for art's sake.

About putting me up -- Harvey & Birch were putting me up for membership. Didn't either of them say so?

Best wishes to you. I hope to find you well very soon. Yours sincerely, A J Munnings

Committee Meeting, July 1917
Present: Forbes, Langley, Rheam
Sec [Rheam] offered to give up subs but it was decided that he should continue to receive one half.
It was decided that it would not be possible to hold RA Show this year.

Committee Meeting, November 24, 1917
Present: Forbes, Langley, Mackenzie
Gotch & Heath were elected to take the vacant places on the Committee.
The Secretary thought he would be able to have accounts ready by end of year, and call General Meeting.

58

Committee Meeting, July 14, 1918
Present: Forbes, Gotch, Mackenzie, Rheam, J B Cornish
The Secretary reported that he had received an application from Mrs Blythe, on behalf of the Newlyn War Hospital Depot, asking if the Committee could place the Gallery including the basement room & store room at their disposal for their work - for the duration of the war. Proposed by J D Mackenzie, seconded by T C Gotch, carried unanimously, subject to a General Meeting of Subscribers and approval of the Trustees.

General Meeting, July 19, 1918
Present: Langley (Chair) J D Mackenzie, Heath, Forbes & Gotch
Mr Gotch explained that he had offered to represent the Hon Sec at the meeting. He read a report from Sec and letter from Mrs Blythe regarding loan of Gallery to Newlyn War Hospital Depot during the war, also a letter from Miss E Hunter dated 18 July on behalf of Mrs Robins Bolitho asking whether the Committee would be willing to allow her the use of the Gallery for a Womans Institute and for headquarters of Newlyn Girl guides.
The meeting having been called to receive the Committee's recommendation to close the Gallery during the war for the depot, it was moved to accept this use...
The question of the appointment of a committee to prepare a scheme for recon-struction of the Gallery after the War was brought forward by Mr Gotch, and after discussion it was decided to bring it up at the next General Meeting.
...That the subscriptions of the artist members continue in force until otherwise determined by General Meeting.
Signed: Stanhope Forbes

Detail from St Hilary, 14 1/2" repeat silk,
from the textile designs of Alec Walker

from *Arts and Crafts in Newlyn, 1890-1930,* by Hazel Berriman

Alec Walker's first contact with Newlyn came about under the most romantic circumstances. Already established in Yorkshire as the manufacturer of 'Vigil' silk, he advertised in 1912, for a poster and advertising designer. Kathleen Earle *replied and arranged to meet him in London with a portfolio of her work. 'Kay' had been a student at the Stanhope Forbes School of Painting in Newlyn since 1910 and had already received commissions for illustration and poster work. Alec was so impressed by her account of the lively Newlyn art colony that he travelled back to Cornwall with her the same day to see for himself. He was welcomed into their midst and immediately felt at home...

[Kay Earle was co-founder with Alec Walker of their firm Crystéde in 1920, after their purchase of Myrtle Cottage, Newlyn [the 'Myrtage' of old, a boarding house for lady art pupils attending the Schools of Art in Newlyn] and then Sambo's Row, the latter of which they converted into their fabric workshops. Kay, a talented designer, worked to her own patterns, as well as producing illustrative and promotional material for their rapidly increasing market internationally. In the first craft exhibition at Newlyn Art Gallery in 1924 she showed leatherwork and dolls of personal design and in 1925 she exhibited paintings. Her younger daughter, Polly Walker, in a letter to the current editor, mentions that her mother also exhibited (unspecified works) in the 1930s, after the break-up of the Walkers' marriage, when Polly could recall accompanying her mother to 'Varnishing Day' (the show days for the RA) at the Gallery.]

59

from *Crystéde, the unique textile designs of Alec Walker,* by Hazel Berriman

[Alec] Walker's contacts with artists were strengthened by the move to Newlyn. Now he was living permanently in an environment where aesthetic matters were taken seriously and he could temper the demands of business with his increasing interest in art. There was also a lively social life which revolved around the "bohemian" parties organised by Cedric Morris (1889-1982), his friend Lett Haines and Frank Dobson (1886-1963) who were all living in Newlyn c.1919/20. Other visitors included Wyndham Lewis and Edward Wadsworth who with Dobson and McKnight Kauffer, were involved in an attempt to revive the Vorticist movement after the war. They re-grouped and in 1920 mounted an exhibition at the Mansard Gallery in London, under the title *Group X*...

Walker's closest friendships were with Harold Harvey (1874-1941) and Ernest Procter (1886-1935), whom he had known since his early visits to Newlyn before the War. Harvey, born in Penzance, was the only truly Cornish artist in the Newlyn group. Having studied under Norman Garstin and at the Atelier Julian in Paris, his painting in the 1920s was moving away from the traditional plein-air subjects of the pre-war Newlyn School towards more contemporary interiors, which give a fascinating glimpse of the drawing rooms, bedrooms and kitchens of middle class 'suburban' Newlyn, particularly his own house Maen Cottage, and reflect his admiration for 17th century Dutch painting. Harvey's subjects were friends and relatives, most frequently his wife Gertrude, who was herself a talented artist...

Kathleen Earle and Alec Walker
on their engagement day, 1918.

Committee Meeting, 12th February 1920
    Present: Forbes, Garstin, Langley, Gotch (Chair)
    Minutes of the committee meeting of Feb 14, 1918 were read & confirmed.
    Resolved that Mr Tregenza's estimate for repairing the storm damage to the roof namely 7 pounds odd be accepted subject to Mr Gotch being satisfied with what Mr Tregenza undertakes to do.

Committee Meeting, Wheal Betsy Cottage, 6 August 1920
    Present: Forbes (Chair), T C Gotch, R T Dick (acting sec)
    Mr Forbes brought forward a proposal from Messrs Lanham Ltd to allow that firm to hold an Exhibition of Pictures for one month at the Gallery -- they being prepared to risk 25 pds on making it a success.

    Points raised in the discussion were -- first, that the Art Control must remain in the hands of the Committee -- responsibility for payment of rates, taxes and liability as regards Exhibits must be taken by Messrs Lanham.
    The Commission on sales had better remain as before, 10% to members 15% to non members -- part of this commission to be paid to the Committee.
    The Entrance Fee and Entertainment Tax to be decided on.
    That Mr Cock be asked to meet the Committee on Monday, August 8 at 12 o'clock -- & that his proposal in detail be brought before a General Meeting of the Artist Guarantors.

A General Meeting of the Artists Subscribers was held in Mr Stanhope Forbes' Studio, The Meadow, Newlyn on August 9th 1920
    Present: S A Forbes (Chair), T C Gotch, L S Barclay, F G Heath, R M Hughes and R T Dick (Acting Sec)
    At the invitation of Committee, Mr Cock, Principal of the Firm of Messrs Lanham Ltd attended the meeting and laid his scheme for co-operating with the Artists for holding an Exhibition of Pictures in the Gallery for 3 months as an experiment and with a view of considering a permanent arrangement -- this proposal was to guarantee fifty pds on behalf of Messrs Lanham Ltd, the Artists Subscribers to guarantee twenty-five pds -- the loss or profit on the Exhibition to be shared two thirds by Messrs Lanham Ltd and one third by the Artist Subscribers -- the art control to remain in the hands of the Artists Committee absolutely, but for the benefit of all concerned be trusted that work of interest to buyers would preponderate. Mr Cock would write the Overseers of Madron and arrange about the rates for the period of the Exhibition...Mr Cock was prepared to make himself responsible for the business end of such an experimental Exhibition but the Secretarial work must be outside his province -- Mr Forbes explained in detail the position from the Artists side...Mr Cock having retired -- Mr Gotch moved and Mr Dick seconded, "That the necessary steps be taken to enter into an agreement with Messrs Lanham on these terms." This was agreed to.
    Mr Gotch proposed and Mr Dick seconded "that one guinea be determined as the subscription due for the period of the War and that the Annual subscription be again adopted and due in November this year."
    Owing to the continued illness of Mr Rheam and subsequent delay in closing the accounts it was agreed on the proposition of Mr Dick seconded by Mr Gotch that a new account be opened.... The appointment of a Secretary and Treasurer was left in the hands of the executive committee.
    Signed: T C Gotch

General Meeting, 9 October 1920 Passmore Edwards Art Gallery
Present: T C Gotch (Chair), Lamorna Birch, F Heath, R M Hughes, A Hayward, Stanley Lloyd, & R T Dick (Secretary)

...Lamorna Birch shall take Gotch's place on the Committee as Mr Gotch was resigning owing to his proposed absence from Newlyn for six months.

Langley notified his desire to retire from the Committee. Hayward and Stanley Lloyd were elected members of the Committee...

It was agreed that steps should be taken at once to ask those interested in the welfare of the Gallery to become Fellows -- the executive committee to take action.

The balance sheet for the first weeks of the Experimental Exhibition was submitted by Messrs Lanham showing a credit balance of £4-1-9. This was considered so far satisfactory but it was pointed out that without some much more remunerative source of income it would be impossible to paint and decorate the Gallery or keep it in a proper state of repair.

Dick reported that he had received from Rheam the balance standing to the credit of the Passmore Edwards Art Gallery...transferred into R T Dick's name, and showed a credit balance of £48-12...

Committee Meeting, Dec 8th 1920
The Meadow Studio
Present: Forbes (Chair), Garstin, Hayward, Lloyd and Dick (Sec)

Mr Cock attended the meeting and submitted the Balance Sheet of the three months experimental Exhibition.

Sale of Pictures £113-12-0
Attendance   516
Total receipts (of attendance) £44-2-3

Subscribers £ 38-16-1, showing a credit of £5-5-10 after deducting the rates now due for half year ending March -- the balance was divided as agreed, two thirds to Messrs Lanham Ltd and 1/3 to Gallery. It was agreed that this was a very satisfactory conclusion to the experiment.

The future was then discussed and Mr Cock showed that he was willing to meet the Committee in every way and that if they decided to continue the arrangement on say a half and half share of risk and profit either including or excluding the Academy Show day he was prepared to consider it but in the later case he should have a percentage of the takings....but he thought that the fairest arrangement was to include this show, he taking the good with the bad. He was quite prepared for the Committee to have the appointment of caretaker subject to his agreement...and he was quite with the Committee as to closing the Gallery for the Winter. Dick proposed that Mr Stanhope A Forbes, R A be invited to hold a private view in the Gallery of his important work, "The Burning of the Royal Exchange, 1839" but that the Committee could not incur any expense. It was considered that this would be a great advantage to the Gallery...

The Secretary reported that the Gallery was in urgent need of re-painting outside and that he had obtained an estimate of twenty pds from Mr Peak - Tolcarne. He was instructed to have this done.

It was decided that the Secretary should draw up an Annual Report. The Chairman agreed to lend him assistance with this.

Garstin was very much in favour of a public meeting being called to discuss the future running of the Gallery but no decision was come to.

General Meeting, Friday January 14th, 1921, Gallery

Present: Garstin (Chair), Forbes, Lamorna Birch, Heath, Hughes, Hayward, Naper, Lloyd & Dick (Hon Sec)

...Agreed that Garstin should write an appreciation of our late Secretary H M Rheam to be added to the minutes.

...the Secretary had received a letter from Mr Cock dated January 8th 1921 saying that after careful consideration the firm had decided that it would not be possible for them to take over the business management of the Newlyn Art Gallery in future -- on the proposition of Garstin, seconded by Birch it was agreed that the Secretary should ask Lanhams to reconsider that decision.

The Secretary reported that three applications had been made to him for the post of caretaker...the Secretary considered that the terms the Gallery could with our present membership afford to offer -- ie, the dwelling room, free rates and taxes and £1 a week when an exhibition was in progress would be accepted by these applicants...[barring one] who might be under the impression that the £1 a week was to be paid all the year round.

Garstin's resolution

At the General Meeting of the members of the Passmore Edwards Art Gallery at Newlyn held at the Gallery on January 14th, 1921, a resolution was unanimously voted that an expression of sorrow and concern upon the death of Mr H M Rheam for so many years Secretary of the Gallery should be conveyed to Mrs Rheam and her family, and that a record should rest in the minutes of the meeting expressing this recognition of the valuable service he had rendered to the institution.

Committee Meeting, Morvah House, Paul Hill, February 4th, 1921

Present: Forbes, Garstin, Lamorna Birch, Lloyd, Hayward & Dick (Sec)

Arrangements with Lanhams discussed at length, Cock's letter adjudged to be trying to move more responsibility on to the Comm & stop further criticism.

The Sec should call on the firm at St Ives, agree to their withdrawal from the management arrang, but prove to them that the Comm fully appreciated the spirited manner & genuine interest in the Newlyn Colony shown by them, & far from thinking that it was only the ulterior motive in making a profit & selling their materials the Committee would continue to sell their materials anyway. Also the artists would continue to ask Lanhams to collect such pictures as the artists of St Ives would send to future exhibitions; this was understood always done at the expense of the artist. If Mr Cock would re-consider & continue as our business agent, the Secretary would call another meeting.

C Richards offered caretaker's post, his connection with the Gallery & his father before, assuring the Committee that he fully understood. He was also a disabled soldier.

It should be minuted that Forbes, R A had accepted the Committee's invitation to hold a Private View of his picture, "The Burning of the Royal Exchange", this had taken place (Fri & Sat past). Attendance was very great on both days & that undoubtedly the interest in the Gallery has been greatly awakened by this, thanks of the Committee are due to Forbes.

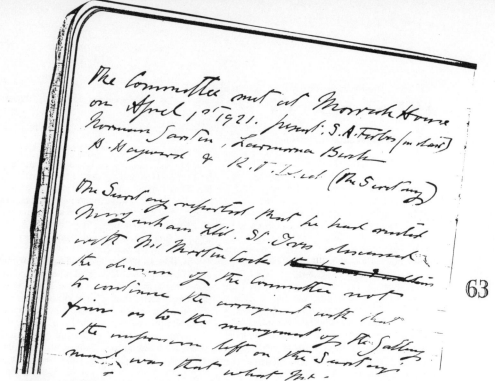

Committee meeting at Morvah House, 1 April 1921

Present: Forbes (Chair), Garstin, Lamorna Birch, Hayward & R T Dick (Sec)

Mr Cock confirmed as agent for the next exhibition, receiving a commission on sales made from St Ives artists, for whom he arranged collection & delivery.

...Private View of next exhibition should be held on Friday 22 April, pictures to be at the Gallery on the 18th. Mr Forbes would write to Mr Pike's quartet to give us some music that afternoon, & that tea should be provided. Mrs Garstin & Miss E Hunter should be invited to join the entertainment comm with Garstin, Hayward & Dick.

Forbes, Garstin & Dick should form a sub-comm, meet at the Gallery and check on such renovation and restoring of the walls as would be done in the time available & at a reasonable cost, as near 5 or 6 pounds as possible.

Committee, April 16, 1921

Present: SJ Birch (Chair) Forbes, Garstin, Lloyd, Hayward, Dick (Sec), Miss Hunter rep resenting the Entertainments Comm

Final arrangements for Private View, and whether in view of the critical position of the national affairs it should be postponed. Mr Garstin said that in view of the decision of the Railway men & Transport Workers on the previous day that they would not join the Miners he thought that serious as the position still was, the necessity to alter our arrangements... did not now arise. Agreed to issue invitations at once & carry on.

The Comm were all pleased with the white walls of the Gallery & that the brown dado would well be left as it was for the present.

Hayward to get out a notice asking for silence during the Music.

The Secretary would worry round about coal - the invitations would go out that day.

The Sec reported that he had been on the telephone with Messrs Lanham with regard to St Ives' pictures and Mr Cock was not very sanguine as to their sending more than one or two -- he seemed to think it was unreasonable to insist on the forms being completed -- It was decided that the Sec should telegraph to the Sec of the Arts Club -- St Ives -- asking for a special effort to be made to send pictures on Monday.

from The Cornishman & Cornish Telegraph, April 27, 1921

ART AT NEWLYN

Musical At Home at the Passmore Edwards' Gallery

Shall the Opie Memorial Art Gallery at Newlyn be given a fresh lease of usefulness as a means of culture, pleasure and profit--profit in the widest aesthetic and material sense? If so, it must be established on a firm financial basis. That is the crux of the position, as indicated by the speakers at the Gallery on Friday afternoon, when there was a happy blend of paintings, music and tea to celebrate the opening of the Spring and Summer Exhibition.

After the first musical number by Miss Violet Nunn, Miss Stewart, Mr Barrie B Bennetts and Mr C G Pike--a dreamy quartette of Schubert's--Mr Norman Garstin thanked their fellow artists of the musical world, and took the guests into his confidence as to the past, present and future of the Gallery. He reminded them the Gallery came to them as an unexpected, unsolicited gift "out of the blue." ...he gave, but did not endow, leaving the recipients to find means for their maintenance. It was a laudable ambition, but in their case it caused them some perplexity and trouble for they had to raise funds to enable the pictures they painted, to be exhibited at the Gallery.

...[he] explained how the Gallery had been maintained. First, there were trustees (about a dozen, whose number has dwindled to three or four); there were about twenty-six artists and about seventy associates, who subscribed a guinea per annum. That enabled them to start without worrying about the commercial side of things; but time has altered the situation.

...[He said] Art is the antithesis of commerce. When commerce enters that is the end of art. The public might regard them as merely artisans who offered commodities for sale, with the gallery as their shop. That was not the fact. In commerce a businessman offers to the public a commodity which the public wants; an artist is an artist because he does not paint something because it is wanted, but because he wishes to express his own point of view in form and colour and thought. That is so with all artists whether their self-expression takes the form of painting, music, speaking or writing. But for the artists who express themselves through these media we should be as dead and voiceless things, inarticulate as stones. Yet it has happened that the true artist has often met with scant appreciation during his lifetime. Great men have died without the knowledge that after death they would be greatly esteemed throughout the world... All the artist can do is to be true to himself and hope that his work will be understood and some day have its worth properly valued. He believed that at Newlyn they had taken their part in the activities of life--in the higher and more spiritual side of life... if the Gallery was to continue to be a centre of Art, they must face the fact that the number of artists at Newlyn had dropped from twenty-six to fifteen, and the number of associates from seventy to twelve.

At this point Mr. Garstin stopped abruptly and effectively, for the figures he quoted were as striking as they were regrettable. It was left to the Mayor (Mr Benning) to boldly and strongly appeal for more guinea-subscribers to enable the exhibitions to be continued.

Money is needed for annual repairs and care of the building--not a large sum, but similar help to that originally given. There were enough present to lengthen the list Mr Cornish had written up to its old proportions...

It was not for Mr Norman Garstin to strike the business note which so jars upon his artistic sense; but it is open to him to point out that apart from the pleasure we have all had at seeing the pictures emanating from Newlyn studios before they have been sent to the Royal Academy, the Institute of Water Colours and other exhibitions, these resident artists have distributed Cornish scenes and figure studies of Cornish people all over the country and to the Colonies overseas--pictures which have acted as eloquent advertisements of the charms of our unique county, and largely owing to the feast of alluring colour, set forth on canvas, thousands of visitors have brought their gold to Cornwall and left it here.

It is no answer to say that the artist came to Newlyn because the Cornish coast is beautiful and its people interesting, and that they exhibited their works from other motives than the desire to attract visitors to Cornwall. The artist lives to paint "the thing as he sees it" because he has the inward call; but nonetheless he has done Cornwall valuable, yeoman, practical service; and therefore guineas contributed to the upkeep of the Opie Gallery are an investment rather than a gift.

As to the pictures shown--there were scores on the walls... One would have liked to mention one's favourites, but it is perhaps as well to give the space to publishing the fact that the Gallery needs support and that the exhibition is now open daily, and should be visited by all who love art and nature as interpreted in art...

HERBERT THOMAS

A party of Forbes School
students on beach
at Sennen Cove

HOW THEY PAINT THEIR PICTURES: THE REALISTIC SCHOOL.

BY FRED HALL.

E Lamorna Kerr, by
Augustus John, 1913-4.

Stanhope Forbes, RA, also a gardener

Gertrude Harvey, 1920s

Harold Harvey, 1920s

Ethel & R Morson Hughes, 1934

Charles Naper, 1930s-40s at Trewoofe

Ella Naper, 1930s-40s at Trewoofe

Max Chapman, 1938

Alec Walker, daughters Bridget & Polly
St Mawes, 1948

The Cornish Loan Exhibition of 1936 [See Chapter VI]

Wallace Nichols, Custodian to the Gallery, 1940s-50s, minding the Exhibition

A tea party at the Kerris home of Paul Feiler,
on the occasion of the visit of the New York
artist, Mark Rothko to West Penwith in 1958.
Peter Lanyon facing camera at rear. On right hand
side from L to R Mrs Rothko, Mark Rothko, Paul Feiler

Mr. Charles Simpson on his motor-cycle.

Theresa Gilder, 1980
Working on 'The Lovers'

Jill Garnier, in the 1960s

Geoffrey Garnier, in the 1960s

Passersby, beware! What are they selling?
(Front, L to R) Bernard Evans, Michael Chalwin, Ken Symonds,
(Back, L to R) Peter Smith, Anthony Frost, Ray Ambrose

Clockwise from top:
Liz Knowles, Organiser
Graham Bazeley & Asst, Sponsors
Fred Yates in France
L to R John Emanuel, Alexander
MacKenzie & Denys Stephens
Richard Cook
Tony O'Malley

Committee, May 10, 1921
Present: Garstin (Chair), Lloyd, Hayward, Dick (Sec)

As a result of the Private View 23 people had agreed to become Fellows and had already paid their subscriptions. Garstin reported two more and these together with the thirteen old ones made a total of 38 Fellows.

The Private View cost £2/17/10 &1/2d.

The Sec asked for and obtained authority to take action if it was possible to have a small exhibition of freshly gathered wild flowers in the Secretary's room. This it was thought would be of great interest to visitors and in no way detract from the pictures.

The Sec reported that doing up the lower rooms and put them in habitable condition had cost £13/10/0, that the white walls of Gallery £6/12/0. The first account was paid and to meet the other and the painting of the outside of Gallery he had £42/17/7 on hand.

The walls of the Lobby & Secretary's room should be white, when the position of finances allowed.

Hayward raised the point as to the duration of the Exhibition -- he thought a definite period should be stated when asking Artists to exhibit -- Garstin was opposed to short exhibitions. Nothing decided on.

65

Committee, Aug 12, 1921
Present: Forbes (Chair), Lloyd, Hayward, & the Secretary

Financial matters difficult. Unpaid bills amounted to 41/pds odd, & about 43 pds to meet these. There had been a loss on the Summer Exhibition so far, no doubt owing to Coal Strikes, and sales had practically ceased -- this statement at first appeared rather startling -- but the chairman pointed out that the income from our subscriptions would cover such a loss and Lloyd agreed that if our income covered our expenses all was still well...

...the Committee were very surprised at the Gallery being closed at 5pm and the Secretary made the best explanation he could: it must have arisen through the RA Show day, Porter stating that admission would be 8d from 1 to 5pm and the next bill carrying on the time 5pm as the latest hour of opening -- The Chairman hoped the Secretary would go into this as he found that workmen and no doubt caretakers also considered nowadays that 5 o'clock was time to go home, but that these hours were just those that many people would choose to visit the Gallery.

Committee meeting, Nov 12, 1921
Present: T C Gotch (Chair), Forbes, Garstin, Lamorna Birch, the Hon Treas J B Cornish and the Hon Sec, Dick

...new trustees are needed owing to the great number that have died and a list of names was prepared of gentlemen who might be approached.

The Secretary was instructed to retain the names of all Artist Subscribers who had not tendered their resignation and to recover if he could their subscriptions -- legal steps should not be taken.

General Meeting of the Artist Subscribers & Trustees, Gallery, Dec 9th, 1921

Gotch (Chair)

The Chairman welcomed the presence of the new trustees thanking them for undertaking this responsibility at a time when the Gallery was in process of being resuscitated and suffering from lack of Funds.

...Forbes spoke at some length on the annual report (read out previously) supplementing the points made, drawing attention to the number of years the Artists had as he thought successful control on the exhibitions. He saw no reason why success should not follow in the coming years and he looked on the new Trustees as a great help -- there were many ways in which such help could be given, not in the management of the Exhibitions -- which was solely a matter for the Artists to deal with -- but as they had helped in the past. ..he then passed on to the proposal to hold an Exhibition and sale of pictures in aid of the Cornish Miners Distress Fund...

...Gotch made clear a point in the report -- especially as the new Trustees would be able to let others know, he wished them to realise, that Loan Exhibitions from the Tate Gallery and other national collections, loans of pictures by modern artists, etc -- could be arranged and would be of great interest to Fellows and visitors to the Gallery if the money could be found to pay carriage and insurance of such to and from the Gallery.

Mr Phelps raised a point on behalf of the Trustees as to the adequate insurance of the building... Hon Sec should arrange for the Insurance to be raised from £1000 to £3000. Mr Phelps thought the present premium too high.

Mr Dick's term of office as Hon Sec having expired and he having decided not to stand for re-election, the difficult question arose as to a successor. Mr Dick thought that the only solution was a paid Secretary, but taking the income of the Gallery as £100 per annum from all sources out of which rents, rates, taxes, caretaker and upkeep had to be paid, it was quite impossible to offer an adequate salary.

...it was agreed "that Mr R T Dick be asked to retain his position as Hon Sec for three months with power to obtain a paid Assistant Secretary at £20 per annum." Mr Dick reluctantly agreed to this as the work entailed had really been more than he had time to give, one of his reasons for his having undertaken it at all was that on his designing and presenting a Frieze to the Gallery (which at the time was thought to be necessary to fill the blank space above the pictures) he had been voted a life member and therefore had for the first twenty years paid no subscription.

At this point Mr LeGrice on behalf of the Trustees that a greater interest and more financial support would be forthcoming from the residents in the District if two or three - Subscribers not Artists - were elected on the Committee...A very lengthy discussion took place: Mr Forbes, Mr Garstin and Mr Gotch all made it quite clear, each from their individual point of view that a laymember or members of a Committee might be a very serious interference with the management of the Gallery as an Art Institution. Heath also spoke. Mr Forbes also pointed out that it might happen that the laymembers would grow in number and outvote the Artists -- Mr LeGrice desired it to be quite clear that he only brought forward this suggestion in the belief that it would help the Artists.

... Mr Boscawen proposed that the Trustees say to the Artists that they, the Trustees, give their consent to the Artists to co-opt if they so wish, one or two lay subscribers on their Committee. Mr LeGrice seconded this. Mr Bailey thought the request for this power should come from the Artists...but that Mr Forbes objection was met by the power to co-opt, clearly defined the position such members would have on the Committee -- that their services would be limited in any way the Artists thought best -- that the period of their term of office would be limited -- that they would have no rights as to re-election or election on any future Committee. [long discussion and debate] The consent was conveyed to the Artists there and then verbally. The Chairman on behalf of the Artists accepted this power to act -- if they so wished...

from Mary Jewels Exhibition programme as described in the Newlyn Art Gallery Newsletter, 1977, by Frank Ruhrmund. This article first appeared in *Cornish Life*.

...The extent of her vision and versatility is astonishing. Propping her paintings against the leg of a magnificent dining table at which Lord Asquith first sat -- there is nothing precious about Mary Jewels, she has no studio as such, but paints in almost every room in the house, "Wherever it's warm" -- she and her sister [Mrs Cordelia Dobson, formerly wife of Frank Dobson, sometime Professor of Sculpture at the Royal College of Art and one of Britain's leading sculptors] recently led me through the whole gamut of her work, from a delightful landscape "Paul Churchtown", painted in 1923, to a canvas on which the paint was scarcely dry...A self-portrait disclosed what a classic beauty she herself possessed when young. A painting, incidentally, that was not at all flattering, its veracity being witnessed by a photograph of herself taken at the time, and a splendid bronze head of her by the sculptor Frank Dobson that was actually fashioned in the very room in which we were sitting.

Mary Jewels in the 1930s.

Minutes of the Extraordinary General Meeting, 4 April, 1924
    Gotch (in the Chair)
    ...That Paras 2, 3 and 6 of the Constitution of the NSA be amended by adding in Para 2 after the words "or both such Arts" the words "and Arts Craftmanship", that Para 3 be amended by adding after the words "or the Art of Sculpture" the words "or Arts Craftmanship", that Para 6 be amended by adding after the words "or both such Arts" the words "or Arts Craftmanship"...
    Same day, immediately following: the General Meeting
    ...The following recommendation was to the Joint Meeting of the two Committees who had these appointments to make in June next, "That the two offices of Secretary and Caretaker be combined if found practicable."

From the Minutes of the Joint Committees of PEAG & NSA, July 23 , 1924

...the Asst Secretary (Miss Churchill-Tayler) stated that if she took up her residence at the Gallery, inside sanitation would be required. The committee agreed that the request was reasonable...

...The Asst Secretary applied for permission to destroy certain old papers belonging to the Gallery. The Committee gave instructions that all unnecessary papers, and bills prior to 1918 should be destroyed but that all papers of value or interest printed or otherwise, should be carefully preserved.

An application was submitted from Mrs Drews, Art Gallery Terrace, that a tree in the Gallery gardens which obstructed her view of the Laregan River should be removed. The Committee gave instructions that the bushes in the garden should be trimmed, but they refused permission to have the tree cut down.

From the Minutes of the Joint Committees of PEAG & NSA, September 16, 1924

...further efforts should be made to have the electric light installed & also some idea of what the cost of providing toilet accommodation for visitors on the upper & lower floors would cost...

...It was proposed to charge 1/- entrance on all week-days except Fridays & Saturdays when 6d entrance fee would be asked.

Joint Meeting of the Committees, Sept 26, 1924

Forbes (in the Chair)

...Mr Forbes suggested that picture postcards of works exhibited at the Gallery should be on view & for Sale: and it was agreed that Artists should be asked if they would allow this to be done & if they would be ready to bear the expense of having their pictures photographed...Mr Dick offered to see Paul, the photographer...

...Miss Tayler offered a carpet for the Secretary's Room & a curtain for the staircase window...

Minutes of the Committee of Selection appointed to deal with the Winter Exhibition of Arts & Crafts

November 12, 1924 at 12 noon

Mrs Gotch (in the Chair), Mrs Naper, Mrs Garnier, Mr Procter, Dick (Hon Sec & Hon Treas)

"That the Secretary be empowered to ask those Exhibitors in cases where he had any doubt as to their exhibits not being their main occupation to ask them to sign a certificate embodying the words applicable from the Finance Act, 1923."

The Western Morning News, December 3, 1924

ART EXHIBITION

Christmas Show at Newlyn Gallery
...The private view on Friday, in spite of bad weather, was well attended, and a good many sales were effected. It is the first time in the history of the Gallery that handicrafts have been exhibited, and it is most gratifying to see the excellence and variety of the work shown.

...W Reynolds-Stephens, PRBS, has sent a beautiful little bronze statuette called "Joy", while his wife, an eminent embroideress, has on view a small embroidered panel of "The Vine," designed by C A Voysey. Omar Ramsden*, one of the leading silver craftsmen of the day, shows several pieces of chiselled silver, and another up-country artist, Miss Ellin Carter, a case of her fine leather work.

The Lamorna colony exhibit some beautiful jewellery by Ella Naper and Joyce Bertram, figurines of animals in pottery by Kate Westrup, and raffia and leather work by Mrs Lamorna Birch and her daughters. The Leach pottery, made at St Ives, makes a brave show of its handsome ware, while the St Ives Handicraft Guild have a number of their handwoven goods on view, as well as some beautiful baskets.

Miss H V Adamson shows illuminations, Mr Reginald T Dick has a stall of his "Pumcetto" pottery--as effective in a garden as indoors, also enamels and copper work by the Newlyn Art Metal Industry; Alec Walker displays hand-block printed crepe-de-chine scarves, and Miss Earle handmade dolls and leather work.

The two embroideries by M W Freeman of "A Flying Dutchman" and "The Vikings" deserve special praise, the latter being an original design by this well-known West country artist. Ernest Procter has sent a charming wall mirror and painted wooden ornaments, while Gertrude Harvey's hand-knitted bags are delightful in design and colour...

The Cornishman, December 3, 1924

LOCAL ART

The World on Canvas
Newlyn Exhibition
The exhibition of Newlyn artists was opened at the Passmore Edwards Art Gallery on Friday, and an innovation was the introduction of a craft section.

Stalls were arranged on which were shown examples of leather work, copper repousse work, raffia, beaten silver, pottery, etc., and these added considerably to the interest of the exhibition for many people.

One very noticeable feature was the total absence of large canvases, and this absence perhaps accounts for the lack of sea pictures which are often so much in evidence. This was rather regrettable, for a good oil of the sea will never fail to appeal, whether such a picture be "fashionable" or not. Most of the exhibits of the artists were small in size, and there was a decided increase in the number of etchings, line drawings, pencil sketches, etc., while the ultra-modern and problem types were scarcely represented; I say "scarcely" because one or two among the black and white drawings had just a suspicion of "What does it mean?" about them. But the faint suggestion was handled in a happy way...

STALLS AND CASES

Stall H was occupied mainly by the Leach Pottery of St Ives, where articles produced by Mr Bernard Leach were on view. These are, of course, all made by hand entirely from local materials, and appeal not only to the connoisseur but to the casual examiner. The chief endeavour of this Pottery is to produce with home materials a handmade, high temperature stoneware of personal design resembling in craft the Chinese early and Korean work of the Sung and Korai periods, but Mr Leach also produces Galena slip-ware of the old Devonian and Staffordshire type, which he regards as the backbone of English pottery.

69

[* Omar Ramsden, RMS, artist in silver, appears as an exhibitor at the Newlyn Art Gallery from its initial exhibition of crafts (1924). He continued to show his work at the following exhibitions: Summer, Christmas 1926; Summer, 1927; Summer, 1928; Summer, Christmas, 1929; Summer, Christmas 1930; Summer, Christmas 1931, Summer, 1932; Summer, 1933, etc to 1937. In 1935 he was elected to membership of the Newlyn Society of Artists.]

Two unidentified & undated photographs, Newlyn Archives, Top : Painting and craft exhibition, between 1927 - 1930 (Georg Jensen silver in foreground), Curator possibly R T Dick; Bottom: Probably the first craft exhibition, Winter, 1924.

The Newlyn Boy Scouts.

A LECTURE

in aid of the above movement, on

ROBERT LOUIS STEVENSON,

FROM A PAINTERS POINT OF VIEW.

will be delivered

by

T. C. Gotch Esq. R. B. C.

at the

PASSMORE EDWARDS ART GALLERY, NEWLYN,

on Friday, January 19th. at 5. 30 p.m.

ALFRED SIDGWICK Esq.

IN THE CHAIR.

Admission 2s. and 1s.

lets can be obtained at
The Newlyn Art Industries Showroom.
Messrs. R. Colenso & Sons, 3 Causewayhead, Penzance.
And at The Passmore Edwards Art Gallery.

Minutes of the Annual General Meeting, March 6, 1925
Gotch (in the Chair)
...The following dates for Shows were then decided on:
Show Days: March 20th & 21st
Spring Show: April 4th to May 2nd
Summer Show: July, August & September
Christmas Show of Arts & Crafts: Nov. 28th to Dec. 19th
...The Hanging Committee was then elected; it being suggested, and agreed to by all present that members votes should be taken by Voting Papers, early in March for the whole year. In case of absence, the next on the list would be invited to serve. It was decided that the Hanging Committee thus chosen should co-opt one or two craft members to act as well for the Craft Shows.

A corner of the village of Newlyn, which furnishes scenes from which the artists
who live there make many of their pictures.—(Daily Sketch.)

A Village That Is Noted for Its Artists and Its Fish

The scene in the Passmore Edwards Art Gallery at Newlyn, where the exhibition was held. Among the pioneers of the Newlyn School of artists was Stanhope Forbes (the son of an Irish railway manager). It was at Newlyn that he painted " The Health of the Bride."—(Daily Sketch.)

from *The Western Morning News* Saturday, March 21, 1925

WESTERN ART FOR LONDON

Brilliant Studies from Newlyn
Upholding splendid traditions

Yesterday visitors were given an opportunity of inspecting the work of the Newlyn artists destined for this year's Royal Academy, and hundreds of people took advantage of the invitation, the gallery in which the pictures were hung being thronged with admiring art lovers.

Newlyn artists are making praiseworthy endeavours to maintain the high reputation for conscientious work which has been built up by the many famous artists who have been members of the colony, and this year, although there is much that is foreign in the subjects, pace has been kept with modern ideas, and the work generally is good...

Artists' Aims

There are something like 50 pictures on view, and most of them, if not all, will be despatched to the Royal Academy on Monday. The subjects are as varied as they are interesting. In some cases colour and decorative design seem to be the chief objects aimed at; in others praiseworthy efforts have been made to produce pictures faithful in every respect to the subject.

It was difficult, however, to point to any one in the gallery and say "this is a great picture." Stanhope Forbes' painting of Penzance Railway Station on a busy day is a marvel of cleverness, and will no doubt be greatly appreciated by the Great Western Railway authorities as a magnificent advertisement, but some people will fail to see the same beauty in it as a work of art...

Another striking picture which will probably exercise the minds of the critics is Mr Ernest Procter's "Helston Floral Dance"...Mr F G Heath...Mr S J Lamorna Birch...Mr Harold Harvey...Mrs (Dod) Procter has produced a powerful picture out of a very simple subject. A girl sitting in a waiting attitude, chin resting on hand...Mrs Gertrude Harvey...Miss Midge Bruford...two small works by Mr S H Gardiner...Mrs W J Garnier...Mr G S Garnier...

from *The Cornishman* March 25, 1925

WHAT THE BRUSH CAN DO

Its Work at Newlyn Exhibition

The exhibition of the work of the Newlyn artists, which opened at the Passmore Edwards Gallery, at Newlyn on Friday, is one in which variety in work is noticeable, and the spring of new art, which was tapped, small but impulsive, a year ago, has swollen to the dimensions of a fair-sized stream...

And so I ask: what is the true calling of the artist? Is it not for him to render beautiful scenes of nature as the average mind sees them, but does not know it sees them until such scenes are presented to it by means of the selective eye of the true artist?...

TOESTRAP

From the Minutes, PEAG Committee September 16th, 1925
...It was decided that an afternoon "At Home" should be given on October 9th to the Fellows of the Gallery and Mrs Crosbie Garstin, Mrs Stanhope Forbes, Miss Frazier and Mr Barrie Bennetts had very kindly consented to arrange a musical programme...

from *The Cornishman*, Dec 2nd, 1925

SKETCHES New Class of Painting at Newlyn

The Growing Craft Section

The exhibition of pictures and craft work ...at present is notable, chiefly, for two features: The really excellent and representative collection of etchings and other dry-point illustrative work; and the completeness of the craft exhibition, and the utter finesse shown in its exhibits...

...The crafts exhibition is surely the most complete that has ever been arranged; the stalls, mainly, are kept down in size, so that it has been possible to obtain representativeness. The hand-woven scarves and materials, the hand-printed silks and stuffs of Miss P Barron, Mrs C. Harrison, Miss J Strangeways, Miss Denbigh, Miss H Jacobs and others; there is wonderful work by the pupils of the Weaving School of Crippled Girls...The jewellery and enamels by Mrs C H Johnson, Mrs Naper, the Newlyn Enamel Studio, and Miss H Seabourne are better than ever before. There is lots of leather-work, some of it made with a delightful Moroccan filigree effect and the pottery shown has improved in quality and increased in quantity. Mr Bernard Leach's stall has given pride of place to three large plaques, amber coloured, with dark coffee coloured designs; they are beautiful examples of the potter's work, and have been fully described in *The Studio*. They are of English slip-ware type, but the designs, on at least two, surely carry with them just a breath of a dream of the Orient...

TOESTRAP

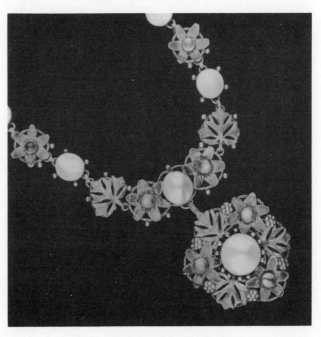

Necklace, designed and made by Ella Naper.

1925 Year's summary:
Gate money £69/3/8;
Pictures sold £192/4/0 (an increase of some £60 over previous two years)
Arts & crafts sold: £356/12/9

From the Minutes of the Joint Annual Meeting of Trustees, PEAG & NSA March 1, 1926
...Mr. Forbes was very strongly in favour of developing the full possibilities of the Gallery for social purposes: the providing of these cloakrooms was the first step to that end. As regards lighting the Gallery, he was quite in favour of gas being installed. This could be done at a small cost...

from *The Cornishman* First notice: March 24th, 1926

A DELIGHTFUL EXHIBITION

Colour-Magic

A feature that at once strikes the visitor to the spring exhibition by members of the Newlyn Society of Artists...is the symmetry in the range of sizes; a small thing, perhaps, but it gives one a favourable impression of the show as a whole, and the impression increases as one's study of the pictures proceeds.

GS GARNIER, RSGA, BWS

On the left, as you enter, are the aqua-tints, drypoints, and etchings of Mr G S Garnier and Mr F G Heath. Mr Garnier seems to show better work year by year, and his execution can be glowingly warm or most chillingly cold...Mr Heath is rather concentrating on etchings...They are clever and pleasing but there is not the delightful individuality in them that one always sees smiling from his sun-bathed oils, which have very often been the salt of the Newlyn exhibitions...

STANHOPE A FORBES, RA

...so representative a group of the excellency of his work would be difficult to find. There is no staleness nor monotony here...

ERNEST PROCTER

...The patchwork effect of last year has gone, and the artist is up-to-date in a different way. Mrs Dod Procter is also uncannily clever; and such works as "The Three Graces", "The Mischievous Boy," and the girl in a chair will probably all be accepted at Burlington House as representative of the ablest conceptions of new realistic and decorative art.

SJ LAMORNA BIRCH

...Mr. Birch has made Lamorna Cove a vast bowl of sunlight ["Morning Fills the Bowl"]...The picture is full of the beauty of a white world which winter boasts when she dons her mantle and waits in silence for the awakening summons of spring.

GARSTIN COX, ARWA.

...goes readily at his job, to judge by "the Pixies'Glen"...

TOESTRAP

Second Notice: March 31st, 1926

Some notable pictures

In our first notice of the Newlyn Pictures...we were only able to describe a few of the works...

Although we miss the outstanding works by such artists as the late Mr Walter Langley, Mr H M Rheam, Mr B W Leader, Mr Sherwood Hunter, and others who have crossed the shadowy frontier, there are still with us several of the pioneers including the doyen of the Newlyn Colony, Mr Norman Garstin. Unhappily... he is at the moment seriously ill...and represented in the gallery by a small but eloquent painting, "A Calm Evening"...If Mr. Garstin could not be met in his old haunt,...a life-like portrait of himself from the brush of his talented daughter, Miss Alethea Garstin, [also represented him]...

Mr T C Gotch...Mrs M Stanhope Forbes...Mr Harold Harvey is neither a veteran nor a novice...One has the feeling that Mr Harvey stands with one foot in the new ateliers and the other in the old Newlyn when he studied with Mr Stanhope Forbes...Mr J G Sykes...Mr R M Hughes...expresses his individual conception of Nature and Art [which] may challenge our criticism but wins our esteem and respect. Mrs E Hughes...Mr T Maidment...M Richey...Alison Rose...Mr. G S Garnier...CH Thompson...C W S Naper...M Bruford...F M Evans, a gifted veteran who still exhibits memorable work.

On the whole the tendency is to produce smaller pictures for which there is greater demand, rather than the massive paintings which used to entail the services of many models and involve great expense to the artist. A small picture, however, may be given a place on Academy walls and find a home in some drawing room or on some library wall. There were many such pictures at Newlyn, and some which we shall expect to see on the line at Burlington House or the Paris Salon.

from Bernard Walke, *Twenty Years at St. Hilary*

...On one of my visits to the Knights [in London] I remember going with Harold to a dinner given by A J Munnings at the Garrick Club in honour of Lamorna Birch when he was elected an Associate of the Royal Academy. The dinner was everything that a dinner should be -- good food, good wine and good company; the only thing lacking was the presence of the guest of the evening. Lamorna Birch had gone that night to a dinner at the Chelsea Arts Club. A J had invited all his friends but had forgotten to send an invitation to Birch until it was too late.

MR NORMAN GARSTIN

Mr Norman Garstin, whose death is announced from Penzance, as having occurred on Tuesday, was a well-known member of the art groups of Newlyn and St Ives, and a frequent exhibitor for some years at the Academy and the Water Colour Society shows. The son of the late Colonel William Garstin, of the 83rd Regt., he studied art in some of the Paris studios, and after a period in South Africa, which brought him into touch with the late Cecil Rhodes, came home and settled in Cornwall to devote himself to painting. He was a man of intensely individual impulses and opinions, and incurred unpopularity at times through his views on war and other topics. But he was a stimulating teacher and a shrewd critic, and had a true eye for a picture with old architecture and historic atmosphere, as well as a brush capable of rendering his intentions with rich effect...He figures in the present Academy exhibition in the form of a portrait by his daughter Alethea, who held a joint exhibition of work with him at Walker's Galleries two years ago. One of his sons, Dennis, was killed in Russia in 1918; his other son, Crosbie Alfred Norman, after some years of adventure overseas and varied service in the European War, has made a name as a contributor to "Punch" and has written nearly a dozen volumes of verse and travel and fiction.

from *The Cornishman* Dec 1926

A NEWER EXHIBITION

The widening appeal of the Newlyn Gallery
Art That Attracts

In the exhibitions at the Newlyn Art Gallery of recent years there has been a marked and steady improvement, inasmuch as there has been a continuous and obvious attempt to make the collections attractive to a wider public. The concentration on making the exhibition one of pictures only has disappeared: the sponsors of the gallery have taken the broader-minded view, and they have backed up the exhibits on canvas and paper with an infusion of the very real and very beautiful art that can be found in other branches of work.

But not only in the arrangement, the conduct, of the exhibition, has there been shown a determination to interest the public; in the paintings, etchings, engravings, there is work from famous brushes and famous styles that has a natural and easy appeal to the commonplace human, and that yet gives us the genius of touch, the perfect balance of colour, and the convincing reality of the artist, in the true sense of the word. The ultimate and present attractiveness of the present Christmas show is, in fact, a combination of improvements.

GS GARNIER, RSGA, BWS

TC GOTCH, PRPC, RI
STANHOPE A FORBES, RA
GARSTIN COX, ARWA
SJ LAMORNA BIRCH, ARA, RWS
THE LATE NORMAN GARSTIN

The more that one sees of Mr Norman Garstin's paintings, the more one realizes what a gap his death has caused in the local colony. There are four works of his, in the gallery now, in his facile, flowing style; two glimpses of the quiet upper reaches of the Severn, with the water in "The Severn at Quatford". and "Sunny Morning at Quatford" excellently handled. "The Farmyard" is not a large canvas but there is a spaciousness in its dealing which is restful and real.

ALETHEA GARSTIN
ALFRED HARTLEY, RE, RWA
FRED HALL

FURTHER ARTISTS: There are works hung by H V Adamson, F Roskruge, M Duncan, F M Unwin, F Perrott, B Leach, S Armstrong, J Ellis, PR Craft, RBC, RCA, G Foy, W Burne, K Airini Vane, JK Moir, F Milner, B Waters, M Grylls, R M Hughes, S H Gardiner, ABWS, F G Heath, E Gray, MS Forbes, E Fradgley, G Harvey, M Bruford, A Rose, M Richey, E Bunt, S Bamber, F M Evans, D Sykes, F M Unwin, and JG Sykes.

CRAFTS are shown by R Gillett, MA Hall, H Le Gallez, M Spanton, A West, M Robinson, E Roskruge, H V Adamson, L Bose, The Notary Binders, E Oldham, P Colman-Smith, H Thompson, MH Ballance. H Bulkley, L Heath, M G Hetherington, P Nesbitt, M Oldham, A Pollard, SE Sykes, P Webb, E Westrup, P Yglesias, E Bradbury, K Westrup, L Denbigh, I Turner, FL Welch, WH Creswick, R Davenport, C H Harrison, Newlyn Art Medal Industry, O Ramsden, RMS, E Naper, Newlyn Enamel Studio, HM Seaborne, the Misses Ash, M Hall, I Low, M Waters, D E Webb, K Radshaw, H & J Birch, H Bond, E Denyer, K Laity, D Raven, MA Rickard, E A Seaward, G Stewart, P E Webb, AM Wood, The Lamorna Pottery, The Leach Pottery, Fishley Holland, and A M Pearce.

TOESTRAP

1926 Year's Summary
Show Days, 19 & 20 March
Spring Exhibition, 3 - 24 April & 20 - 29 May
Summer Exhibition (Arts & Crafts) 3 July - 18 Sept
Christmas Sketches and Crafts Exhibition, 27 Nov - 22 Dec
  Gate money £75/18/3
  Pictures £254/5/6
  Crafts £592/2/10
'satisfactory and distinct improvement all round!'

MODERN NOTE IN ART

STRIKING PICTURES AT NEWLYN

Vivid Contrasts in Style

The orthodox and unorthodox schools of painting meet in vivid contrast today and tomorrow at the Passmore Edwards Gallery where the local Society of Artists' public exhibition of pictures intended for the Royal Academy and other spring shows is being held.

Mr and Mrs Procter sound the modern note with canvases that completely forsake conventional ideas; but the Newlyn School is noted for its versatility and works hung this season make their appeal to a wide range of tastes.

The leader of the colony is Mr Stanhope A Forbes, RA, who in "The Courtyard, Pendeen Manor," a place of much historic interest, gives one of those remarkable realizations of the beauty of ancient Cornish buildings for the painting of which he is famed...

THE CORNISH RIVIERA

Though a Lancashire man, Mr Lamorna Birch practically makes his home in Cornwall, which has brought him fame, culminating in the new honour of ARA. He shows several oils this year. "The Cornish Riviera" is an exquisite combination of landscape and seascape. On the hills between Penzance and Gurnard's Head Mr Birch felt the beauty of springtime in Cornwall and, looking back over Mount's Bay, the Great Western Railway and St Michael's Mount, he was impressed with the magnificent view that so many thousands of people admire. Tones and values are perfect in a wonderful picture...

THE MODERN SCHOOL

Mr Harold Harvey...

Mrs Dod Procter's "Morning Lady" partially clad and reclining in sleep on a couch is one of the large and instantly arresting oils...

Mr Herbert Truman, St Ives, strikes a new note in his picture of gulls...Mr CH Thompson, St Buryan, another sea picture...showing how two artists can portray the beauties of the deep from entirely different view-points.

IRRESTIBLE CHARM

Miss Alethea Garstin's water-colour "Commandeering Horses for the War, Brittany, 1914" has irrestible charm...Other pleasing water-colours are from Mrs Hughes, who sees beauty in trees; Mrs Harold Harvey, a student of flowers; Mr S H Gardiner ("The Land's End Road") Miss Dorcie Sykes (marigolds), and Mr J G Sykes.

For an artist so young as Miss Joan Manning-Sanders "The Pedlar" is a good character study.

...Altogether there are 60 pictures, and other artists represented in the gallery are Alison Rose, AF Walke (St. Hilary Vicarage), Mary E Richey, M Bruford, C W S Naper, M Lenny-Smith, H Adamson, C Vyvyan, and B Waters.

Wonderful Work of child of Thirteen
Study Which May be Seen at Royal Academy

From our special correspondent

NEWLYN, CORNWALL, Friday: A painting which set all the distinguished members of the Hanging Committee of the Newlyn Artists' Society agog with excitement when they gave it a good place on the walls at their annual spring show is the work of a surprising girl genius of thirteen years, who has hitherto been regarded as a precocity, but now seems to have passed definitely into the ranks of great artists in the making.

After studying her portrait of the old pedlar "Dungy"--a well-known local character, by the way--I drove out the four miles towards Land's End to find Joan Manning Sanders at home.

She is a big-built girl with a head of glorious auburn hair, a head which recalls the Rossetti portraits of Mr William Morris. She is just an unaffected child who, in normal circumstances, would be at school instead of attempting unusual masterpieces.

The astonishing thing about her portrait is its maturity of expressiveness. It is not a photograph, but the representation of a living personality...

...I learnt that two years ago, when she was only eleven, Joan's drawings caught the eye of the Rev Bernard Walke, the vicar of St Hilary, near Penzance. He has a beautiful church. He was seized with the idea that Joan could do a series of twelve symbolical paintings for his church, and she has, in fact, just completed them. They are in the church and have attracted widespread attention from connoisseurs.

GIRL ARTIST A GENIUS

1927 Building Minutes *

14.1.27 Mr Sherwood Hunter asked for drawings and full specifications for the suggested additions of bathroom and lavatory plus renovation of passage, floors of extension, flue of fireplace, the join of new building to old.

25.1.27 Mr Sherwood Hunter to proceed with work by agreement with Mr J B Cornish.

2.3.27 Mr Sherwood Hunter's estimate approved, for £130 , and he is empowered to go ahead.

*[Editor's note: It was at this point that a small annexe was adjoined to the rear right of the building. No plans or drawings exist for this small addition, and therefore it was not included in Chapter 2 as one of the major re-vamps of the Gallery interior. In later years this small addition has been employed as offices on the upper floor, and as the 'boiler room' or back kitchen on the lower floor. This usage remains the same now at the upper level, while the lower space is office/storage with projected plans to form a small kitchenette.]

Clockwise from top left:

Lamorna Birch

Ernest Procter, Reginald Dick, & Eleanor Hughes

Dod Procter's 'Morning'

Photos from *Daily Sketch* & *Western Morning News,* 1927

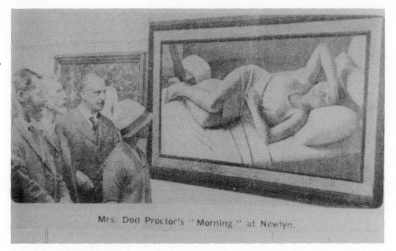

Mrs. Dod Proctor's " Morning " at Newlyn.

SUMMER EXHIBITION OF PICTURES & CRAFTS, 1927

The Western Morning News, July 20, 1927

FINE WORKMANSHIP ON VIEW

NEWLYN ART AND CRAFT EXHIBITION

The extending relationship between arts and crafts is exemplified at the exhibition being held...Pictures by notable painters are open to public view side by side with the crafts of those whose artistic faculty gives dignity and individuality to design and beauty to the workmanship of their own hands. A feature is the clever workmanship of a Devon blacksmith. At the present rate of development the time may come when the crafts section at Newlyn will be entirely Cornish.

Craftsmanship only is the subject of this article; the pictures will receive notice later.

The pretty Lamorna coloured pottery...

Miss Ravenscourt, a London exhibitor, also specializes in pottery, and the Newlyn Enamel Studio (Mr Reginald T Dick) makes a feature of pumcetto...

Hand-wrought ironwork has a resourceful exponent in...Mr. JAR Stevenson of West-hill, Ottery St. Mary...

Hand-woven clothes are displayed by Mrs. Luned Hamilton Jenkin of St Ives. In her Harbour weaving-room may be seen fleeces as they come straight from the sheep of the Pyrenees or the Shetland Isles...

Georg Jensen,* the Danish sculptor and silversmith, has a case of lovely silver ware, including a wine jug and rose bowl.

Miss Ellin Carter, RBC, Miss EM Dobito, London and Notary Binders have exquisite examples of bookbinding...

*[Newspaper cuttings from the period confirm the showing of silverwork by Georg Jensen at the following exhibitions: Summer, 1927: Arts & Crafts Exhibition; Autumn Exhibition, 1927; Summer, 1928; Autumn & Christmas, 1928 -- craftsmen not individually named but 'familiar ones' said to be there; and Christmas Show, 1930.]

Miss E. ELLIN CARTER
ART LEATHERWORKER

Gold and Silver Medallist
Exhibitor, Paris Salon & London
Caskets, Covers and Bags of every description suitable for Gifts and Presentations. Work may be seen on Tuesdays, Wednesdays and Thursdays.

128 CRAWFORD STREET, W.1

from *The Cornishman*, November 30, 1927

...Upwards of two hundred visited the exhibition on the first day, and business would appear to have been brisk; if the rush continues the artists and craftsmen may be hard put to it to make supply meet demand...

from *The Western Morning News*, 1 December 1927

100 PICTURES OF MERIT

Interest and a general standard of merit that is very high are always assured at shows held in Newlyn Art Gallery, as the exhibits are passed by a committee of artists, with Mr Stanhope A Forbes, RA, as leader. Moreover, the membership of the Newlyn Society embraces so many prominent painters and craftworkers that there is never difficulty in arranging a thoroughly representative and attractive exhibition.

Between now and December 22, the Society are certain of a great many visitors to the gallery for the Christmas show of sketches and crafts...

1927 Summary of year
Show Days, March 18 & 19
Spring Exhibition April 9 - 23 & May 28 - June 11
Exhibition of Arts & Crafts 2 July - Sept 17
Summer Ball -- Marina Winter Gardens: 235 in attendance
Xmas Show of Sketches & Crafts 26 Nov - Dec 22
   Gate £95/2/0
   Pictures £518/9/0
   Craft £640/10/8

from the article 'Mary Jewels' by Frank Ruhrmund, 1977

...It was, in fact, Augustus John who first focused national attention upon her in 1928 when he persuaded her to exhibit in London. Writing in the magazine Vogue at the time, he said: "She shows landscapes that are remarkable in the intensity of their earth-feeling. They blaze in the sight and are almost menacing in their hint of place-magic. The colour and design of her paintings convey something of the sensitiveness and wonder of primitive vision. If Mrs Jewels avoids sophistication her paintings will be of refreshing interest..."

...She has been called a "primitive", a term she dislikes intensely, "Makes me sound like some sort of savage..."

Minutes of the PEAG, January 10, 1928

Gotch (in the Chair)

Geyser in bathroom not satisfactory; get Mr Sherwood Hunter back. Heating is needed in the Gallery before another winter.

It was decided to have the words "Art Gallery" painted in two foot red letters on a cement ground....and the copper panels designed and executed under the superintendence of Mr J D MacKenzie to be overhauled....

from *The Western Morning News* , March 23, 1928

SPRING SHOW OF PICTURES

To-day and to-morrow pictures intended for the Royal Academy and other spring exhibitions ...will be on view at the Passmore Edwards Gallery, Newlyn. the opening hour this morning is 11:30 and to-morrow it will be 10 o'clock.

Exhibitors number 69, an advance on last year...Much of the work is on modern lines...

from *The West Briton*, March 29, 1928

WAR OF THE ELEMENTS

ERNEST PROCTER'S STRIKING STUDY IN NUDE

...one single room containing the lot...with so many as 69 exhibits, the walls are apt to be too full. Also, as the committee decide the position of pictures in accordance with their relative effect, the works of individual artists are separated and require to be sought. Perhaps this is a point in which St Ives scores, as individual studios contain nothing but the owner's works...St Ives shows a fair number of watercolours. At Newlyn there are a few only...Practically it is an oil exhibition and a good deal of it tends to keep pace with modern treatment. The nude, too, is very much in evidence...

...Perhaps the most arresting picture is "Earth, Water, Fire, Air" of Ernest Procter, Int Soc P. It represents the war of the elements, symbolised by nude figures...It is bound to provoke discussion, for there are those who "come to bury Caesar, not to praise him." Yet even to those who understand it least there is a strong appeal in the large conception of character in the faces of the figures...

At an exhibition, 1927: L to R (unidentified woman), Dod Procter and Midge Bruford (*Daily Sketch*)

from *The Western Morning News*, August 13, 1928

ARTS AND CRAFTS IN CORNWALL

FINE EXAMPLES AT NEWLYN EXHIBITION

...The Leach Pottery, St. Ives, started in 1920 by Bernard Leach with the object of producing with local materials a hand-made, high-temperature stoneware of personal design, resembling in craft the early Chinese and Korean work, is well represented. After eight years of experiment the pottery has begun to standardize both in stoneware and slipware, and it is obvious from this selection that a very successful attempt has been made to revive the characteristics of pre-industrial pottery...

JEWELLERY AND SILVERWARE

The jewellery and silverware are a striking feature of the exhibition. Miss H M Seaborne (gold medallist) and Mrs E Naper show the jewellery, Miss Seaborne's being the larger collection...

The silver is shown by Mr O Ramsden, RMS, and Mr G Jensen...The minute decorations on Mr Jensen's pieces tell of very careful moulding. Among his exhibits is a miniature of a fruit bowl embellished with a hanging grape pattern, which was executed for the Crown Prince of Sweden...

Fruitbowl with grape motif, designed by George Jensen in 1918, used on numerous bowls, candlesticks and bottle trays at the end of the First World War.

Listing from the Exhibition Programme of Pictures & Crafts July 12 - September 22nd 1928

BASKETS
H Le Gallez, P Hewitt, N Pascoe, M Spanton
BOOKBINDING
E M Dobito, The Notary Binders
BOOKPLATES & WOODCUTS
H V Adamson, E Oldham
EMBROIDERY
R M Carr, M H Freeman, F Horne, H I Low, G L Matthews
HAND-WEAVING
Barclay Workshops for the Blind, L Denbigh, The Kingsley Weavers, D & I Turner, F L Welch
HANDWROUGHT BRASS & COPPER
I Cooke, The Newlyn Art Metal Industry
HANDWROUGHT PEWTER
P Hewitt, E A Seaward
HANDWROUGHT SILVER
G Jensen, O Ramsden, RMS
JEWELLERY
E Naper, H M Seaborne (Gold Medallist)
LACE
The Misses Ash
LAMPSHADES
K Bradshaw
LEATHERWORK
B Craig, E Denyer, E M Dobito, E M Harvey, E Matthews, M G Newman, M A Rickard, E A Seaward
MINIATURES
J Pakenham
PAINTED FABRICS LTD
Disabled Soldiers & Sailors
POTTERY: The Leach Pottery, Ye Peasant Pottery, Devon
"Pumcetto" (Newlyn Enamel Studio), Wayside Potteries (St Agnes), R Wilson
SHETLAND WOOLLIES
A M Pearce
WOOD CARVING & INLAID WOODWORK
Romney Green, B A, R T Morton Nance
The Model of the Mausoleum of Halicarnassus (358 BC) was made by Mr William Harry of St Just

Minutes of the Committee of the PEAG, September 17, 1928

Arising out of the Minutes, the Hon Sec reported that the final payment for the bathroom annexe had been made to Messrs Sherwood Hunter Ltd, a new ceiling of beaver board had been put up in the dining-room, the outside of the building had been painted & necessary repairs done to the roof, and "Art Gallery" in large letters had been painted on the rear of the building, & the copper panels at the front, had been thoroughly cleaned and oiled with olive oil. Mr Peake's bill was submitted for the above, which the Hon Sec was instructed to pay...

from *The Western Morning News*, 24 November 1928

WORKMANSHIP OF HIGH STAND-ARD

...There are 104 sketches hung, and most of them are being shown in public for the first time. Whilst many of the exhibits are of subjects not directly connected with Cornwall, there are...paintings which typify the grandeur of the Duchy...

Lamorna Birch has sent a very beautiful selection...

TC Gotch's group of eight sketches presents a wide variety of subjects and atmospheres...

GS Garnier's "Gweek" is one of the outstanding pictures of the exhibition...

Stanhope Forbes gives a delightful glimpse of farm life...

RC Weatherby shows two striking Indian canvases...

Garstin Cox has two nice canvases, "Harvest Time" and "Springtime"...

...Most of the exhibits under such headings as basketry, book-binding, book plates, embroidery, hand weaving, hand-wrought brass and copper, pewter and silver, jewellery, lace, leather work, pottery and wood-work are familiar to those who make a habit of attending this exhibition...The exhibition should solve the Christmas present problem for all who attend.

1928 Summary of year
Show days 23-24 March
Spring Exhibition Easter April 7 - 21 & Whitsun May 26 - June 9
Summer Exhibition July 11 - Sept 22
Christmas Show Nov 21 - Dec 19
  Gate £127/9/6
  Paintings £530/7/6
  Craft £668/19/9

from *The Artist*, March 1990

CHRISTOPHER WOOD: THE LAST YEARS 1928 - 1930

...Falling somewhere between Naturalism of the '20s and Abstraction of the '30s, he is now regarded as one of the most important painters of the Modern Movement. Charming and attractive, Wood died in 1930 at the age of 29 under the wheels of a train in Salisbury Station. The tragic circumstances of his death have wreathed him as an artist in an aura of mystery and romance while his strong expressive paintings continue to be admired by generations...In 1928 he spent some months in St Ives and West Cornwall where he found the atmosphere and scenery and the influence of Alfred Wallis and his close friends, Winifred and Ben Nicholson most inspiring. for similar scenic atmosphere he was attracted to the coast of Brittany...

from the Minutes of the PEAG February 5, 1929

Forbes (in the Chair)

...An Ideal boiler has been installed by Maritime Recovery Company and heating is now good.

...Cowell, Drewitt & Wheatley, the architects, have reported on the lantern and the increasing subsidence. Necessary work has been carried out but there is much left to do...

Joan Manning Sanders' paintings going to Varnishing Day at the RA, 1929 (*Daily Sketch*)

from *Western Morning News*, November 25th, 1929

WOMEN ARTISTS OF NEWLYN

Prominent Exhibitors at Christmas Show

...A glance around the walls reveals most of the familiar names, although there are one or two absentees, noticeably those of the Procters and Miss Joan Manning Sanders. The latter's pictures are now very difficult to secure, for since her success at the Academy, every exhibition wants an example of her work, and as other studies demand a good portion of her time, this young artist is unable to keep up with the demand.

Though, as usual, the exhibition has produced some very excellent Cornish landscapes, the women members of the society have come to the fore with still-life subjects, and a feature of the exhibition is the number of remarkably fine flower studies...

from *The Daily Mail* March 21, 1931

NOTABLE NEWCOMER AT NEWLYN EXHIBITION

From OUR OWN CORRESPONDENT

Penzance, Cornwall, Friday

Most of the veterans are represented as well as several newcomers...Mr Stanhope Forbes, RA...Mr Lamorna Bird [sic] has gone to Aberdeen for inspiration and as a result...Mr TC Gotch...Mr Garstin Cox...Mr Morson Hughes...Mr Frank Heath...A newcomer this year is Mr Job Nixon, whose picture has the position of honour. It is a large canvas and has attracted considerable attention. He calls it "Gipsies." In the foreground is a typical Romany encampment...

from *The Western Morning News* March 20, 1931

...In "Gipsies" Mr J Nixon has been most daring in his colour selection, and although there is some evidence of grouping in the figures in the left-hand corner the general composition is of unconventional type. the drawing is of a character that one associates with certain phases of modern pictorial art...

from *The Cornishman*, March 25th, 1931

ACADEMY PICTURES

A Newcomer to the Newlyn Gallery
What He and Others Have Painted

There is little that is outstanding, and a good deal that is excellent in the spring exhibition of pictures...Most of the exhibitors hope that what they are showing in this gallery will get hung in the Royal Academy, and some of them probably will. That is what is known as a safe prophecy.

There is a new star in the firmament which radiates round the Newlyn Art Gallery; the Procters are not there and even if they were, many eyes would still turn to the painting by Mr Job Nixon, who lives somewhere near St Buryan, but is no native there; for Mr Nixon, at the very start, has put the biggest splash of colour in the gallery that the gallery has ever known. With just one picture he has loaded up the end of the gallery with such a gamut of colour that you stare. He has surprised even the artists, though they may not admit it: but the amazing thing is that he seems genuinely to have pleased them: genuinely to have excited admiration from the best of them. Colour, of course, is exciting...

from *The Cornishman*, Thursday, May 7, 1931

DEATH OF FAMOUS CORNISH ARTIST

Mr T C Gotch of Newlyn

We regret to announce the death of Mr T C Gotch, of Newlyn, one of the most distinguished artists of that famous colony, which occurred in London on Friday, at the age of 77.

Mr Gotch had gone to London for Varnishing Day, and the private view. His picture had been placed in a good position on the line, but unhappily he did not live to see it.

He was taken to Brompton Hospital suffering from pleurisy...

from _The Cornishman_, 6 July 1932

ART AT NEWLYN: Rare Collection of Mr Gotch's Works

...To make room for the works of Mr Gotch some of his colleagues have not sent so many as they have done previously. Mr Stanhope Forbes, RA, has only two...Mr SJ Lamorna Birch, ARA has three clever works...Mr G Garnier, ARWA, SGA has some amusing little works...Mr Job Nixon, ARWS, ARE, NEAC has only one of his etchings...Mrs Nixon is also showing a painting. Three artists from St Ives have sent along works: Mr Moffatt Lindner, Mr Borlase Smart, Mr John A Park...Miss Dorcie Sykes, Mr Garstin Cox, Mrs Maude S Forbes...To all lovers of homely studies the picture of Mr PR Craft, RBC should have a direct appeal...Mr R Morson Hughes...Miss JC Moncrieff Bell...EG Cresswell. The crafts include some wonderful designed work by Mr. Omar Ramsden, RMS, and works by Miss P Yglesias.
PENWITHIAN

from *Northamptonshire Advertiser* 25 March 1932

ROYAL MESSAGES TO LOCAL EXHIBITION

Prince of Wales Honours Work of Thomas Cooper Gotch

In the town which gave him birth, homage was paid to the name of Thomas Cooper Gotch, a great painter and a great man. It was a proud day for Kettering and the assemblage gathered for the opening of the memorial exhibition of Gotch's works at the Alfred East Gallery was a testimony to the reverence with which the name of the son it honoured was regarded...

from *The Cornishman* , 23 March, 1933

CORNISH ART NOTES AND MEMORIES

Artists, like other folk, move with the times. A few decades ago, in quaint little studios at Newlyn, the founders of the "colony" who had discovered the people who lived the "sheltered life" (except when at sea) in cottage homes and harbour scenes, created great canvases which compelled attention at the Royal Academy and other Exhibitions...To-day there are still masters of the art of painting among us, some dating from the days before Mr Passmore Edwards presented the Opie Memorial Gallery to the fraternity; but, being practical folk, they use smaller canvases, and mirror Cornish beauty scenes and other pleasing subjects on a scale which will appeal to buyers with smaller incomes and residences than in the days before the war, and before rival attractions robbed life of much of its leisure and restful charm. Sometimes young blood splashes in riotous colour or weird subjects, perhaps to attract attention, as we sometimes should through a megaphone; but at the Newlyn Gallery such veterans as Stanhope Forbes, RA, and Lamorna Birch, ARA show that they can catch the magic of the countryside of quiet streams, shimmering rivers, farmyards, and dreaming valleys, and tempt those who love both art and nature to covet these canvases to adorn their homes, or to add to the charm of such public galleries as have funds at their disposal.

****

Few of the Newlyn pictures this year are bizarre in subject or treatment; few are extravagant in size...

****

...One canvas has a pathetic appeal -- "A Cornish Waterway" -- by Garstin Cox, who recently passed away in the prime of life, after great strain and a short illness. It was painted in the neighbourhood of Mylor, and has caught the beauty of a tree-fringed waterway; but it makes one desire to see an exhibition of his "Sunshine Pictures," signed by "Garstin Norman Cox," which caused a lady who had watched his career to write that he had "added lustre and honour to the name given to him" as a tribute to Norman Garstin, who was then a notability -- some forty years ago...

One would like to dwell on Captain Borlase Smart's "Spate on a River at Invergordon"; on Mr. Fred Hall's poetical studies of rural beauty and charm --"Jubbergate, York" and "Winter Feed"...

...H.T.

West Cornwall landscape miniature (actual size) H Gluckstein (Gluck)

from *Manchester Guardian* July, 1933

NEWLYN SUMMER EXHIBITION

Concentrated Cornwall (From a Correspondent)

From No 1 to No 101 it is almost "Cornwall, Cornwall all the way," and much of it landscape. The Newlyn "school" at one period was going away from direct Cornwall, and only reflecting the exquisite shades of sea, sky, meadow, and cliff in paintings that were of any subject but local ones. Not that Mr Stanhope Forbes, RA, ever proved unfaithful to his fishermen, boats, and jetties, but his younger followers were off and away and the brush of the revolutionary was daubing paper and canvas with geometric enigmas that only the deeply lored in the cult could understand.

Like futurist poetry, futurist art seems in a decline. Newlyn Exhibition, which opens this week, is as simple to understand as nature's landscape. The cliffs, the sea...An influx of new artists has opened out some fresh pastures. Mousehole looms as prominently as Newlyn this year owing to an immigration of artists; St Ives is "going strong"; other hamlets are creeping up in "artist" importance...

The village folk are proud of the exhibition this year. It is more like the old times; they can recognise relatives or familiar local figures; familiar places. This is what they like. "Beautiful, aren't it, my dear?" "'Iss, Mr Farbes be in great heart, it do seem." "Did 'ee see that pretty piece by Mr Birch?..."

VI: 1935-44

from the Bulletin and Annual Report of the Russell--Cotes Art Gallery & Museum, Bournemouth, June 1935

Percy Craft and Mrs Craft
Mount Vernon, Belle Vue
Newlyn, 1897 approx.

PERCY ROBERT CRAFT--ACTOR AND ARTIST (1856-1934)

The son of John Craft, this somewhat delicate youth divided his attention between private tuition, and life in the saddle at his home at Milton in Kent, until he was sent to University College, London.

When his father died, he started life as an actor with an Old Stock Company run by Boughton of Plymouth, playing twelve different parts per week. These were the days of triple bills! His early memory was so retentive that he was able to learn his words whilst dressing and shaving. This faculty was partially destroyed by successive attacks of influenza.

Whereupon Craft entered the field of pictorial art, studying at Heatherley's and the Slade School under Sir Edward J Poynter, PRA, and Professor LeGros, and winning gold, silver, and bronze medals. For many years from 1882 his work was to be seen in the Summer Exhibitions of the Royal Academy and at other well-known Exhibitions.

His migration down south to join the well-known Cornish School around Penzance and St Ives about 1889, produced one of his best-known oils, "Heva! Heva!" Through street and court we 'Heva' hear, and he was there in the role of peacemaker during the riot of the fishermen in 1896.

It was at this period that he visited the East and obtained the material for many of his later works in water-colour and pastel, and probably, for the brilliant scene in oils now in our gallery...

In 1905, he returned to London where he continued to work (with an interruption caused by volunteer service -- he over military age -- in the Royal Army Medical Corps during the Great War) until his death late last year...

from *Journal of WASL,* 1990

...Ernest Procter died in 1935 and soon after Dod Procter gave up her studio in London and returned to live permanently in Newlyn. After election to the RA [1942, when she became the second woman RA in the century, following Laura Knight's election in 1936.] she toured the Canary Islands in 1938...later (in the 1960s) she often travelled with another of her artist friends, Alethea Garstin...In the inter-war period Dod Procter was one of the most successful women artists of the day...

Minutes of the NSA, April 4, 1935

...Election of Crafts Selection Committee: Mr Dick proposed that Mrs Naper, Miss Churchill Tayler and himself should form the Crafts Selection Committee with power to co-opt.*

...Mr Forbes then proposed that though Mr Harold Harvey, a non-member of the Society, already had two pictures hung in the Spring Exhibition, he should also be invited to show his picture "The Dresser".

[* This same group of three were re-appointed and re-confirmed at each AGM, serving until 1939.]

Minutes of the Joint Committees of PEAG & NSA, October 2, 1935

...LOAN EXHIBITION On the proposal of Mr. Forbes, seconded by Mrs. Naper, it was decided that the Loan Exhibition should be held in the Summer of 1936...The Committee for the Loan Exhibition: Mr Stanhope Forbes, RA, Mr SJ Lamorna Birch, RA, Mr CH LeGrice, Mrs Naper and Mrs Hughes.

...ELECTRIC LIGHT: Provided that the assembled committee had the right to authorise the withdrawal of the sum from War Loan, it was decided to use a sum not exceeding £50 for the purpose of putting electric light in the Gallery and in the flat below, the motion being proposed by Mr LeGrice and seconded by Mr Stanhope Forbes, RA...

from the Minutes of the Annual Meeting, NSA, March 5, 1936

...The Crafts Committee for the year was appointed as follows: Mrs Naper, Miss Churchill-Tayler and Mr Dick...On the Secretary raising the question of getting new crafts, Mr Borlase Smart said that it was for the Crafts Committee to go into this and endeavour to obtain new craftworkers. Passed unanimously.

...A proposal sent by letter by Miss Adamson concerning greater wall space to be given to Craft Members was discussed and unanimously rejected...

from the Minutes of the Cornish Loan Exhibition Committee, June 4th, 1936

...Posters: It was decided to accept Messrs Roach's estimate of £11 for 1,000 car slips; £1.5.0 for 100 posters; and £1.5.0 for 200 Show Cards, to be printed in yellow and black as the poster, a proof of which was approved.

...Exhibits: Mr LeGrice reported on his choice of exhibits from Mrs Pendarves; Mrs Naper on hers from Mrs Cade, and Mr Forbes on his from Major Williams, Viscount Clifden, Lord St Levan, Lord Falmouth and Miss Borlase.

from the Minutes of Arranging Committee, June 25th, 1936

...Arranging Committee: that Miss (Hilda) Quick should be co-opted to serve on the Arranging committee.

...Press Day: Press Day was fixed for Thursday, July the 16th

...Labels: Mr Garnier should be approached as to making the labels for the exhibits.

FOREWORD to the Exhibition programme of the Cornish Loan Exhibition of 1936

Ever since some forty years ago, when Mr J Passmore Edwards gave an Art Gallery to the artists of Newlyn, a constant series of Exhibitions have been successfully held by the Newlyn Colony, in which not only the work of the painters and craftsmen of this district has been shown but to which also many famous artists of our time not associated with Cornwall have contributed.

These Exhibitions have so far been confined to contemporary art, and it occurred to some of us recently that it might be well to try a new departure and to give a display on our walls of the work of the artists of the past, many examples of whose skill we knew were to be found in private possession in the Duchy.

This project met with the entire approval of the painters of the district as well as that of the Trustees of the Passmore Edwards Art Gallery, and it was decided to approach the various owners of Art Treasures in Cornwall and ask for the great favour of their loan. Our request received a most generous response, and through the kindness and consideration of the possessors of such treasures we have been able to assemble a collection the like of which has never yet been seen in Cornwall.

It was, moreover, as generously decided by the Newlyn Artists to give up the best time of the year to this Show, so that the largest number of people might have the opportunity of inspecting this unique Exhibition.

The works which our Gallery, therefore, is now showing were executed and fashioned by artists and craftsmen who have long since passed away but many of whose names are still revered by all art lovers, and we painters of to-day feel privileged in being able to offer the hospitality of this our Gallery to our confreres of the past and to accord them a hearty welcome to Newlyn.

STANHOPE A FORBES

The First LOAN EXHIBITION of the ART TREASURES OF CORNWALL held at The Passmore Edwards Art Gallery NEWLYN, PENZANCE

JULY 20th to SEPT. 5th, 1936

Lenders:
Mrs C H Bailey
Mrs Bainsmith
Lieut-Colonel E H W Bolitho, DSO
Miss Borlase
Dr Branwell
J A D Bridger, Esq
J G Burgess, Esq
Miss Cade
Viscount Clifden
Mrs Cornish
Miss C de W Lane
Marquise de Verdieres (aka Phyllis Gotch)
Mrs Doherty
Mrs Dunstone
Viscount Falmouth
Colonel Findlay
Mrs Stanhope Forbes
Stanhope A Forbes, RA
Geoffrey S Garnier, Esq
Norman Garstin
Mrs Norman Garstin
Mrs T C Gotch
Mrs Grant
Mrs Hankey
A W H Harvey, Esq
G H Johnstone, Esq
C H Le Grice, Esq
W Leslie, Esq, M D
Moffat Lindner, Esq
F A Magor, Esq
Mrs McAlister
Mrs Ella Naper
Bernard Ninnes, Esq
Lieut-Colonel Paynter
J S Pendarves, Esq
Sir Arthur Quiller-Couch
Miss Foy Quiller-Couch
Miss Hilda Quick
Mrs Quick
Sir Hugh Molesworth St Aubyn, Bart
Mayor & Corporation of St Ives
Lord St Levan
Alfred Sidgewick, Esq
John Symons, Esq
R W G Tyringham, Esq
Lord Vivian
Sir Courtenay Vyvyan, Bart
J Millar Watt, Esq
Miss Emily Westrup
Major John Williams

Minutes of the Joint Committee Meeting of PEAG & NSA
    January 14, 1937
    Mr Holman (in the Chair)
    ...Mrs Nichols read her report on the Loan Exhibition, explaining that there was a balance after all accounts had been paid of £7.14.1...

Minutes of the Annual Meeting of PEAG & NSA 11 March 1937
    Borlase Smart (in the Chair)
    ...Ella Napper then proposed that Borlase Smart be appointed to take Mr Birch's place while he was away in New Zealand.
    ...The Chairman desired to congratulate the Newlyn Society of Artists and Mr Stanhope Forbes upon the Loan Exhibition [of 1936] and said that it had done a lot for Art in Cornwall.

88

Letter from Max Chapman, Artist, to his cousin, Bernard du Sautoy in Penzance, 1995*

...The picture concerned [that I exhibited] was a large anti-war allegory, somewhat anachronistically informed by the Italian Renaissance influence of my art-school days. The year must have been approximately 1937/8. The size of the work (if my memory serves) was 8 ft x 4 ft, the largest picture of that year's exhibit.

More usefully, the Gallery at that time was being looked after by the poet and historical novelist, Wallace B Nichols and his wife. (These are personalities I had thought to bring to your attention, Bernard, in my rambling jottings to you. and will do one day...).

Clearly not a work to attract a private buyer -- and in the absence of any interest shown by public collections (despite much hype unloaded by the West of England edition of the News Chronicle (!) -- its then future became a matter of hearsay, probably through some friend of a friend. whoever that might have been was good enough to give the work sanctuary in his house in the Midlands --where its remains were last seen hanging on a stairway wall of his bombed-out house! Two other pictures of mine, both murals, one in Chelsea, one in the City, were targeted by Nazi bombs!

*Max Chapman [born 1911] painter of abstracts, portraits, figurative subjects in oils and emulsion, printmaker, collagist, art critic & illustrator, worked in Newlyn from 1936 to 1939, returning after the war for a few years, while exhibiting generally in London and abroad.

'Allegory' by Max Chapman, exhibited at Newlyn, 1937-8

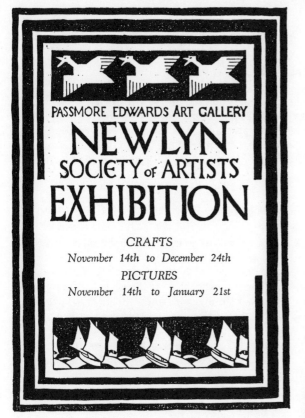

PASSMORE EDWARDS ART GALLERY

NEWLYN
SOCIETY of ARTISTS
EXHIBITION

CRAFTS
November 14th to December 24th
PICTURES
November 14th to January 21st

ADMISSION : SIXPENCE [1937]
CATALOGUE : THREEPENCE

Letter from Keith Gardiner to the Editor, 1995

...My father [Stanley Gardiner] was born in Reading in 1887, and apprenticed to a decorator. By attending evening classes, he won a scholarship to Reading University to study fine art. There he studied under W S Collingwood, one-time secretary and associate of Ruskin. He then went on to Arbroath Academy in Scotland to work in oils. With his wife, Bertha, he moved to Cornwall in 1923 to a cottage and studio in the Lamorna Valley. Over the rest of his life he exhibited at the Newlyn Art Gallery, also the Walker Gallery in Liverpool and the Royal Institute of Oil Painters. At one point he had a one-man show at the Fine Art Society in New Bond Street. From 1927 to 1949 he exhibited at the Royal Academy. Stanley Gardiner was an accomplished watercolourist, and made all of his own frames and mounts. He also made the picture frames for other local artists, including Stanhope Forbes. He died in Cornwall in 1952.

Stanley Gardiner painting *en plein air*, Porthcurno, 1938

PICTURE BY 'BUS DRIVER

Shown At Newlyn Exhibition

FINE MARBLE BY VICAR

...Its most interesting feature is the tug-of-war that has been going on for some time in that society between the old school and those who like to think themselves a little more modern, and it is represented on the one hand in pictures in which the subject is the thing the artist has striven to impress upon the viewer, and left the technique to be found by those who have the eye to see where it has been subtly applied, and on the other in pictures in which the subject is treated as a mere back cloth against which to show a method.

Among the former Mr Stanhope Forbes, RA, the veteran president of the society easily takes first place with a very fine portrait of an elderly lady. He has caught the serenity of her years remarkably well, in pose, in expression, and in his handling of the flesh tints.

While the society very often exhibits some of the best work in the Westcountry it has in this exhibition a little oil of old Newlyn by J Pappin, a "Western National" omnibus driver, and a Scillonian landscape by Lighthouse-keeper L C Hicks.

Vicar-Sculptor

A feature of the exhibition is a fine marble by Rev A G Wyon, who is now becoming almost as well known as the vicar of Newlyn West as he is as a sculptor. The subject is taken from Thomas de Quincey's "Suspiria," the story of the three semi-divinities, the mother of sighs, the mother of tears, and the mother of darkness, who plague man's heart until they have unfolded the capacities of his spirit. The three divinities are represented by three lovely feminine nudes in white marble. They hover above the world, which is represented by a sphere of Mexican onyx, a stone of remarkable beauty which appears to reveal its inner depths, and round the base romp a number of cherubs, representing mankind in infancy, blissfully unaware of the trials that life will subsequently unfold to him. The work is a beautiful conception of the literary theme, and has already attracted much attention in important exhibitions.

from The Western Morning News & Daily Gazette, Monday, November 14, 1938

Minutes of the Annual Meeting of PEAG & NSA, January 19, 1939

Mr Forbes (in the Chair)

... in view of the deficit it should be recommended to the Newlyn Society of Artists at the forthcoming AGM that they should raise their annual subscription by four shillings...it should be proposed at the AGM that subscriptions to the Newlyn Society of Artists should be payable in the current year and that failure to do so should constitute forfeiture of membership. Mr Wyon and Mr Nichols were instructed to prepare the wording of this resolution...

Minutes of the Annual Joint Meeting , February 4, 1940

Mr LeGrice (in the Chair)

...It was decided not to print the Balance Sheet this year, but that it should be available for examination at any time by the Fellows...

...that the usual catalogues should be printed in 1940 but it was left to the Secretary to use the unused Entrance Forms and change the dates to save the expense of printing...

...The Secretary said that she did not wish, in view of the situation to take any commission on sales this year. She was thanked for her generosity in this matter and her offer was gratefully accepted...

...The Secretary (Mrs Nichols) also said that she was willing to consider the question of her salary...but it was unanimously decided that she should be paid as long as it was possible...

Minutes of the Joint Committees of PEAG & NSA, February 12, 1941

Mr LeGrice (in the Chair)

...The Balance Sheet of the Gallery was read and explained by the Treasurer, showing a deficit for the year and a serious position unless something could be done to put the Gallery on its feet for the interim of the War.

Pilgrim Trust Grant...Mr Nichols had approached the Pilgrim Trust for a grant, and he was happy to be able to inform the joint committees that he had succeeded in obtaining a grant of One Hundred Pounds. The money had actually been received...

...No AGM should be held this year but that the Gallery Accounts should be open to inspection by any of the Fellows who so desired.

...Forms...it was decided to use a postcard instead of the usual forms for the coming year.

...to hold the Show Days as normally...to get into touch with Mr Fuller of St Ives and arrange the dates so as not to clash with Show Day at St Ives...the Spring Show from the 5th of April to the 26th of April and from the 26th of May to the 7th of June, and that the Summer Exhibition might start on the 5th of July, but this latter date was left to the Secretary.

...On the motion of Mrs Naper it was unanimously decided that no Annual General Meeting should be held this year...

Geoffrey and Jill Garnier
[Geoffrey in uniform of
Home Guard] World War II

Minutes of the Joint Meeting January 8, 1942
   Mr Holman (in the Chair)
   ...the Chairman requested the Secretary to write a letter of sympathy on behalf of the Joint Committees to Mrs LeGrice on the death of her husband.

from Wilhelmina Barns-Graham [Letter, 1994]
   ...Newlyn was the first Gallery I joined in 1942 having arrived in St Ives in 1940. The curator's desk was opposite the entrance slightly to the left of the main gallery, and I think the stairs linking to the lower galleries was fairly narrow, normal house-type stairs in Cornwall...

   Far too many works were packed in, the walls covered with mediocre, small traditional and academic work with here and there a more professional, distinguished painter. A feeling of brown-ness. One has to remember this was war time...

   ...The period before the 1940s must have been vastly more interesting -- and it seemed to hit a dull unimaginative period in 1940s and into the 1950s . It certainly is much more lively now and in recent years.

91

Minutes of the Joint Committees of PEAG & NSA, January 18, 1943
   Rev Allan G Wyon (in the chair)
   ...Special Exhibition: It was proposed from the Chair, and seconded by Mrs Hughes, that a small committee should be appointed to organise an exhibition of old scenes of Newlyn and District, this to be held on behalf of some charity together with the Gallery, the proceeds to be halved between them. The following committee was appointed: Mrs Dod Procter, RA, Mrs LeGrice, Mrs Hughes and Miss Garstin, with power to co-opt.

Minutes of the AGM of PEAG & NSA, 1944
   Mr Forbes (in the Chair)
   ...a letter of appreciation and thanks to Mr Robinson and Mr William Peak for their generous action with regard to the Special Exhibition held the previous year.
   ...Vote of thanks: Mrs Hughes proposed a Vote of Thanks to Mr and Mrs Nichols for their untiring work for the Gallery and the NSA.

George Lambourn
'Test Pilots',
1943

ONE ARTIST'S WAR

from *George Lambourn (1900-1977)* biographical notes published by Newlyn Art Gallery in 1982, on the occasion of an exhibition of paintings and drawings. The monograph by John Halkes

...In 1936 on a tour of the west country in his open Sunbeam -- he visited Mousehole, a small fishing village on the western shore of Mounts Bay...When a disused school came up for auction he bought it for £400 and converted it into a studio home...

...At the outbreak of the second world war and at a crucial stage of his career, he joined the Red Cross and in early 1940 he went to France with an ambulance unit attached to the British Expeditionary Force...The destruction, the plight of the wounded and the refugees made a lasting impact. He was Mentioned in Despatches in the withdrawal and returned from France to paint some startlingly uncompromising images on the horrors of war. "Those They Left Behind" a dark painting of a row of bodies in a Calais cellar Dressing Station was purchased by the Imperial War Museum.

In July 1940 George Lambourn joined the British Volunteer Ambulance Corps and commanded No 1 Section as it deployed to Northern Command. His pending application as an official war artist was cleared at around this time and he was able to do a series of watercolours of the military installations. (Three of which are in the collection of the Imperial War Museum.)

When the need for this ambulance corps came to an end he was directed to work on the shop floor at Hawksley Ltd: an aircraft factory at Gloucester. Most of the works painted then were sold off by auction for the 'Aid to China Fund' with the exception of the large painting "Test Pilots".

An event occurred at this time which was to shape the next four years of his life. He decorated the canteen and recreation area at the factory and this was so successful that he was offered a YMCA appointment with the newly formed Combined Mediterranean Forces. His task was to follow the allied armies to set up and decorate canteens, theatres, libraries and rest centres. His first men were twelve Italian prisoners of war who were later joined by British soldiers who were no longer fit for active combat.

From 1942-1946 George Lambourn's 'private army' followed the war from North Africa through Italy to South Austria. Gradually decorating became secondary to the role of therapy for troops although this was not army policy and was something which just evolved. Officially the title was 'Army Decorating Section' and in the minds of most people it was a team doing a special job. But George Lambourn knew the value of practical work for men suffering from battle shock and fatigue...For many, too, it was an opportunity to learn a new skill which would serve them well back in civilian life. His dedicated team spared no effort; towards the end of the war they ran weekend painting schools for soldiers and had created a chain of civilised havens through the length of Italy, not to mention major exhibitions in Rome and Graz...

He returned to Mousehole in 1946...the large building [St Clement's Hall] was spartan and demanding...He turned the large school hall into the 'Merlin Theatre' and had the local men and women involved in Shakespeare. The theatre was to last until 1951...*

[*This school-turned-theatre was subsequently converted into the St Clement's Gallery, Mousehole (owned and managed by Janet Bennette , who latterly was to become an administrator at the Newlyn Art Gallery). More recently it is employed as an artist's studio by a Royal Academician who is also a member of the NSA.]

VII : 1945 -1954

from the Minutes of the Joint Committees of PEAG & NSA, February 8, 1946

Lamorna Birch, RA (in the chair), Mrs Naper, Mrs Hughes, Miss Garstin, Mrs LeGrice & the Rev AG Wyon

...Mrs Hughes proposed that a sub-committee should be elected to deal with the decoration of the Gallery and to deal with the matter forthwith. Mrs Kerr, Mr Charles Simpson and Mr Weatherby were elected to this committee with power to co-opt others...

from the Minutes of the AGM of the PEAG & NSA, March 29 1946

The Rev AG Wyon (in the chair)

Votes of thanks:

...to Mr Carle for his generously advertising the Exhibitions in his Cinema free of charge.

...to the sub-committee elected for the decoration of the Gallery...there and then dissolved.

Tea Committee: It was decided that the Artists were to entertain the Fellows to tea (on the Show Days) and Mrs Oldham and Mrs Cooper were elected to serve on a tea committee for the year.

from the Minutes of the Joint Committees of the PEAG & NSA, January 17, 1947

The Rev AG Wyon (in the chair)

Secretary's Commission: It was proposed by the Chairman that the Secretary's Commission on sales, which had been forgone by Mrs Nichols during the War, should be restored to her from, and including the current year.

Lamp Post: The request from the Penzance Corporation to be allowed at a rental of One Shilling a year, to place a lamp post in a corner of the Gallery Premises was refused unanimously and the Secretary was instructed to write to that effect to the Borough Engineer.

Minutes of the Joint Committees of the PEAG & NSA, April 24, 1947

The Rev Mr Wyon (in the chair)

Radiators: Mr. Simpson volunteered to see Messrs Nicholls of Penzance about the radiators, oil burning, which Mr Hoyton had recommended for use in the Gallery, and if these were approved he would order same, two of them.

Report: It was unanimously approved that the Annual Report of the Gallery should again, after the lapse during the War, be printed and distributed to Fellows & Members.

Minutes of the Joint Committees of the PEAG & NSA, October 8, 1947

Lamorna Birch, RA (in the chair)

Plaque: The suggestion made by Mr Nichols that a bronze Plaque in memory of the late Stanhope Forbes should be placed in the stone oblong beside the entrance door was discussed and unanimously approved. It was proposed by Mr Hoyton that this plaque should be executed by Mr Wyon and that the cost of it should be raised by private subscription among the Members of the Newlyn Society of Artists and the Fellows of the Gallery, and that it should not be paid for by any kind of public subscription.

The Rev Allan Wyon preparing the plaque of Stanhope Forbes for the exterior of Gallery, 1948

94

Minutes of the AGM of PEAG & NSA, March 19, 1948

Lamorna Birch, RA (in the Chair)

...no picture should be hung which had been on the walls during the previous two years.

...the article about the Gallery in *The Cornishman* should be reprinted to the number of 500 copies and sold in the Gallery for sixpence. [Reprinted below.]

Cornwall's Home of Art

NEWLYN ART GALLERY

Reprinted by courtesy of "The Cornishman."   *PRICE SIXPENCE*

from THE CORNISHMAN, Thursday, December 11, 1947, by Wallace Nichols

The foundation stone of the Art Gallery at Newlyn, the name of which, to speak more accurately, is "The Opie Memorial Gallery" was laid on the 22nd of May, 1895, by the late J Passmore Edwards, at whose charges it was built...Unfortunately he did not endow any of his gifts.

The Newlyn Art Gallery is unique in that it is the only gallery of its kind in England. That is to say, it does not belong, as do most art galleries, to the local corporation, but is in the hands of a number of trustees. Also its exhibitions are of works by contemporary artists, and it does not house a permanent collection. It was given to the district at the time when Newlyn School was in its provocative beginnings, and was erected to enable the group of artists then working in the neighbourhood to show their work to the public.

Contrary, however, to what seems to be the prevalent local opinion, it does not belong to the Newlyn Society of Artists, which is an entirely separate body, and the Gallery is not run by the Society.* But under certain clauses in the constitution of the Gallery the Society is allowed to hold its exhibitions in the Gallery free of charge provided certain conditions are fulfilled. But the two bodies, the Newlyn Society of Artists and the Passmore Edwards Art Gallery are quite separate, with a different committee and a different balance sheet.

The Gallery itself is run, under the trustees, by certain appointed agents, and up to the present, for the convenience of working, the two secretaryships, that of the Society and the Gallery, have been held by the same person. Not being endowed, the finances of the Gallery are made up from two sources: the annual subscriptions of Fellows, and a donation from the Newlyn Society of Artists. The admission fees go to the Society and not to the Gallery. It is another misapprehension that the Society has the right to hold its exhibitions in the Gallery, but it only holds them there provided it fulfils certain conditions laid down in the Gallery's constitution, and the Gallery can be, and has been, let for other exhibitions, and can be hired. But there are conditions as to that: it cannot be hired for any purpose other than one connected with the arts. That is to say, it cannot be hired for a public meeting, a political meeting or a religious gathering.

***

The Newlyn Art Gallery has a remarkable history, one probably not to be paralleled by any other Gallery in England of the same size and local association. On its walls were first hung many pictures which are now in various great public galleries all over the world, including the Tate Gallery in London, and the people of Penzance and its district have had the privilege of seeing these pictures for the first time. They should be proud of the fact, but seem to be unaware of the importance of what is in their midst, for the majority of visitors to the Gallery are strangers and not residents. During the tenure of the present secretary people have visited the Gallery from all parts of the world, some of them coming to Penzance solely for that purpose, among them Dutch, French, American, Danes, Norwegians and even Indians and Chinese. Only recently one of the most eminent of contemporary Norwegian artists was sent by his government especially to see the Gallery. Its fame, therefore, is world-wide. And yet it is difficult for the Gallery to secure fifty of the inhabitants of the district to be annual subscribers.

The subscription is one guinea, and this entitles the subscriber to an invitation to all private views, and to free entrance at all times to the exhibitions of the Newlyn Society of Artists, and also to a dozen complimentary tickets for giving away to friends. There are usually four exhibitions each year.

***

The Gallery, of course, is associated with the fame of the Newlyn School, and a word or so about that may not be amiss, for the present generation seems not to understand what is meant by it. It was not a school in the sense that it was a teaching centre, though Stanhope A Forbes had for many years a school of painting. But what is meant by "The Newlyn School" was a method of painting which in its day was new and quite revolutionary. Until Frank Bramley, Walter Langley and, above all, Stanhope Forbes himself, and their earliest associates in the little village of Newlyn, began to paint in their particular way, nothing like it had been seen in English art, and "The Newlyn School" must be understood in something the same sense as for instance, "The Dutch School,", "The Venetian School" and so on. Now in what did this newness of method consist?

***

It was simply that the landscape painted was done entirely out of doors from first to last, and was a faithful transcript from Nature done on the spot. Previously, even in the case of so great a landscape painter of Constable, the practice had been to make sketches on the spot, but to work up the picture itself in the studio. Directness of painting was sacrificed to a traditional gloss and arrangement. Today this direct painting is the rule rather than the exception, and it is difficult to remember that it is a method little over sixty or seventy years old in England. It had its origins in France, and it was in France, under the great French painter Bonnat, that Stanhope Forbes learnt to paint his landscape solely in the open-air and to paint directly from Nature.

When his early work, and that of his Newlyn associates, was first shown in the Royal Academy, the result was revolutionary. It was derided by most of the critics of the day, and was considered as "immoral" as the most advanced work of Picasso, for instance, is today. It is not easy to get back into the common outlook of the late 'eighties' and early 'nineties' and to understand how this new freshness of painting seemed like a slap in the face to the public of that day.

***

These early and revolutionary pictures were first shown in the Newlyn Art Gallery, and thus it has a part in the very history of English art. These pioneers should be remembered with honour, even though contemporary painting has largely abjured their principles. Stanhope A Forbes, Elizabeth Forbes, Walter Langley, Frank Bramley, Henry M Rheam, T C Gotch, Fred Hall, Norman Garstin, A Chevallier Tayler, G Sherwood Hunter, H S Tuke, and many others. Later artists who have worked in the neighbourhood and exhibited their pictures in the Newlyn Gallery include Sir Alfred Munnings, the present President of the Royal Academy, S J Lamorna Birch, Dame Laura Knight, Harold and Gertrude Harvey, Ernest Procter, Dod Procter, Charles Simpson, R C Weatherby, R Morson Hughes and Eleanor Hughes and, again, many others. Art has by no means ceased to function in West Cornwall. Only a year or so back a picture which was exhibited on the walls of the Newlyn Gallery was bought for the Chantrey Bequest, and now hangs in the Tate Gallery, London, as part of England's national collection.

During the war years, as was only to be expected the Gallery carried on with some difficulty, but its policy of remaining open was fully justified. More than one Service-man and Service-woman expressed themselves as grateful for the spiritual oasis which they found there. Since the war its activity has increased, and the year 1946 was one of the most successful in the whole history of the Gallery. It has a past of which Newlyn and Penzance should be proud, and its future should be fostered by the appreciation and support of the whole neighbourhood....Wallace Nichols

*[Editor's footnote: This arrangement, in practice, was to begin to change within five years of this article; by 1959, the NSA was licensed to 'run' the Gallery.]

Minutes of the NSA, December 8, 1948

Lamorna Birch, RA (in the Chair)

...*Forbes Exhibition:* ...it was decided to hold the Stanhope Forbes Memorial Exhibition from May 28th to June 18th; ...the Tate Gallery should be approached concerning the loan of "A Health to the Bride" ...the pictures should be fetched from the Faugan by St Loy at the Society's expense...that the Arts Council should be approached about financial help towards the framing of the pictures...

unattributed cuttings, May 30, 1949

IGNORE MODERN PAINTERS SAYS SIR ALFRED

Meets old friends at Penzance

Sir Alfred Munnings, President of the Royal Academy, talked to old friends in the Queen's Hotel, Penzance, last evening, recalling the days he spent painting at Lamorna and the old friends of those times.

With him and Lady Munnings were Mr S J Lamorna Birch, a fellow RA; Mrs Lamorna Kerr, who is also a painter, Mr James Lennox Kerr, the writer; and their young son, Adam Kerr...

FORBES MASTERPIECE IN CELLAR WHILE MATISSE IS 'HUNG PRECIOUSLY'

Sir Alfred Munnings: Make a Row

...[he] spoke out angrily at Newlyn on Saturday at circumstances that put Stanhope Forbes's masterpiece "Toast to the Bride" in the cellars of the Tate Gallery, while "absurd" pictures by Matisse were hung with lavish wall space as if they were "worth 10,000 pounds apiece"...

"I think the best thing Newlyn people can do is to hire three or four coaches on one of those expresses and march in a body to the Tate, like the women who wanted a vote, and make a row about it."

...Among those present at the opening of the exhibition were Mrs Mary Rowe, who, as Miss Stephenson, was Forbes's model for the bride in his picture "Toast to the Bride." and Mr John Henry Tonkin, who was his model in his picture "The Lighthouse". The exhibition contains 85 examples of Mr Forbes work...

Top: Sir Alfred Munnings on Gallery steps, Reverend Allen Wyon in doorway at rear.
Middle: Stanhope Forbes Memorial lecture by Sir Alfred Munnings (standing), seated (L to R) Colonel E H W Bolitho, Lord Lieutenant of Cornwall, Mrs Maude (Stanhope) Forbes, and Lamorna Birch.
Bottom: The plaque admired by Sir Alfred Munnings, Lamorna Birch and Mrs Houghton Birch.

PRINTED BY GUIDO MORRIS
SAINT IVES

Holiday
Sketching Group

SEASON 1949

Eric Hiller (left),Charles Breaker (right), & Marjorie Mort (left of CB)

Directors

ERIC HILLER

CHARLES BREAKER

from the Introduction, New Art Centre Exhibition: 1977, by David Brown

...By late 1948 some of the members of the St Ives Society of Artists were becoming apprehensive of the growing number of their colleagues working in more advanced styles, and at suggestions that exhibitions no longer be jury-free. Tension developed and as a result 20 of the more adventurous members resigned. At a meeting at the Castle Inn on on 8 February 1949, 19 people, including Bernard Leach, resolved to found the Penwith Society of Arts in Cornwall, making Herbert Read president...Furthermore the painters and sculptors would be divided into two groups, A and B, one essentially figurative, the other abstract...

The Penwith Society's rule on the division of artists into figurative and non-figurative caused irritation and in 1950 six members, first Hyman Segal, and then others including [Peter] Lanyon resigned. Lanyon began to show his work, as did John Tunnard and John Armstrong at about the same time, at the Newlyn Gallery and these artists were an invigorating force among the Newlyn Society of Artists...

Minutes of the Artists' Meeting following the AGM, March 17, 1950

Lamorna Birch, RA (in the Chair)

Hanging:...there should be three hangers for each exhibition. The following were elected to serve on the Hanging Committee for the forthcoming year: Charles Simpson, Mr Hoyton, Mr Cobb, Mrs Hoyton, Mrs Kerr, Mrs Dod Procter, Miss Garstin, Miss Duncan and Miss Bruford, three to serve at each hanging as already arranged.

Festival of Britain: The Gallery and the NSA having been approached by the Borough of Penzance to co-operate in an Art Exhibition in Penzance during the Festival of Britain, the Rev AG Wyon and Mrs Nichols were appointed to represent them on the Borough Council's Committee for this purpose.

Minutes of the NSA, July 10, 1951

Mr E Bouverie Hoyton (in the Chair)

Winter Exhibition: After much discussion it was finally decided to continue the present (Summer) Exhibition until the 15th of September, and instead of the usual Winter Exhibition to hold a Christmas Fair, the arranging of which should be in the hands of Mrs Procter, Miss Garstin and Mr Hoyton, the choice of exhibits to be left to their discretion, and they would also seek out suitable craft-work for exhibition. The two small walls of the Gallery should be reserved for sketches (unframed but mounted) and that there should be a large Christmas Tree, with the exhibits on the tree all of one price...

Minutes of the Joint Committees of PEAG & NSA, Stanley House, Alverton, January 11, 1952

Charles Simpson (in the Chair)

The Committee received with sorrow and regret the news that Mrs Nichols was so dangerously ill that she could no longer exercise the functions of curator and secretary. The Committee agreed that Mr W Nichols should be appointed as temporary deputy curator for a period not exceeding six months from Jan 1, 1952...

The Committee then discussed the possibility of improving the amenities of the Gallery and the prestige of the Society and the suggestion that a merger should be made with the St Ives Society of Artists if this would be generally acceptable.

It was unanimously decided to send if necessary a sub-committee of three to meet St Ives representation and to explore the possibilities of association. The sub-committee to consist of the Rev Wyon, Mrs Kerr and Mr E Bouverie Hoyton and that Mr Hoyton should act as temporary President of the Society until the AGM.

Minutes of the AGM, March 21st 1952

E Bouverie Hoyton (in the Chair)

...The Rev Mr Wyon proposed that the Society should have, and proceed to the election of, a President. Mr Lamorna Birch, RA was elected unanimously...

Mrs LeGrice, on behalf of the Trustees expressed her deep appreciation of the work of the late Mrs Nichols as Secretary and Custodian, and also to Mr Nichols for his constant and voluntary assistance...

Minutes of the Joint Committee

Held at the Gallery immediately following the AGM

Present: Lamorna Birch, RA (President), Mrs Dod Procter, RA, Miss A Garstin, Mr C Simpson, Mr Hoyton, Mrs LeGrice & the Rev A Wyon

...The Joint Committee interviewed the two candidates for the vacant post of Secretary & Curator.

Mrs Hunt was appointed by ballot to the post under the following conditions:

(a) She undertook the duties of Secretary to the NSA at a salary of 50 pounds p a.

(b) She was to serve at the same time as curator & custodian of the Gallery at a salary of 50 pounds p a. Making her total salary 100 pounds p a in all.

(c) She would reside free of rent, etc in the flat attached to the Gallery with the provision that the large room in the basement being at the disposal of the Trustees or the Artists Committee whenever it was needed.

(d) That her appointment could be terminated at 6 months notice on either side. Notice being given in any quarter day.

S J 'Lamorna' Birch, RA
elected President of Newlyn
Art Gallery, March 21, 1952

100

from the Minutes of the NSA, June 20th, 1952

Mr E Bouverie Hoyton (in the Chair)

Gallery Affairs: Mr Hoyton read a letter from Messrs Cornish & Birtill relating to the legal agreement between the Trustees and Mrs Eileen Hunt as curator...It was agreed that the sum of 5/- weekly should be allowed for the cleaning of the Gallery. The amount of Commission on the sale of pictures was then discussed, and it was decided to raise the present rate of 10% to 12 1/2%, 10% to go to the secretary and 2 1/2% to the Gallery, the amount of 20% for non-members to remain unchanged, 10% to the Secretary, and 10% to the Gallery...

...Means of increasing publicity were then discussed...the sale of pictures had been good, attendances could be greatly increased. It was decided to lop back, or cut down, the trees obscuring the building.

...Mrs Kerr suggested that a box for a chair fund might be placed in the Gallery, and the Secretary was instructed to do this.

from the Minutes of NSA Meeting, September 3, 1952

Bouverie Hoyton (in the Chair)

Christmas Fair: notices for the Fair should be sent out as soon as possible to enable craft workers to have time to prepare...It was decided to have a White Elephant Stall as last year...Miss Freeth to become a co-opted member of the committee for this exhibition.

Exhibition of children's art: ...Mr MacCarthy and Mr Alex Mackenzie had made enquiries about the possibilities of holding an exhibition of Children's Art in the Gallery...must find out what the position is regarding the sale of such work, and whether we should be liable for Entertainment Tax if the work shown was not for Sale...if no entrance fee could be charged, a rental should be asked, and any publicity should be arranged by the promoters of the exhibition.

Telephone: Mr LeGrice having passed on correspondence from the Telephone company, with a list of subscribers who might possibly share a party line, the Secretary was asked to approach the possible ones, as there was little hope of getting a private line for some time.

from the Minutes of the Joint Committees of the Trustees & the NSA, February 13, 1953

Charles LeGrice (in the Chair)

Report on Gallery Building: Mr Drewitt explained the estimates for the repairs to the Gallery...First priority repairs (structural) would cost about 65 pds, Second priority repairs (necessary) about 105 pds, and third (redecoration, badly needed but not essential) about 125 pds. Mr LeGrice said that if the property was put into good repair, this should be maintained, otherwise the Society might lose the use of the Gallery altogether.

Repair Fund: Ways & means of raising money were discussed...the Press, the Fellows & the AGM should be informed...local societies such as the Photographic might be glad to hire the Gallery or the large room downstairs...

Programme: As the boys' art exhibition had been successful it was decided to have further similar shows...possibly those on loan from the Arts Council during the intervals between the NSA Exhibitions...Mr Graham Binns of the Arts Council was willing to attend the next Committee meeting to give advice about an application to the Council for help with the repairs.

Gift Pictures: Mrs Kerr suggested that the artists were asked to give some of their own work for sale in aid of the Repair Fund, and this was agreed. Prices were to be kept low, five pounds and under, and these pictures would be shown during the RA show.

Minutes of the NSA, 24 March, 1953

Mrs E Lamorna Kerr (in the Chair)

...The application to the Arts Council was discussed, with the aims of the Society, the year's programme and suggestions for raising money for the repair fund.

...It was decided that the Society should try to secure the co-operation of young painters in the district. Mr Hiller proposed inviting three local artists, Jack Pender, Alexander MacKenzie and Dennis McArthy. Mr Armstrong seconded this.

...Mr Armstrong proposed that competitions should be held during the summer exhibition with gift pictures as prizes, competitors choosing a number of the most popular pictures on show. The competition should be well publicised and results published at the end of the exhibition.

...Mrs Crosbie Garstin and J Morgan Hosking should be approached about the possibility of holding concerts or recitals in the Gallery.

...Invitations to the Friday evenings were to be sent with notices of exhibition dates, and would start on Friday, April 10th. Mrs Kerr proposed that members should pay 1/- and be allowed to bring a friend...

Elizabeth Lamorna Kerr,
'Mornie' at Flagstaff Cottage
Lamorna, 1952-3

unattributed cutting, 1953 by Denys Val Baker

PAINTINGS MADE DIRECT FROM NATURE

...And Newlyn has good reason to be proud of its artists, from Stanhope Forbes and his friends onwards. Norman Garstin, Lamorna Birch, Harold and Laura Knight, Ernest and Dod Procter, the Harveys; these are a few names that come to mind, along with those of two gifted painters whose recent deaths have robbed the Newlyn Society of two of its foremost members, S H Gardiner and R C Weatherby.

But no art colony, or artist for that matter, can live on the past: and perhaps Newlyn paid official farewell to that with its big 1951 exhibition of the work of some of its famous earlier painters -- notable inclusions being Stanhope Forbes's 'Health of the Bride' and Dod Procter's 'Morning'.

Dod Procter is still busily painting and her work and that of others of the older generation -- such as Charles Simpson, Lamorna Birch, and R Morson Hughes -- bear excellent testimony to the high standard of what might still, loosely, be called the Newlyn School. At the same time, many other painters have come to work in Newlyn, or near Newlyn.

One thinks of the etchings of E Bouverie Hoyton and the paintings of his wife, Inez E Hoyton, with their unusual colours; of the paintings and drawings of David and Jean Cobb, with their strong focus on the sea and ships; of the excellent drawings of Geoffrey Garnier, and the striking paintings of George Lambourn (apparently a more politically conscious painter than most); of the exquisite carvings and sculptures of Barbara Tribe, and many more.

A word is also due to Charles Breaker and Eric Hiller, who, apart from their own paintings have built up a thriving summer art school at Newlyn, to which students come from all over the country. Then there are Newlyn's two stormy petrels, John Wells, the abstract painter, and Mary Jewels, a natural primitive painter...Neither of these painters is much favoured for exhibition at the Newlyn Gallery, yet both have achieved reputations with the art critics -- John Wells with his intricate, carefully evolved designs of colour and space and perspective; Mary Jewels with her vivid almost childlike paintings of Newlyn fishing boats and Cornish houses.

(Incidentally, Newlyn might well pay greater tribute to Mary Jewels, for she was born in Newlyn and describes herself as "a true Celt loving my Cornwall": entirely self-taught, her work has been greatly admired by the late Christopher Wood and Augustus John.)...

Minutes of the NSA Committee July 18, 1953

Mrs E Lamorna Kerr (in the Chair)

...Mr Hiller proposed forming a Loan Fund so that work could be started before long, members and fellows to be asked to loan sums free of interest, which would be repaid as funds were collected from dances and other functions...

...Miss Bruford asked if artists whose membership had lapsed needed to submit work again if they wished to rejoin, and it was decided that this must be done...

Minutes of the NSA Committee October 26, 1953

Mrs E Lamorna Kerr (in the Chair)

...The fancy dress dance to be held on Friday, November 20th was discussed and judges chosen for selecting prize-winning costumes. Mr Lamorna Birch RA to present the prizes to the winners. All details were in the hands of the Dance Committee...

...no repairs had been started...

from the *Newlyn Notebook* of Michael Canney, Mary Jewels & Cordelia Dobson

The Tregurtha sisters were genuine relics of an older Newlyn, but touched by a certain metropolitan sophistication. Conversations would range over visits from Mr Asquith to friendships with Lawrence of Arabia, Ben Nicholson and Christopher Wood, or Augustus John, who admired and collected Mary's paintings it was said. Cordelia had retreated after her divorce from Frank Dobson, leaving Mary to act as her lifeline with the outside world and the gossip of Newlyn and St Ives. Vine Cottage was the communications centre for information about the two colonies. Cordelia was the mistress of total recall, from what Henry Moore was wearing at a nineteen-twenties arts ball, to what Sacheverell Sitwell said to the butler when the Dobsons came to visit. Mary's pictures were, I thought, less good than her conversation, but at their best they may indeed have influenced Christopher Wood.

102

The Newlyn Society of Artists

Secretary's Report [Eileen Hunt]

The year 1953 was a lively and enterprising one for the Society, although all the new ventures were not entirely successful.

...The Life Class was not well enough attended to pay for itself, and had been discontinued.

The Arts Council turned down the Society's application for assistance with repairs to the building, but a Loan Repair Fund had been started by Members of the Society and Fellows of the Gallery. The sum of £250 had been raised, the President Lamorna Birch having started the fund off with a donation of over £70. After some delay repairs had now begun starting with essential work on the roof.

...The closer co-operation with other Societies suggested last year had been achieved, Miss Misome Peile, chairman of the Penwith Society, and Mrs Wilkins, Secretary of the St Ives Society, being most helpful.

103

Minutes of the NSA Committee February 12, 1954

Mrs E Lamorna Kerr (in the Chair)

...it had been worth holding [the Fancy Dress Dance] in spite of the small margin of profit. A good foundation had been laid down for another dance as this one had proved a success socially.

...As repairs have still not begun...a sub-committee should be formed with full powers to act in the matter, Mrs Kerr, the secretary and a member appointed by the Trustees to form the sub-committee...

Christmas Show:...the value of an exhibition at this time of year queried, in consideration of the lack of craftsworkers and apathy of the public. The possibility of discontinuing this exhibition but keeping open from early spring to late autumn without the customary break was suggested by the secretary and adopted.

'The Lanyon-Canney Years' Letter from Jeremy Le Grice (Worpswede), 1995

In the early 1950's the Newlyn Gallery tended to be regarded as a bastion of vague neo-impressionism particularly practised around Lamorna.

Due to the (inevitable) accident of Peter Lanyon disagreeing with the ideologies of the youthful Penwith Society, he transferred his considerable energies and enthusiasms to the Newlyn Gallery around 1953. He personally attracted painters to West Cornwall from London and around the country, many of whom exhibited at the gallery during the later 1950s...

Minutes of the AGM of PEAG & NSA March 26, 1954

Lamorna Birch (President) Mrs E L Kerr (in the Chair)

...Mr John Armstrong wished to rent the large room below the Gallery for a period probably of at least a year, and it was agreed that details should be arranged with the Trustees & the Committee.

Committee: The appointment of a committee of 12 members, including officers, proposed at last year's AGM was confirmed according to the Constitution. Mr Charles Simpson and Mrs Procter were the two retiring members. Mrs Procter was re-elected, and as Mr Simpson was not able for health reasons to attend meetings, Mr Peter Lanyon was elected in the vacant place.

The President: Mr Birch said that if the Society was to prosper, artists must send their best work to Newlyn. He expressed the sorrow of the Society at the deaths of Mr George Manning Sanders, Mr Seal Weatherby and Mrs Reginald Dick.

from the 'Newlyn Notebook' of Michael Canney
...During the time of Eileen Hunt's curatorship, John Armstrong painted the Bristol Council House ceiling mural in the lower front room at Newlyn Art Gallery. Armstrong was living in Lamorna and working there. The mural, which was on canvas, was so large that it had to be wound around three giant rollers, from which it was unwound as needed and painted, a section at a time. It was eventually "marouflayed" (stuck) to the Council House ceiling where it still is...

Minutes of the NSA Meeting, April 13, 1954
Mrs E Lamorna Kerr (in the Chair)
...A final draft of the [appeal] letter to be sent to the Press. Miss Bruford suggested that an appeal might go to A J Munnings, and to Laura and Harold Knight, and Mrs Kerr thought Mr Birch would send them a personal letter...
...Miss Freeth had offered to re-paint the front door of the Gallery and the Committee accepted this offer gratefully, leaving choice of method & materials to Miss Freeth. Mrs Kerr suggested that as Miss Freeth had helped considerably in many ways, the Committee might co-opt her as a member...
...Miss Garstin proposed that the Secretary should be given a whole day off in each month...

Minutes of the NSA Meeting, July 2nd, 1954
Mrs E Lamorna Kerr (in the Chair)
...*Artists Materials* Although Messrs Winsor & Newton's had not agreed to supply the Society with materials direct, the correspondence had resulted in more adequate stocks being held by the local agents.
...*Evening Hours* The question of opening during the evening was discussed but not adopted, as it was thought not worth the work involved.

Minutes of the NSA Meeting, October 28, 1954
Mrs E Lamorna Kerr (in the Chair)
...*Small Picture Exhibition* The exhibition of small pictures was discussed and it was decided that the size must be limited to approx 10 x 14 inches, framed. The posters advertising the exhibition were to be printed...
...*One Day Sale* The one day sale in aid of Gallery funds was discussed and on the proposal of the Secretary it would be held on 4th December, the last day of the exhibition.

'Looking to sea' by Marjorie Mort

4 UNKNOWN CORNWALL

touch with ancient things, and with strange memories, with a people whose thoughts and visions are marvellously remote from those of the crowded populace.

No ordinary train : no ordinary journey. You start beneath the smoky glass and hideous iron tracery of Paddington ; in less than six hours you are in the midst of a land

LAMORNA : MR. BIRCH'S HOUSE ON THE SKYLINE

of mystery ; a land so beautiful and so alluring that the love of it and the longing for it will remain with you always.

Look at the passengers. They, too, are out of the ordinary. There is my cheery friend, John Birch—" Lamorna Birch "—dispensing traveller's hospitality with a persuasiveness that is quite irresistible. Here is a group of chirpy young women, of the type that grows so freely on camp stools—recruits for

105

Page from *Unknown Cornwall*, a drawing by Charles Simpson.

Minutes of the NSA Meeting, February 3, 1955

Mrs E L Kerr (in the Chair)

Mr Wyon expressed the sense of loss left by the death of the President, Mr S J Lamorna Birch, and of sympathy with Mrs Kerr and her family. Members stood for a moment in silence.

...Mr John Armstrong was appointed Vice-Chairman.

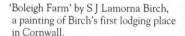

'Boleigh Farm' by S J Lamorna Birch, a painting of Birch's first lodging place in Cornwall.

Newlyn Society of Artists

Ballot for Hanging Committee

Please place the mark X against the six members you wish to elect on the hanging committee for the current year. The result will be announced at the AGM...

Bruford, Miss M F
Bell, Miss I M
Bland, Miss S J
Barnes, Mrs Garlick
Breaker, Charles
Bedell, Miss E
Duncan, Miss M
Garnier, Geoffrey
Garnier, Mrs J
Garstin, Miss A
Hiller, Eric
Hocken, Miss M G
Hoyton, E Bouverie
Hoyton, Inez
Hambley, Arthur
Johns, Mrs D
Kerr, Mrs E Lamorna
Law, Denys

Lawrenson, Miss D A
Lanyon, Peter
Mort, Miss M
MacKenzie, Alexander
Procter, Mrs Dod
Barkins, Miss M E
Pennington, George
Peile, Miss Misome
Simpson, Charles
Sefton, Mrs Ann
Singleman, Mrs B
Tomlin, Geoffrey
Waters, Miss Billie
Wyon, Mrs Eileen
Tunnard, John

106

(Members living out of the district have not been included on this list.)

[Ed note: In effect this list represents the local members of the NSA of 1955; there was always a fair number of distant ones, residing elsewhere, or not available due to travels.]

Minutes of the Finance Sub-Committee, August 17th, 1955

Charles LeGrice (in the Chair)

Income: ...the minimum sum required for the annual income was £150, since salary and rates were about £95 per annum, and an indefinite amount had to be allowed for repairs and maintenance. After some discussion it was decided to suggest to the Committee of the NSA that either the commission on the sales of pictures should be increased from 12 1/2% to 15%, or the annual £1.1.0 subscription be raised, and the extra amount go to the maintenance fund.

The possibilities of letting the large room below the Gallery, and of drafting a letter to circularise residents of the district asking them to become Fellows, were discussed, and it was decided to meet shortly to decide on the best course. Ways of attracting in more visitors were suggested, including an outside frame to hold representative pictures, tubs of flowers, and a large notice board...

Minutes of NSA Meeting, 15 September 1955

Mrs E L Kerr (in the Chair)

Col Williams'* Talk: [on August 31 past]... had been a great success financially and socially, the sum of £35 had been raised after paying expenses. It was suggested that a certain amount should be put towards a Chair Fund...

...Mr Wyon said that he had been a Fellow of the Gallery for over 19 years and that as he was retiring and leaving the district he would now have to resign from his liaison office between the Trustees and the artists. Mrs Kerr expressed the gratitude of the committee for all Mr Wyon had done...

*[Col J H Williams, a well-travelled Cornishman, was the author of *Elephant Bill, Bandoola,* & *Big Charlie,* all books about elephants; he was popularly known as 'Elephant Bill', and much loved by his artist friends and neighbours.]

Secretary's Report [Eileen Hunt] 1955

During the last year the Gallery was open for 27 weeks in comparison with 26 in 1954 and 21 in 1953, but for the first time in the last few years there was no increase in the sales of pictures or admissions. The fine weather affected this as all other Galleries, and kept everyone out of doors.

Visitors...on the whole, found the mixture of traditional and contemporary styles of painting interesting and stimulating. Pictures by Peter Lanyon, Alex Mackenzie, Jack Pender and Clifford Fishwick sold as well as those by Lamorna Birch, Dod Procter, Alethea Garstin, Charles Simpson and Denys Law. More local residents visited the Gallery regularly, local children had been very interested, and several schools had sent classes down to each exhibition.

Personal contacts make more difference than is perhaps realised, quite a number of sales had been made through what were initially social channels, and members could do more by bringing in their own visitors and helping to publicise the Gallery whenever possible.

More help is needed in seeing to publicity, display and so on. When visits to printers, deliveries of posters, payments to banks, arrangements for crating pictures, all have to be seen to before opening the Gallery at 10 o'clock in the morning, it is not surprising that there have been a few occasions when the door was opened a little late. A good many stray callers who come out of hours pleading to be let in as it is their last day when generally a call could easily have been made at the proper time.

As an experiment the Gallery was opened for a few hours on Good Friday, on a Sunday, and on one or two evenings, but the attendances were negligible. If members were sufficiently keen and the scheme was well advertised it might be possible to make one certain evening every week an open night.

The building has now been put into repair as far as the essential priority repairs were concerned. The repair fund was almost exhausted but there is a lot of re-decorating needed. The roof and guttering has been carried out...a new fireplace put in the flat to replace a broken one...The outside appearance and garden are still in bad shape. If this had ever been put in order it would be possible to maintain it, but while the fence was down and boys playing football and cricket on the green ran in and out it was impossible to keep well, and while the Gallery is open it is difficult to keep an eye on the back...

Until last year when the weather defeated us, over £200 had been added each year to the takings, which had gone from £156 in 1950, and £170 overdrawn in 1951 to £746 in 1954 and £632 in 1955, and perhaps this year we shall do better still...

Minutes of NSA Meeting, January 26 ,1956

Mrs E L Kerr (in the Chair)

The Dance: The result of the [November] dance was discussed...it was worth holding if it paid expenses, so it had done, without making much profit. Mr Hoyton suggested holding several dances in the Gallery.

Gypsy Market: The result of this [10 December, 1955] had been a profit of £70 which was considered satisfactory.

RA Exhibition: ...so few artists were sending up to the Royal Academy that it would be inadvisable to hold an exhibition.

Minutes of NSA Meeting, March 16, 1956

Mrs E L Kerr (in the Chair)

...Mr Armstrong had resigned from membership and from the Committee, having left the district, and Mrs Hunt had decided that she must resign at the end of the required six months.

...Mr Lanyon suggested that the Gallery could not be run on a voluntary basis and that it is essential to get grants from some source...

...The question of letting in more members was discussed but it was decided that it was essential to keep up a certain standard of work...

Minutes of the AGM of the NSA, March 22, 1956
Mrs E L Kerr (in the Chair)

The chairman read her report... She said the Society would be very sorry to lose Mrs Hunt, and she herself wished to resign from the Chair and would not seek re-election...Miss Garstin proposed a vote of thanks to Mrs Hunt, saying what a pleasant atmosphere she had created in the Gallery, and how much she had increased the sale of pictures, during her five years as Curator...

Minutes of NSA Meeting, April 26, 1956
Denys Law (in the Chair)

Accounts ...Mr Kemp suggested combining all three accounts, and after discussion it was decided to use the Gallery account for paying in Fellows' Subscriptions and the Society account for all other purposes...

Post of curator ...the position should be advertised in *The New Statesman*...

Guest Artist Miss Garstin proposed inviting Mary Jewels to send a group of 4-6 paintings to the summer exhibition...

from West Briton, (undated,est October, 1956)
'Gallery's New Curator'

Two years ago Mr and Mrs Michael Canney spent their honeymoon in Mousehole. During the past week they have returned to West Cornwall -- but this time in charge of the Art Gallery at Newlyn.

Mr Canney, who has taken over as curator from Mrs Hunt, is the son of the Rector of Redruth, Canon W R Ladd Canney. His wife, Madeleine, has many relations in the district.

At the moment they are busy settling in at the gallery and making preliminary arrangements for the Arts Ball which will take place in mid-December.

from WEST BRITON, November 22, 1956
Exhibition Twice Usual Size

Newlyn Artists

That a close bond exists between the farmer and the artist was suggested by Mr L Graham White, chairman of West Penwith Rural Council, who opened an exhibition of works priced up to ten guineas at the Passmore Edwards Art Gallery, Newlyn, on Saturday. The exhibition included drawings, paintings, sculpture and pottery.

Mr White said he had been a farmer most of his life, but he was not one of those to whom the prefix "rich" might be added. He was a true farmer as distinct from a gentleman farmer. The distinction was that a true farmer ate what he could not sell, and a gentleman farmer sold what he could not eat.

As a farmer he had an eye for the beauty of nature apart from a professional eye. The farmer and the artist were both very close to nature. Both combined the skill of the hand with a knowledge of the tools they used. The farmer and the artist...work with the skill of our hands - our workshop is the open air...

SIXTEEN NEWCOMERS

The exhibition this year is double its usual size, and includes works of more than 16 artists who have never shown at the gallery before and some of whom have a national reputation...

from *The Cornishman,* undated
NEWLYN ARTS BALL

Rock 'n' Roll Display & Picasso Decor

...There was plenty of rock 'n' roll atmosphere about the decorations. The curator and Mr Charles Breaker had given everything a Picasso flavour...The prizewinners were Myth & Legend -- 1 Mrs Pat Pickles as 'Prince Charming' and in General fancy dress -- Mrs Franklyn Pool as 'A Girl of the Twenties'. A competition which offered a painting by the late Mr Lamorna Birch was won by Miss J Franklyn Pool. The master of ceremonies throughout the evening was Mr J Lennox Kerr* and the dancing provided by Russell Pengelly and his band.

*[Ed Note: The novelist & travel writer-husband of E Lamorna Kerr]

"Tereska" by Jeremy LeGrice has a quality of directness and depth and the same firmness and impatience of unnecessary details are reflected in the artist's group, "The White Jug Still Life."
E Bouverie Hoyton
Denys Law
Lionel Miskin
Marjorie Mort
Jack Pender
George Lambourn
Karl Weschke
Dod Procter
"Fish" who exhibits several of her charming cat studies, also shows a pleasing view of St. Ives in pencil.*

Among a large number of "moderns" John Tunnard, Ithel Colquhoun...

Some excellent sculpture is exhibited by Barbara Tribe and Michael Butler, and pottery by Bruce Taylor, Patty Elwood, Barbara Tribe, Peter Lanyon, and the Penzance and Lamorna Potteries. A kitchen table and chair in Oregon pine by Robin Nance, an innovation at Newlyn, is also shown.

[Ed Note: Anne Harriet Fish, Mrs Sefton, caricaturist and social satirist, creator of 'Eve' of *The Tatler,* during the 1920s and 1930s.]

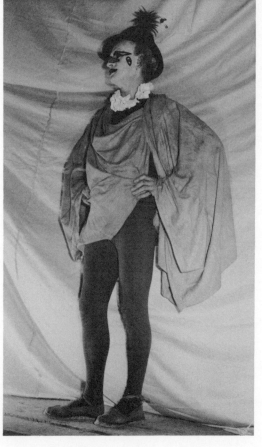

Three Arts Balls, 1950s-60s
Top: 1956, Theme: Rock 'n' Roll
Left: L to R Eric Hiller, Charles Breaker, Pat & Bill Pickles
Right: An Arts Ball aficionado, Charles Breaker

Michael Canney teaching *en plein air*, Jeremy Le Grice at left.

from the *Newlyn Notebook* of Michael Canney

Phyllis Gotch, otherwise known as the Marquise de Verdieres Bodilly, daughter of T C Gotch, was originally married to a French nobleman, and latterly to Judge Bodilly in Hong-Kong. The Marquise who features frequently in Gotch's paintings as a flaxen-haired nymphet, retained her fairy-tale appearance into old age, complete with fancy dress & golden slippers. Extremely persistent, she maintained that not only was Gotch the most outstanding artist at Newlyn, but that he and his wife founded the colony. Fantasy was her forte!

She lived at Wheal Betsy, a house with C F A Voysey overtones, above Newlyn. There she established a shrine in Gotch's studio, where not only his pictures were stored long after his death, but also his hat, his last cigar, his walking stick and coat, and a tall-boy full of letters and other papers, dating back to the early Newlyn days. There was even a letter from Whistler. At some time, in the thirties, I think, she master-minded a fisherman's protest against the destruction of old Newlyn, when the locals were persuaded to vacate their picturesque cottages for new & hygienic council houses, inconveniently placed high above the village.

As a result, a fishing boat, *The Rosebud*, sailed to Westminster with a petition, signed by locals and artists, and it was said that the Marquise sailed with it. It was something of a 'cause celebre' at the time, and the Marquise if one was to believe her, became a local heroine. Both Dod Procter and Alethea Garstin, however, thought the Gotch's had pretensions. Personally I found the Marquise had a certain fey charm although I could not rely upon her stories.

from the *Newlyn Notebook* of Michael Canney

A flamboyant figure, "Bouverie" Hoyton added colour to the Newlyn scene. An ex-Rome scholar and Head of the Penzance Art School, he was given to grandiose and even outrageous statements, but he did provide a useful link between the older Newlyn members and the newcomers. Friendly for a time with Nicholson & Hepworth and possibly Gabo, he later came to regard them as subversive 'modernists' whose aim was to jettison the traditional artists, but he was not alone in this.

Sutherland, a fellow student at Goldsmiths' came and stayed with the Hoytons when he was studying tin miners at work in Geevor mine, and the first public display of an abstract work by Nicholson in West Cornwall took place at Penzance Art School in a travelling exhibition. 'Bouverie' could therefore be said to have acknowledged the presence of 'modern art' in a traditional area, although firmly traditional in his own work. It also seems likely that he was responsible for employing John Tunnard and Bernard Leach at Penzance Art School, and also approached Barbara Hepworth, but without success.

Letter from Jeremy Le Grice (Worpswede)

'...The appointment of Michael Canney as curator in 1956 consolidated the transformation of the appearance of exhibitions. The pleasure he took in the company of artists, his powers of observation, mimicry and anecdote, together with a reckless sense of humour and excitement in the earlier days of his job, sharpened the atmosphere considerably.

' I was fortunate to be able to observe this at close quarters when, during the winter '56/57 I used the lower front gallery as a studio (whilst preparing for Slade entrance). In those days access from the main gallery was via a tortuous metal winding staircase and the ground floor presented a domestic scene of nappies drying in front of a one-bar electric fire, news of the Suez crisis over a crackling radio and Madeleine juggling baby-food, cups of coffee for complaining, disorientated artists or quietening vociferous poets -- Sydney Graham and Arthur Caddick appeared to take the place on as a retreat from the pubs.'

'FOR MADELEINE MICHAEL AND SIMON'

[This poem was written late at night at Newlyn Art Gallery on one of Sydney's many visits. He also did drawings with Roger Hilton at the gallery, but these were unfortunately destroyed.]

Now after midnight, Madeleine
And Michael and the abstract man
And I myself who write this down
Talk here in the sleeping town.

Let the abstract distances
Make their love there in the dark.
And the baby, Simon sleep
And never never loveless weep.

So across the starless sky
The dark proportions come and go.
Face to face the lovers lie
Once or twice before they sigh.*

Simon boy, on every breath
You take so smally now tonight
The dark intelligences ride
And from those you shall not hide.
                    *First draft -- "Before at last they turn and sigh."

Drawing of W S Graham
by Tony O'Malley, 1960

from *The West Briton*, Spring, 1957

150 EXHIBITS TURNED AWAY

Newlyn Art's "Best Ever"

"Almost unique" was how Mr Charles Le Grice described the Newlyn Art Gallery of 1957, when on Saturday he officially declared open the Spring exhibition of the Newlyn Society of Artists.

Speaking of the history of the Gallery he said that it was started in 1895. "Ever since then finance has been our difficulty." From the beginning it had been kept in a state of repair by the Fellows of the Society. "We can only hope that more people will become Fellows again."

During the war years, the building became sadly neglected, and when the war ended, their major concern was to get the building back into a good state of repair. That was a big job. With the help of the architect (Mr G B Drewitt), they had got the building looking rather much better inside and outside.

With the newly-painted walls of grey, the pictures showing to full advantage by the light traps in the roof, Mr LeGrice said he had never seen the gallery looking quite like this before...[he] felt it was a great pity there was not more space available...about 150 exhibits had been turned away...The artists were, however, lucky to have a gallery like that at Newlyn. Everyone must be made to realise that...

from The Cornishman, April 11, 1957

Newlyn Art Gallery's Revival

Exhibition of Merit

Serious Competition of St. Ives

Those who have not visited Newlyn Art Gallery for some months will find it very much changed. The public section has been entirely re-decorated with improvements instigated by the curator (Mr Michael Canney).

Going through the entrance, the visitor sees the foyer, now part of the exhibition space, framed through the door in the facing wall of deep red. The gallery and foyer have now been repainted a restful shade of grey, while overhead, lamps are trained on to the walls.

The Spring Exhibition, to be opened on Saturday by Mr C Le Grice, is without doubt the best for many years, not only because of the quality of the painting, but also because of imaginative hanging. There is a fair balance between   representational   and non-representational schools, with the addition of some new names, and if the present improvement continues, the Newlyn Art Gallery will be well on its way to being a serious competitor of the two main galleries at St Ives.

Principal work of the exhibition is Peter Lanyon's *Saracinesco* 1957, a six feet by four feet abstract canvas recording his emotional experience in this Etruscan hill village high up in the Italian mountains...This work is in the same class as some of those he showed recently in his successful one-man exhibition in New York.

Nearby hangs Michael Canney's *Chapel at Tredavoe* an abstract in which the artist conveys impressions with diverse shapes of contrasting and toning colours...Of John Tunnard's pictures, the most interesting is his "Painting" an outstanding example of a combination of varied shapes and textures...

Two concerts are to be held in the gallery in the near future, the first, by Newlyn Male Choir on May 3, followed by one by Mousehole Male Voice Choir on May 17.

Letter from Charles LeGrice, Trustees, to MRL Canney Esq 29 April, 1957

Dear Mr Canney,

As promised, I had a talk with the County Valuation Officer on Friday, and he cannot imagine how the Gallery can be treated as "charity", when its main, and really only objective, is to assist <u>financially</u> the local artists!!!

He was most pleasant about it, but far from hopeful, because he points out that the Art Gallery is quite unlike a gallery which is merely used for exhibiting pictures. He promised however to look into the position further, and write to you.

He did tell me "un-officially", that St. Ives now pays a considerable sum in rates...

from the Minutes of the Committee Meeting, May 30th, 1957

Charles Breaker, [Elected to the Chair]

...sign-posts to the Gallery...the Council had approved the erection of signs in four places...the cost of each sign approximately 33/-...approved the placing of signs on posts at Newlyn Bridge, near Newlyn War Memorial, at the junction of Alexandra Road and the Promenade and near Lariggan Bridge...

Hanging Mr Lanyon raised the question of hanging space allotted to members and non-members. Mr Hoyton said it was his view that members' work should get preferential hanging, in view of the annual subscription that they paid. Miss Garstin pointed out that for this they already had the benefit of having at least one picture accepted, and did not feel that any further preference could be given. Mr Hoyton pointed out that there were cases where people had been turned down for membership by the Committee, but had two works hung by the selection committee. Miss Garstin pointed out that the decision of the hanging committee was final.

The Chairman asked that in future hanging committees should bear in mind any decisions of The Committee with regard to membership. Mr Lanyon suggested that pictures should be shown 'on the floor', but the Chairman pointed out that such pictures would have been rejected for the exhibition, and it would not be fair to members. It was agreed that any such pictures should be kept out of sight.

Spiral Staircase The Secretary was instructed to offer a tender of £10 for the spiral staircase belonging to the Public Library...

Letter to Alan Bowness re Early Newlyn Exhibition from Michael Canney, June 1, 1957

...Thank you for your letter regarding the latest developments on the Early Newlyn front. I am personally a bit disappointed that it has not turned out as we originally envisaged...Some people may refuse to lend works if it is no longer an Arts Council show, but I think that will not apply to the majority. Alethea and I are going to have a big drive in this area to find work, not for ourselves alas, but Early Newlyn painters! She will drive me around to see people...

I do hope that Mr James does realise just how precarious the financial position of the Society still is, and what a lot we have attempted in such a short time, with so few people doing the work, and such slender resources to draw upon. I am giving up my only holiday this year to put on the Early Newlyn Show, so I pray that we shall not lose on it. I cannot afford a cut in my salary, at £150 pa as it is now!!!

I shall miss writing you muddled letters at the Arts council, but hope to see you in Town from time to time. Thank you for all your help and understanding comments. Very much appreciated, all round...

from the *Newlyn Notebook* of Michael Canney about Alethea Garstin

"As good as Vuillard" was how Patrick Heron described the work of this sympathetic and talented artist. Painting on a remarkably small scale and with a limited and sober palette, Alethea Garstin achieved more than most. Like her friend, Dod Procter, she had an individual voice and delivery and a questing manner, the latter due perhaps to her poor eyesight. Just to be with her was a delight as she had a gentle sense of humour and a rare ability to describe people and events. She could also recall early members of the Newlyn school with great clarity. It was she who took paints to Alfred Wallis when he was incarcerated in Madron workhouse. This was typical of her generosity & her recognition of his genius. Her own gift for describing a boulder, a chicken, and palm-leaf, a rusting fishing boat, with a mere touch of the brush is less well known than it should be. Her paintings are miracles of economy and understatement.

from *arts review* (undated, Summer 1956 or 1957)

PAINTINGS AT NEWLYN

There can be few exhibitions in which the traditional and the advanced elements in British painting can be seen in one Gallery, and in such amiable proximity, as in the current Summer Exhibition of the Newlyn Society of Artists. It is moreover, further evidence of the outstanding importance of West Cornwall as an artistic centre.

Patrick Heron, Paul Feiler, Peter Lanyon, John Tunnard, Dod Procter, Alethea Garstin, John Wells, Bernard Leach and Clifford Fishwick are all well-represented, together with many youthful painters of promise working in the area.

"Tachism" and "Action-painting", no longer the prerogative of St Ives, have made their appearance at Newlyn, in an extremely pleasing vertical composition by Michael Broido, and in the apparently mildewed *Celtic Twilight* of Dorothy Bordass.

The restrained and precisely constructed paintings of John Wells and Alexander Mackenzie, and the sculpture of Denis Mitchell, appear as a rebuke to the apparent excesses of "L'Art Autre".

There is no easy category into which one can fit the latest work of Peter Lanyon, nor that of Karl Weschke, whose painting owes much to Lanyon. Although echoes of many contemporary movements are evident in the painting it is not in any way eclectic, but is, on the other hand, probably the most fruitful and original line of approach to landscape-painting that we can see today.

114

WEDNESDAY, AUGUST 21, 1957.

The exhibition of British contemporary sculpture which the Arts Council of Great Britain is opening in Penlee Park, Penzance, today.

PENZANCE HAS OPEN-AIR DISPLAY OF SCULPTURE

from *The Cornishman*, Thursday, August 22, 1957
BRITISH SCULPTURE

Ideal Setting at Penzance

Not for a century had sculpture in this country been so esteemed the world over as at the present time, said Mr Philip James, director of Art at the Arts council, when he declared open an exhibition of sculpture in the grounds of Penlee Park on Tuesday evening...he paid special tribute to the help received from Miss Barbara Hepworth, Mr Michael Canney (Curator of the Newlyn Art Gallery) and Mrs Halliday.

...The Exhibition visited Cardiff, Nottingham and Southampton prior to coming to Penzance and has been seen by about 150,000 people. After leaving Penlee Park it will make its first appearance at the Cheltenham Arts Festival...

from *The Newlyn Notebook* of Michael Canney
...Particularly encouraging was an important exhibition of modern British sculpture in Penlee Park, which Barbara Hepworth and I organised, so that for a moment it looked as though the old rivalries between Newlyn and St Ives had been forgotten...Although this exhibition was of interest to the "cognoscenti", it could not equal the excitement aroused by the "Early Newlyn Exhibition" [see 1958] in which the dead and dying of Newlyn staggered out to see their ancestors and relatives in the paintings of Forbes, Bramley, Langley, Garstin, Gotch & others. The gallery had never seen such crowds and many who came had never been in the gallery before, although they had lived in Newlyn all their lives. The exhibition subsequently went on tour, and it was this exhibition that really put Newlyn's art on the map again...

from the Minutes of the NSA, October 25, 1957
Charles Breaker (in the Chair)
...*ICA Show:* The Chairman suggested that the Society might show the pictures by chimpanzees that had been shown at the ICA. The Committee felt it might be unwise to do this, but agreed that the Society should try to get other travelling shows by the ICA during the year...

from the Minutes of the Committee, November 29th, 1957
Charles Breaker (in the Chair)
...Mr Peter Lanyon proposed a vote of thanks to all who made the Arts Ball a success, and who worked on the decorations. The Secretary stated that all was not satisfactory in the matter of gatecrashers at the Dance, and that takings did not tally with the numbers who appeared to be present. It was agreed that next year the Dance might be held at St John's Hall, that the Parade of Costumes in its present form should be abolished, that there should be tear-off tickets for the supper or buffet, that the wine supply had been inadequate and too expensive, and that tickets should be numbered and the Society's Members should watch the door in future...

Letter from Peter Lanyon to Patrick and Barbara Hayman 18 December 1957
You will be pleased to hear that Mary Jewels has been showing lately in the Gallery at Newlyn. She is doing very good work with no paint and very little hope while the big guns roar and batter at Art...

From the Minutes NSA February 7, 1958
...*Spiral Staircase:* In view of the fact that the spiral staircase had cost more to erect than had been expected, the Committee agreed that in future for any structural alterations to be made or anything purchased for the Gallery, estimates should first be obtained.

from the *Newlyn Notebook* of Michael Canney about John Tunnard
As a textile designer, jazz musician, "soft shoe" dancer, and one of the first artists to be bought by Peggy Guggenheim for her distinguished collection, it was surprising that John Tunnard then retreated to Cornwall and turned recluse, communing largely with badgers, beetles and the wild-life of West Penwith. There was however some contact with his students at Penzance Art School, and latterly an agreement to exhibit at Newlyn, and to become an active member of the Newlyn Society of Artists. When Rothko visited the gallery he expressed amazement that Tunnard, who had long been recognised by the avant-garde in the USA was still alive, but he was, and still at work. Restless & original he added an unpredictable and sometimes explosive element during the fifties to what was a rather conservative group of artists, but everybody liked and respected him.

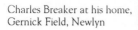
Charles Breaker at his home, Gernick Field, Newlyn

TWENTY CORNISH ARTISTS

An Exhibition sponsored by the Falmouth Art Group, Polytechnic Gallery, March 9th-22nd 1958

Introduction by Michael Canney, Curator, PEAG

For over seventy years artists have been visiting West Cornwall regularly...and in many cases remained to swell the numbers in the colonies of both Newlyn and St Ives.

In the first place, Cornwall, like Brittany, attracted artists owing to the cheapness of living, the picturesque quality of its fishing communities, and the admirable light. The intense enthusiasm for "plein-air" figure composition has gradually given way to an equal enthusiasm for the landscape of West Penwith and its unique coastline.

The influence of Ben Nicholson and Naum Gabo on the younger artists is less obvious today than it was even five years ago, and is partly supplanted by that of "tachisme" and "action painting". There is, however, every indication that the general standard of artistic achievement in West Penwith is as high as ever and that the leading artists are as well known in London and elsewhere as their predecessors were in their day.

This exhibition shows a fair cross-section of the work that can be seen regularly at the Newlyn Art Gallery and the Penwith Gallery at St Ives...The twenty are

Anthony Benjamin: *Landscape*
Michael Broido: *Painting March 1st; Painting March 2nd*
Michael Canney: *Coastal Farm, Land's End; Harbour; Coastal Farm, Pordenack*
Frederick Cooke: *John Dory; Bush Captives; Saphrophytes and Bush Tenants*
William Fisher: *Composition, September 1957; Composition*
Francis Hewlett: *Boy in Bath; Francoise*
Philip Howells: *Still Life; Beach Scene*
Mary Jewels: *Raginnis Farm; St Ives Harbour*
Peter Lanyon: *Still Life with Pitcher, 1956*
Jeremy Le Grice: *Fishing Boat*
Gwen Leitch: *Landscape-Tremedda; Veor*
Alexander Mackenzie: *Reclining Figure; Composition; Composition*
Lionel Miskin: *Landscape; Landscape*
Jack Pender: *Repairing the Trawl; Beach Scene; Dodging the Dahn*
William Redgrave: *The Model, Cora; Shrouded Car*
John Tunnard: *Caddis; Botallack; Engineer's Eye*
John Wells: *Red Harbour Front; Black Sky*
Karl Weschke: *The Horseman*
Nancy Wynne Jones: *Island Figure; Green Man Becoming*
Bryan Wynter: *Painting*

from *Arts Review* April, 1958

Newlyn Society of Artists are pursuing their avowed intention of showing the best non-figurative, in juxtaposition with the best figurative and traditional art, at their Spring Exhibition. Such an exhibition must necessarily appeal to a wide public by virtue of the catholicity of its taste.

Peter Lanyon's powerful imagery is exemplified in a fine drawing of a *Mourner at the Cross*, and he also exhibits a curiously disturbing sea-rocking *Europa and the Bull* construction in plaster. John Tunnard is nearly always well represented in this gallery. He has intuitively predicted the radio telescope and the earth satellite in paintings, long before the event. In the four pictures on view, transparent forms, and lines like springs in tension, are set against menacing skies in which moons circle.

Paintings by Alethea Garstin and Dod Procter, RA, are not only assured but also possess undeniable charm. E Bouverie Hoyton shows his complete mastery of the engraved line in *Sappho,* and there are some excellent non-figurative paintings by John Wells, Alexander Mackenzie and Michael Canney, all of whom work in Newlyn. Young artists are again settling in and around Newlyn, the oldest of Cornwall's art colonies, and there is evidence in this exhibition that the future of Cornish painting on this coast is indeed promising.

Minutes of the NSA Meeting, May 30, 1958
Charles Breaker (in the Chair)
...*Accounts:*...the bank overdraft at the time of audit was £41...Mr Tunnard proposed to cut out posters for the season. Advertising was proving too costly...
...*Hanging Committee:* Mr Lanyon suggested that the committee should be varied as much as possible, and avoid having the same people together. Mr Canney suggested there should be one woman on each committee. The summer committee will be Mrs Procter, Mr Lanyon and Mr Pender, and the winter show would be Miss Garstin, Mr Breaker and Mr Tunnard.

117

from *The Western Morning News,* Saturday 31 May 1958

EXHIBITION SHOWS BEST OF THE NEWLYN SCHOOL

Revived interest in Victorian art

...There are two reasons why this exhibition is being held this year. Firstly, because it is a kind of centenary exhibition to mark the births about 100 years ago of some of the more notable founders of the Newlyn School.

Secondly, it is an attempt to increase what the art world believes is a fresh public interest now being displayed in Victorian objets d'art, and a growing delight in paintings of the Victorian period. The Tate Gallery, for example, has recently opened a Victorian room...

from The West Briton, June 5, 1958

LATE VICTORIAN PAGEANT OF CORNISH LIFE

Remarkable Exhibition of Work by Famous Newlyn Artists

An enormous and ambitious undertaking over the past year reached its climax on Saturday, when an exhibition of the work of Newlyn painters between 1880 and 1900 was opened at the Passmore Edwards Art Gallery, Newlyn by Mr Howard Spring the well-known novelist. The exhibition represents a herculean effort in tracing the work of the painters of that time from art galleries all over the country and also from private collections and arranging for their transport to Newlyn.

Behind this enthusiasm lies another important impetus, the current revival of interest in Victorian art. When applied to Cornwall this interest has a deeply personal and even sentimental significance, for the Victorian men and women who painted here were the pioneers who, moved by the simple directness of Cornish people and the beauty and romance of their land, dedicated their lives to recording it on canvas honestly and with human sympathy.

Mr. Howard Spring, the novelist, opens the 1880—1900 exhibition of paintings by the Newlyn school in the village art gallery on Saturday. Pictured with him are Mr. Michael Canney, curator, and Mr. Jack Pender, secretary of the Newlyn Society of Artists.

"Newlyn School" Exhibition Opened by Mr. Howard Spring

Made Artists and Place Famous

Detail from
Norman Garstin's
'The Rain it Raineth Every Day'
programme cover

from *The Newlyn Notebook* of Michael Canney, [Present: Peter Lanyon, Jack Pender & myself] Noted immediately after Mark Rothko's visit. Summer, 1958.

...Walking around the Gallery with [Mark] Rothko, he said "Look at that little painting!" (a sketch by Denys Law of a Lamorna bluebell-wood). "I wish I could do that! I don't mean that painting, but just go and sit in the woods and paint, with trees, and birdsong. You know, the life of an abstract painter is that of the loneliest artist - all alone in that studio, you and the picture -- no model to talk to -- nothing. It's very hard. Like Courbet when he had to flee from France. You're all alone. Painting is above all a moral activity. Look at Pollock's suicide. It's not surprising. Peter [Lanyon] is, of course, a very religious painter. That sustains him."

"What is it like to be successful now? Too late -- too late. I needed that success when I was thirty five, not now. All I can do is keep on working now.

"We painters have been lucky, publicised by the government. Sure there are a whole lot of completely different artists stemming from Mondrian's stay in New York, but nobody pushes them, not yet. They're not official art like us.

"You think my paintings are calm, like windows in some cathedral? You should look again. I'm the most violent of all the American painters. Behind those colours there hides the final cataclysm. Yes, painting is a moral activity alright. Some people think Gorky was violent, or Bill de Kooning, but there's a latent violence in my art. Look again!"

The West Cornwall Film Society

from *The Cornish Magazine*, September, 1958

...During this first season, a surrealist film show was staged as a special performance [Winter, 1957]. A number of the 'Avant Garde' films of the twenties were booked, the main feature being 'L'Age d'Or', a film long banned in this country for various reasons. At the entrance to the Gallery, an elaborate display of surrealism was staged by Mr Canney, featuring all the usual symbols of the cult, including bowler hats, armless hands and, of course, a stuffed crocodile. The programme, after all, turned out to be rather boring, but the Society was congratulated on its idea...

The fourth season will be opening in the autumn, and it does seem that, at long last, West Cornwall has a, if not exactly flourishing, at least well established Film Society.

Newlyn Society of Artists Lecture, Friday 15th November at 8 pm

An illustrated lecture entitled "The Italian Scene" will be given by Mr E Bouverie Hoyton, R S

A silver collection in aid of the Gallery funds will be made and the Committee hopes that all who attend will contribute as generously as possible to this cause.

from the *Newlyn Notebook* of Michael Canney

Regarded by many as 'rather odd', Ithell Colquhoun was in fact a highly intelligent woman with a wide understanding and participation in the international Surrealist movement. She maintained a connection with Belgian and other artists of her persuasion. Unfortunately she was notorious in Britain for a nude photo of her in an art magazine, which tended to obscure her very real talents as an artist. She was very knowledgeable about 'automatism' and the whole gamut of surrealist techniques, and was one of the last genuine surrealists in Britain. Regrettably she did not really become involved with the Newlyn Art Gallery until the surrealist movement was in decline, but she continued to produce works that could only be described as 'surreal' and exhibited them at the Gallery.

[Like his paintings Peter Lanyon's communications with friends were often full of oblique references and **doubles entendres**. The following humorous 'announcement' by Michael Canney refers to an occasion on which Lanyon and Denis Mitchell mischievously relieved themselves against Barbara Hepworth's garden wall...which then fell down!]

'The Erection of New Chairman 1959'
    Mr Peter Lanyon, the well-known Hornish artist, has become Chairman of the Newlyn Society of Artists after his erection at a Committee meeting of the Society.
    Mr Lanyon is a fortunate choice. Noted for his tact and diplomacy, he has been a friend of long-standing of the celebrated amateur sculptress Barbara Hepworth. He mentions her by name frequently, and takes a great interest in all her activities. Mr Lanyon is a man of many parts. He, and Mr Denis Mitchell, last Hairman of the Penwith Society of Farts in Cornwall, ran a demolition company for a short time, using novel methods of wall destruction. He still retains much interest in demolition in St Ives...

Peter Lanyon

from *Leave Tomorrow Behind* by John Miller
    ...At about this time I was elected a member of the Newlyn Society of Artists. Peter Lanyon was chairman and Michael Canney, the curator...In the thirties a group who were more influenced by post-Impressionism came to work in the area and some of these were still exhibiting when I first became a member...
    ...The Newlyn Society was self-supporting and the younger members frequently helped paint the gallery at the beginning of a season. I can remember decorating the gallery with Jeremy LeGrice, Margo Maeckelberghe, Mary Stork and Helen Dear. Charles Breaker always gave a hand, although from an older generation of artists. Giles Auty, now critic of the *New Statesman,* was exhibiting at that time and Joan Gillchrest began to paint her enchanting pictures of Cornish harbours...
    ...When Karl Weschke had a major exhibition of his paintings at the Grosvenor Gallery in London I was very impressed by his work and we became good friends. Although Karl exhibits in Newlyn and St Ives he has remained very much his own man.
    The avant garde painters at Newlyn when I became a member have now become establishment figures. Bryan Wynter and Roger Hilton, with whom I played chess, have died, but Terry Frost, Paul Feiler and John Wells keep the tradition going with sculptors like Paul Mount and Denis Mitchell...

from Denys Val Baker, *Britain's Art Gallery by the Sea*

Some roughly comparable [to Alfred Wallis' comprehension of Cornwall and the Cornish character through painting] has been achieved at Newlyn by Mary Jewells, another primitive, though a much more educated one than Alfred Wallis. In her case she began painting in 1915 when Cedric Morris gave her a canvas with four tubes of paint and one brush and told her to cover the canvas by the evening. Subsequently she was encouraged by such visitors as Augustus John, who bought a number of her paintings, and Christopher Wood. Like Wallis, she never had any orthodox training, she just had to paint; or as she puts it herself: 'I have been influenced by nobody and entirely self-taught, a true Celt loving my Cornwall, its lovely stone hedges and the beautiful blue sea with puff-ball clouds and little fishing coves and corn in stooks--what could one wish for more?

Lanyon, Wallis, Jewells, all Cornish in origin, all seeing Cornwall with unexpectedly unconventional vision: it makes one wonder how many other Cornish painters exist who have not yet been recognized...I would particularly draw attention to the work of Anthony Benjamin, Alexander Mackenzie, Jack Pender, Trevor Bell, Karl Weschke, Gwen Leach and Keith Leonard...

120

undated letter from Peter Lanyon to Michael Canney
[*about the collection of hanging fees for the PEAG*]
Dear Mugsie,
Wynn Jones   10/ (2 hung)
Oliver   5/ (one hung)
H Clark   5/ (was hung)
Hayman   10/ (un sung)
Delaney   2/ (nickered)
Mr Weschke and Miss Hocken have done their nut independent. Bordass well and happy in transit for Malaya leaves debt of 5 bob which I will not pay. The rest have paid me.
Love to your doll. She's cute. Yrs, George P Lanyon

Letter from Jeremy Le Grice to the Editor (Worpswede), 1995

The tolerance and elasticity of Newlyn were fully stretched in encompassing factions on the one hand entranced by the values of the Royal Academy under the leadership of Alfred Munnings (an 'old boy' of the area) thundering against Picasso in the nineteen-fifties. On the other hand, were loose cannon straying over from St Ives aggrieved by some abstract slight at the Penwith. Increasingly the centre ground was held by Lanyon and his accomplices.

This scene of ferment changed with the end of the fifties. By the nineteen-sixties the pre-war group were elderly and quietened, and a new conformity that tended towards abstraction blanketed the wall-space of the Gallery. Lanyon had fixed his sights across the Atlantic; the catalyst had moved and that phase of Newlyn Gallery history, that particular potency, had passed.

from *The Western Morning News*, Nov. 16, 1959

'ENCOURAGE COUNCIL TO SPEND MORE ON ARTS'

Suggestions that the Penzance Corporation might be asked to spend more money on the arts was made on Saturday when the Newlyn Society of Artists opened its Christmas Exhibition in the Newlyn Art Gallery, where a wide selection of painting and some pottery and sculpture were on display.

Mr Peter Lanyon, Chairman of the Society, presided...and said that record sales for the year totalled £1,700. Admissions had been 4,000. The Arts Council of great Britain had given them the screens in the gallery and for the third year had given them a grant of £200.

An interesting point and one which I have not seen very much done about is that the local authority is empowered to levy up to a 6d. rate, which they can spend on the arts, said Mr La-

nyon. In the case of Penzance this would amount to some £6,000 a year. For the year 1958 to 1959 purchases by Penzance have totalled £9 12s 2d...They paid £17 11s 11d for the hire of exhibitions, rather short of the £6000 that they are empowered to pay...

from *The Western Morning News*, April 11, 1960

3 pictures sold on first day of Newlyn show

Over 200 people attended a cocktail party at the opening of the spring exhibition of the Newlyn society of Artists at the Passmore Edwards Gallery, on Saturday. For the first time, the gallery is to be open on Sunday afternoons throughout the season.

from the Minutes of the AGM, The NSA at the NAG, April 30, 1960

Peter Lanyon (in the Chair)

Chairman's Report:

...He stated that our object as artists was to insist that there was no division in art, in spite of pressure from commercial galleries, who would have us believe that one kind of art was better than another. There was only good art and bad art, and he was happy that the Gallery existed and maintained the traditional, while being able to absorb experimental and wilder paintings.

He said that he thought there was a great need for far more good academic painting and drawing. There was very little drawing shown in the Gallery, and he believed that since it should form the basis of one's art there should be more drawings exhibited. The Lower Gallery, apart from its value as a gallery in which an artist could sell his work, had been a great encouragement to younger painters in enabling them to have a place in which they could see their work all together.

...This year has been the most successful in the history of the Society from the point of view of sales of pictures, sculpture, and pottery, in admissions, and in the general standard of exhibitions and one-man shows.

from the Minutes of NSA Meeting, December 16, 1960

...*Matters arising*...Gulbenkian Scheme: Mr Philip James had not been able to do anything about this picture hire-purchase scheme [Ed note: a picture loan scheme] as yet. He had said that...all the private provincial galleries were running at a loss and that this had surprised the committee. They were reviewing the whole matter...

July 21 - August 31 1960 City Art Gallery, Plymouth

Painters in Cornwall 1960

The Exhibitors

Shearer Armstrong
W Barns-Graham
Anthony Benjamin
Trevor Bell
Peter Blakeley
Angus Brent
Michael Broido
Michael Canney
Frederick Cook
Paul Feiler
Michael Finn

Terry Frost
Leonard Fuller
Alethea Garstin
Jeffrey Harris
Michael Heard
Patrick Heron
Francis Hewlett
Mary Jewels
George Lambourn
Peter Lanyon
Alan Lowndes
Alexander Mackenzie
Margo Maeckelberghe
Jack Merriott
June Miles
Lionel Miskin
Kate Nicholson
Marion Paul
Misome Peile
Jack Pender
Dod Procter, RA
Peter Rainsford
William Redgrave
Adrian Ryan
John Tunnard
Reg Watkiss
James Van Hear
Karl Weschke
Nancy Wynne-Jones
Bryan Wynter

Introduction

TO REPRESENT ALL the painters who are working in Cornwall in one exhibition would be an impossibility, for their number far exceeds the space that is available in any gallery in the West. It is hoped, however, that this exhibition will give some idea of the many different aspects of art in Cornwall.

The tradition of painting in the county goes back as far as Turner, Rowlandson and Opie, but it was not until 1880 that the first colony of artists grew up at Newlyn, and shortly afterwards artists settled at St Ives and Falmouth. Today the painters are not only concentrated in St Ives, Newlyn and Mousehole, but they are also scattered over the peninsula of West Penwith and can be found as far afield as Polperro, Looe and Mevagissey.

Painting in Cornwall today is largely concerned with the landscape, the coast, the sea, and the characteristic harbours and villages with which the county is richly endowed. The traditional approach to the picturesque in Cornwall needs no explanation, but the visitor may find that the 'contemporary' works present something of a problem, especially if he seldom visits exhibitions of modern painting. I believe that this modern painting can be best explained by saying that it deals with, and represents, the artist's total experience of his subject, and not merely one aspect of it. This can include experience which is physical and experience which is connected with the past as well as the present. A modern landscape painter is aware not only of the country around him but of the sky above him and the hidden mineworkings beneath his feet; he recalls the road he has just travelled, the hill he has just climbed. The traditional painter selects one view, at one time of day, and at one particular season, but modern painters are not so restricted. The purely abstract painter, on the other hand, is concerned with problems of pure art, freed from all associated ideas, and this pure art, like music, represents nothing except possibly a mood or a general environment. In spite of this, it would seem that abstract art is not as detached as it would like to be, and in many abstract paintings the light and colour and the atmosphere of Cornwall come across to the spectator very forcefully.

...The first artists in Cornwall were impressed by the comparatively primitive existence led by its people, and it is still true today that the elemental is more obviously present than in most parts of England, and that the feeling of an ancient land and its early inhabitants and traditions are inescapable. The modern artist's imagery of Cornwall is permeated with it, and I do not think that anyone who knows the county could fail to find evidence of it in much of the painting in this exhibition.

Apart from London, there is nowhere else in this country where so many artists are working in such a small area...

Michael R L Canney

NEWLYN ART GALLERY

NEWLYN ART GALLERY

Retrospective
Exhibition of
Paintings

by

ITHELL
COLQUHOUN

———————●———————

Drawings
&
Paintings of
Ghana and
Nigeria

by

KEN SYMONDS

AFRICAN
&
OCEANIC
SCULPTURE

A South Western
Arts Association Exhibition

———————●———————

The Committee of
the Newlyn Society of Artists
have pleasure in
inviting you to the
Private View of these three
exhibitions on Monday, October 2nd
at 8 p.m.

OPEN WEEKDAYS 2 - 5
UNTIL OCTOBER 27

July 1960 - June 1962

TOURING EXHIBITION - SOUTHWESTERN ARTS ASSOCIATION
from the collections of the Royal Albert Memorial Museum, Exeter

[The exhibits were selected and arranged by Michael Canney, Curator of the Newlyn Art Gallery, who also compiled and designed the catalogue.]

'It will be seen from the African and Oceanic works in this exhibition that many of them show a high degree of skill and aesthetic sensibility. The true significance of many primitive works, however, is still unknown to us, and will probably never be fully understood; it is as though we were to look at the frescoes by Giotto in the Arena Chapel of Padua without knowledge of the Christian story. We can, however, recognise that it is part of the great tradition of man's achievement in art, that stretches unbroken from the earliest cave paintings to the art of today.'

Michael R L Canney , Newlyn, 1960

Minutes of the AGM of NSA at the Newlyn Art Gallery, May 6, 1961

Charles Breaker (Chairman)

The Chairman stated that the year had been a satisfactory one...He thought the future of the gallery depended upon a few more artists settling in Newlyn. The question of a permanent collection of painting by artists who lived or who had lived in Cornwall was overdue, and a gallery should be built or found to house these pictures before St Ives took the initiative in this matter. It could be either in Penzance or Truro, but it was certainly needed.

Letter to Michael Canney from Peter Lanyon, 17 June 1961

...Herewith late sub yours truly having just surfaced.

Sorry about it and that I didn't tell you I wouldn't be at the last committee meeting. Who is our new Prince Charming?

I will have a look at my professional conscience in my bath and decide how to approach your other questionnaire and will hope to be present at the next meeting.

IF you restrict members to the "for profit and as their main occupation" idea you will have no members. I think I should leave out profit and replace it with - who practice as their declared occupation and have shown a consistent loss over the previous 10 years! I think professional members should be inspected every so often and their moral and artistic life EG beards, old clothes, and number of mistresses, enquired into. Anyone with a clean sheet should be advised gently to foul up a Bit.

In addition I hope to propose that the rule governing re-showing of a picture should be amended. To encourage younger artists we should have student membership to be held for a limited period after which the student applies in the normal way for full membership.

Holes in sculpture shall not be greater than an equivalent of 75% of the gross bulk of the original block. All paintings must pass the finger test if on canvas, and the hammer test if on board. All welded, brazed and rivetted construction must be equivalent to AID regulations, glass constructions must be toughened on safety glass. No human material will be permitted in the manufacture of paintings.

I like the last one

from the *Newlyn Notebook* of Michael Canney

Dod Procter, RA was a most likeable and intelligent woman, and an artist of rare sensitivity, but she did not suffer fools gladly, and was, I suppose, somewhat eccentric. Of Jack Smith who was living for a time at Sancreed, she remarked -- "Oh! he's that artist who paints babies in sinks with dirty feet", and that seems to sum her up. She had a cracked and perhaps affected voice that suited her opinions, which could be forceful and final. Tales were told of her incredible parsimony, watering down the gin, or ordering a mere half-pint of milk a week. A keen gardener, she had a "cuttings bag" or coat, that she always took to public parks and gardens, where she would acquire cuttings at no cost to herself. Painting very thinly and with great sensitivity, a tube of paint would last her a lifetime. However, she had appalling technical habits, "feeding the paint" as she put it, by rubbing her dry paint with linseed oil to "bring up the tones." Newlyn does not seem the same without her.

extraordinary occasion, in which the entire population of Newlyn seemed to pour into the gallery in order to see themselves, their relatives and their ancestors, in pictures that had now become legendary".

1958- "Life at Newlyn was extremely difficult on such a small income. I
1959 endeavoured to supplement it by working as a part-time coastguard, often at night, and also bought a small fishing boat, but this was not a success. However, the opportunity arose to become a free-lance contributor on the arts in the West Region of the BBC, an area in which I knew nearly everybody of any consequence. This work developed rapidly, and between 1957 and 1977, I contributed some two hundred documentary programmes both on the radio and on television, and in the process became a well-known figure, as many of the programmes were networked nationwide. These programmes not only covered the work and lives of painters and sculptors, but also dealt with ecological and environmental subjects, being some of the first in this field. Whilst this work was fairly time-consuming I still managed to produce a considerable body of paintings and reliefs, and exhibited consistently."

1961 Together with St Ives' sculptor Brian Wall, designs and constructs a steel and perspex display for a travelling exhibition of African and Oceanic sculpture, for the South West Arts Association. This display is featured in the *Museums' Journal* and attracts favourable comment.

1962 Reorganises and re-designs the Fore Street Gallery in St Ives with architect and painter John Miller. The gallery had been acquired from Major Patrick Wylde by Elizabeth Rainsford, who wanted to provide an exhibition space for young artists.
"The gallery had already been showing contemporary work, but this was now extended. Both this gallery, and Elena Gaputyte's Sail Loft Gallery, showed lively mixed exhibitions and one-man shows for several years. These exhibitions had a freshness that was lacking elsewhere, in part due to the introduction of young figurative painters on the St Ives scene. Being commercial ventures, they could show whom they liked and were not subject to the constraints that existed in the society galleries at Newlyn and St Ives. Their importance in the artistic life of St Ives at that time has tended in recent accounts to be underplayed. At Newlyn also, a Lower Galler- had been opened, that gave first one-man shows to a number of artists ~~~ Pearce and Anthony Benjamin".

1956- Thro~ ~~llery in St Ives, and his
1965 work ~~working
in C
or tł
Ala
Pat
Bla

1964- Te
1965 G

8

4 **French Crabbers, Newlyn, from Art Gallery Terrace,** 1956
oil on board; 13¼ × 18 inches
signed, titled and dated '56 on reverse

from MICHAEL CANNEY, Paintings, Construction & Reliefs
The Belgrave Gallery, 1990
1962 [Canney] reorganises and re-designs the Fore Street Gallery in St Ives with architect and painter John Miller. The gallery had been acquired from Major Patrick Wylde by Elizabeth Rainsford, who wanted to provide an exhibition space for young artists...At Newlyn also, a Lower Gallery had been opened, that gave first one-man shows to a number of artists, including Bryan Pearce and Anthony Benjamin.

from *Manchester Guardian,* August 1, 1961

'The Cornish circle'

The visitor to Cornwall may well be surprised at the number of galleries, six in all, within the small area of West Penwith. They provide facilities for the artist which are unequalled anywhere else in the provinces. There are continuous exhibitions throughout the year, and although the standard varies considerably, it is always possible to see an interesting selection of work ranging from the most esoteric non-figuration to modern figurative or traditional painting.

At Newlyn Art Gallery, near Penzance, the present summer exhibition of the Newlyn Society of Artists contains works by Peter Lanyon, John Tunnard, Adrian Ryan, Paul Feiler, and Dod Procter, all of whom have reputations outside the Cornish circle. But the exhibition is interesting for the absence of bias towards any particular school or style of painting, and there are exciting examples of the younger figurative artists who are perhaps reacting against the cool abstraction that dominated art in Cornwall through the influence of Nicholson, Gabo, and Hepworth...
Michael Canney

16 **Quayside, Newlyn,** 1957
oil on collage on board; 13½ × 8 inches
signed, titled and dated '57 on reverse

from the Minutes of the NSA, August 10, 1962

The Chairman (Charles Breaker) read a letter from Mrs Maeckelberghe applying for hire of the main gallery for an exhibition of Belgian painting next year. Mr Pender gave fuller details to the Committee and explained the idea of an exchange exhibition with Belgium at the Feest Palais in Ostend, and the wartime connections with Belgium and Newlyn. The Director of the Belgian Gallery was to select painters for the exhibition at Newlyn and the artists from West Cornwall who were represented in Belgium would pay a hiring fee for the gallery...

Exhibitors
Ithell Colquhoun
Michael Canney
Derek Guthrie
Alan Lowndes
Margo Maeckelberghe
John Miller
Jack Pender
Nancy Wynne-Jones

L to R Charles Breaker, Mayoress Mrs Lawrey, Mayor Mrs Lilian (Crosbie) Garstin, & organiser, Margo Maeckelberghe

kunstenaars uit newlyn

uitwisselingstentoonstelling

2 juni – 23 juni 1963

open elke dag van 10 tot 13 h en van 15 tot 19 h

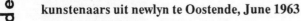

May.		
Sat	18.	Derek ½
Mon	20.	Derek
Tue	21.	Margo
Wed	22.	Derek
Thu	23.	Ithell
Fri	24.	Canney
Sat	25.	Jack
Mon	27.	Margo or Mother
Tue	28.	Canney
Wed	29.	Canney
Thu	30.	
Fri	31.	Canney.

kunstenaars uit newlyn te Oostende, June 1963

from *The Cornishman*

West Cornwall's first exhibition of Belgian paintings has opened at the Newlyn Art Gallery, Penzance, with an exchange exhibition between eight Cornish painters and fifteen painters from Ostend. The mayor of Penzance, Mrs L Crosbie Garstin, who opened the exhibition, stressed the importance of seeing paintings from outside the immediate area, and the happy coincidence of the exhibition at a time when the King and Queen of the Belgians had just visited London.

She also praised the initiative of the organiser of the exhibition, Mrs Margo Maeckelberghe who had arranged the complicated interchange of paintings with Ostend...The germ of the idea of the exhibition sprang from the fact that Belgian fishermen and their families fled to Newlyn during the last war and made their homes there. Moreover, both Newlyn and Ostend possess the now familiar mixture of artists and fishermen's communities in a harbour town...

L to R Derek Guthrie, Charles Breaker & Margo Maeckelberghe

from the Minutes of the AGM, 4 May 1963

...Fellows' representative Major Evans was not present owing to illness, but he was unanimously re-elected.

...The Secretary announced the result of the annual election.

Executive Committee: C Breaker, [Alethea] Garstin, P Lanyon, D Law, J Le Grice, J Pender, D Procter, J Miller, D Guthrie

Hanging Committee: C Breaker, P Lanyon, J Le Grice, R Watkiss, J Pender, J Miller...Derek Guthrie had told him that he would be going away later in the year.

...There was general discussion regarding apathy within the Society and the lack of activities during the winter months, but no solution was reached and no resolution passed. Mrs Maeckelberghe suggested a life class. The Secretary concluded the discussion by saying that the Society did not lack exhibitors or interest in showing in the Gallery. He felt that the Gallery was doing the best job as an exhibiting centre. In this way it served the artistic and local community best of all. Apathy, such as it was, was inevitable in a widespread community of artists. These problems should be referred back to the Executive Committee...

127

from the Minutes of the NSA, August 30, 1963

...Lower Gallery The sales had been very poor there and [the Secretary] wondered whether it might be now put to better use for special exhibitions for invited young painters or indeed for the Society itself. Mr Lanyon thought that Newlyn was up against the independent galleries in St Ives and could not compete with a gallery such as the Fore St Gallery. [He suggested] that the Lower Gallery should have about 50 pictures on view by Members. Every Member could show one picture, but if all Members did not take advantage of this it might be possible for those who did exhibit to have more than one. Hanging fee should be about 5/- for the season...

from the Minutes of the NSA, May 2nd, 1964

...Alethea Garstin asked the new Curator (David Coad) about the request for Biographies that she had received from him. The new curator replied that it was primarily to be of information to prospective buyers and those interested in the Society. She asked how much information was required. The Curator replied as much as the artist were willing to divulge...

...The Chairman (Charles Breaker) presented to the retiring Secretary/Curator Michael Canney, an anglepoise lamp and a cheque for £27. The meeting applauded Mr Canney's good work for the Society over the last seven and a half years...Mr Canney thanked the meeting and said that after 7 1/2 years the Society needed new blood. On looking back, he continued the sales of pictures and of admissions...both had increased and he could see no reason why this trend should not continue.

Charles Breaker
'Newlyn'

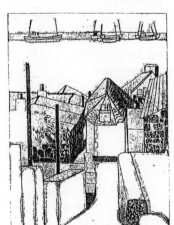

from the *Newlyn Notebook* of Michael Canney

Newlyn Art Gallery, Spring 1959
Stands and screens from Arts Council

Sculpture
left: Brian Wall
distance: Denis Mitchell

Pottery
Bernard Leach
Janet Leach

Paintings
Various, including Dod Procter's Flower Painting
End wall: Peter Lanyon's *Saracinesco*
 (now at, Plymouth Art Gallery)

Entering the Gallery, 1995. The 'new' groundfloor entrance & stairway to the upper floor.

Lamorna Kerr, at 83 years,
visiting
Melissa Hardie, 1987
in Newmill

'Mornie's World'
oil painting by
Annette Johnson, SWA,NS.
A view of Carn Dhu, Lamorna

Watercolour of 'Z542, Newlyn Harbour' by Charles Breaker (1906-1985)
Employed as the poster image for his Memorial Exhibition, 1986

Poster painted by Charles Breaker
for the Newlyn Gallery lecture by
Col J H Williams

from the Artists Series of 32 portraits
by Ken Symonds. 1986 Exhibited at
The Penwith Gallery, St Ives
Upper left: John Wells
Lower left: Barbara Tribe
Lower right: Bryan Pearce
Upper right: Denis Mitchell

Untitled painting by Ernest Procter.
Donated to & sold at Artshare Auction, 1986

The ceramics of Francis Hewlett
Exhibited at Trelissick, 1989

'The Newlyn Exhibition' presented to the Permanent Collection by Joan Gilchrest, 1979

1 John Halkes

3 Professor Charles Thomas

8 Joan Riley, Ray Ambrose & Cecil Riley

13 Eileen Hunt, David Gittings & Charles Breaker

4 John Wells, Terry Frost , John Halkes & friend

9 Peter Ellery & Anthony Richards

5 Janet Bennette & John Halkes

10 Frank Ruhrmund, Lord St Levan in background

6 Ithell Colquhoun & Cordelia Dobson

11 Tom Cross & Bernard Evans

2 Ken Howard, RA

7 Vaughan Tregenza, Margo Maeckelberghe & John Wells

12 Ella Halkes, Tina & Tommy Craske-Rising

14 Joan Gilchrest

IX: 1965-1974

from John Miller to the Editor, Letter, 1994

...I was chairman during the sixties at a time when the gallery had a number of different curators and, at times, none at all! It was a marvellous period though, when members would all come in over weekends and paint the gallery because there was no money and when Gabriel White,[the Director of Art for the Arts Council of Great Britain] who was an enchanting man, would come and have lunch here, walk on the Carn and I would tentatively say, "Do you think you could raise the eight hundred pound grant to one thousand pounds this year?" and peering towards Lamorna Gap he would say, "I think so". In those days the curators lived in the flat on the ground floor of the gallery and this, together with eight pounds a week, light and heating, constituted the salary!

Then came the time when, following the 1966 Building Regulations, as a public building, we had to provide toilets which was when we carried out the alterations which enabled us to utilize the lower front room as part of the gallery. Again, although Alister McLeod worked very hard to raise grant money from the local authorities, and we both went with my plans to London where we got a promise of grants from the Arts council, much of the funds really were raised by functions which the artists undertook. Michael Newman, who was then a director of W H Lane conducted a very serious auction and there were also fancy dress balls and so on. In some ways, because the survival of the gallery and showing space meant that the artists had to be much more involved in these things, it brought them together, but perhaps I am simply looking back with the sentimental eyes of one who is now practically a recluse.

John Miller at work, 1965
Photo by Ander Gunn

from the Secretary's Report (David Coad), AGM, 15 May, 1965

...the Curator started his report by saying that this had been his first year in office and that he felt it had been encouraging, the sales of paintings had increased and admission had risen by a small amount. He regretted to announce over the year the deaths of Mr Peter Lanyon, a long time committee member of the society and indeed Chairman, Mr Eric Hiller, also a past committee member, and Mrs Anne Sefton, who had bequeathed the Society fifty pounds...at the moment there was a memorial exhibition of Mr Hiller's work on show in the Lower Gallery.

The Bazaar had been a success and the Arts Council Film show had for one of the first times made a slight profit. The Arts Ball which had been held in the present financial year had only just covered itself...

from the Minutes of the NSA Meeting, September 6, 1965

[Editor's Note: the curator having resigned, this meeting was for stating the qualities required from the next.]

...Mr Hoyton stated that he felt that anyone who practised Art, would be prejudiced. Mr Jeremy LeGrice suggested that even if they did practise art they could still be a competent curator, and he cited Mr Canney the Curator before the present one as a good example. He felt that it would be too restraining to rule out all candidates who practised art. Mr (Reg) Watkiss added that any applicant would have a definite interest in art if he were an Artist.

...The committee were told of the extra fifty pounds from the Arts Council, to enable the society to advertise at a higher salary.

from *The Western Morning News*, June 13, 1966, By a Special Correspondent

Newlyn reconciles two points of view

THE SUMMER exhibition organised by the NSA is now on view in the PEAG. The Society has a wide membership and includes within its orbit not only the abstract painters, but also a nucleus of traditionalists...The summer exhibition is lively and colourful and by careful and competent hanging, the committee have overcome the inevitable problems which arise in combining the two points of view....In the main, the upper gallery is devoted to the modernists and the lower gallery serves the traditionalists. This is a slight over-simplification, but in essence, this is how they sort out their affairs and the formula works very well.

Near the entrance hang two small paintings by June Miles. Both of them of high quality, and painted by an artist who has a fine feeling for subtle colour. Her pictures have subject interest and superb tonal quality...In the corner of the room is a large abstract canvas by W Barns Graham. Here is a true professional who handles her material with ability...Another West-country painter rapidly making a reputation is Margo Maeckelberghe. Her picture 'Sea Swell and Rain Cloud' is a very successful work which has a fine atmospheric quality. Jack Pender thrives on rich colour. His latest series 'Moorings' give him ample scope to indulge in this...'Interior II' by Jeremy LeGrice is painted on a large scale...many will prefer his more vigorous 'In a Landscape' which is a fine piece of work.

Roger Hilton's 'Paris 35' is well drawn but his second contribution, 'May 66' with its splash of red on a dirty white ground is unimpressive. One expects something better from an artist of his reputation.

The sweeping lines and subtle colour of Karl Weschke's work are powerfully drawn and his under-painting gives his work a delicate quality which is hard to define. He is one of those artists you either like tremendously or you hate, but you can never ignore.

Tony O'Malley's picture, with its rich warm colour, fairly glows on the end wall...A small drawing by John Miller 'Carn Green' has fine colour and is modestly priced...and Roy Smallman, John Milne, Clifford Fishwick, Patricia Fishwick, Marie Yates, Alan Richards, Bouverie Hoyton, Peggy Frank, Stanley Miller, Ken Symonds...Much of the painting in this gallery has a topographical interest. The West Penwith landscape with its fascinating coastline and intensity of light provides wonderful scope for the artist...The sculpture section is small but it includes a splendid little work by John Milne, 'Sculpture 66'...On a centre table in the upper gallery is a fine array of pottery of good design and beautiful glazing. Janet Leach's work is well known, and it is interesting to see the work of the two Saltash potters, Dennis Bullock and Ian Gallagher represented in the exhibition...

from the Minutes of the AGM of the NSA, June 9, 1967

Jack Pender (Chairman)

...The past year was reviewed by the Chairman who mentioned the visit of the Bristol College of Art, The Arts Council Print Exhibition, film shows, jazz evening and brought this right up to the moment, with the success of the Spring Exhibition. He continued with mention of the new curator (Alister McLeod)...Thanks were expressed to Mr Gabriel White and Miss Katherine Kinnear in their absence for their interest in the Society on behalf of the Arts Council and finally to the Committee for their ever willing cooperation for the benefit of the Society...he concluded his review with a brief outline of future policy embodying improvements to the Gallery for which all possible support should be given...

...Mr McLeod then detailed briefly the planned improvements to the Gallery. These would include installing new toilets; re-siting the Curator's office, linking the upper and lower galleries more positively by a new central staircase and making arrangements for heating the building...

131

from the Minutes of the NSA Meeting, January 5, 1968

Jack Pender (Deputy Chairman)

...The Committee agree that the gradual accumulation of work for a small permanent collection would be prudent and add interest to the Gallery...

The Trustees' architect and the Society's architect had agreed upon the first stages of the improvements and the selected builder would start work next week upon their instructions.

It was decided the catalogues for 1968 exhibitions should be the folded card type and be produced by Alfred Chappell (printer) as per the estimate...

...It was agreed that the Bazaar which had deteriorated to a Jumble Sale in recent years was no longer in keeping with the image of the Society or the Gallery and should be replaced as a form of income by some more suitable means...

from the Minutes of the NSA Meeting, November 8, 1968

Jack Pender (Deputy Chairman)

...[The Chairman] praised the hanging of the Peter Lanyon Memorial Exhibition which had been carried out during the day by Margo Maeckelberghe and Ken Symonds with the Curator's assistance...

from the Minutes of the AGM of the NSA, May 30, 1968

John Miller (Chairman)

...The Chairman made his report on the year's activities giving details of the almost completed improvements at a cost to date of some four thousand pounds. The Arts Council, Cornwall County Council and Penzance Borough Council had made grants towards this and further sums had been promised by the Carnegie Trust and the Museums Association, application had been made for these. The auction of gifts of paintings and antiques collected by a tremendous effort and so successfully and professionally auctioned by Mr Michael Newman on the night of the Spring Exhibition Private View had produce the magnificant sum of six hundred and sixteen pounds...

from the Minutes of the NSA Meeting, September 5, 1969

John Miller (Chairman)

...A Christmas exhibition was considered and it was generally agreed these were ill attended and unrewarding...

Letter from Alister McLeod, Curator-Secretary to the NSA, October 6, 1969

Dear Member

The Right Honorable Miss Jennie Lee, Minister of State, Department of Education and Science will be making a brief visit to the Gallery between 4.15pm and 5pm on Saturday, 18th October, 1969.

You are invited to be present and take sherry with the Minister and if you have works now on exhibition it will be appreciated if these can remain in the gallery until after the visit... Yours sincerely...

Before (L) & after (R) the renovations, 1969. Entrance to the Gallery upstairs.

Before (L) & after (R) from SE corner upstairs

Just look at that!

Before(L) & after (R) from NW corner upstairs

From the upper to the lower, after renovations

THE ARTS BALL for 1970 to be held on the night of February 20.
The theme is 'SPACE'
Music by Job Morris

from the Minutes of the NSA Meeting, November 6, 1970
...Dates for the three 1971 Exhibitions were agreed. Spring 10 April - 3 June; Summer 12 June - 5 August; Autumn 14 August - 2 October. The one-man shows to be held in fortnightly periods as previously at a fee of six pounds per fortnight with the exception of those periods that have the benefit of the Society Private View when the fee will be ten pounds for two weeks.

The Admission charge to the Gallery for 1971 will be 5 new pence. Half price reductions will only be allowed for students in school or college parties or children at primary schools. The charge for the Catalogue will be 3 new pence.

134

THE ARTS BALL for 1971 to be held on February 26th.
Theme: 'THE SEA'
Charles Breaker will organise the catering, Peter Ellery the decorations.

ITHELL COLQUHOUN

NEWLYN ART GALLERY

July 12 - 24, 1971

Recent Exhibitions

Newlyn Art Gallery, 1967 :
Constructions and Collages.

Czechoslovakia, 1967-8 :
Paintings and Collages in
Poesie-Fantasmagie Exhibition.

W. Berlin, 1969 :
Paintings in **Fantasmagie International**
Exhibition.

Apeldoorn, Holland, 1969 : Ditto.

W. Berlin, 1969 : Paintings.

Hamburg, 1969 :
Constructions and Collages.

Bristol, 1970 :
Paintings, Constructions and Collages.

Montages

1.	Portrait of a Dignitary	1970
2.	Sun-Child	1971
3.	Cyclops	1971
4.	Shaman	1971
5.	Ripples	1971
6.	Night and Day	1971
7.	Eye of Horus	1971
8.	Open Entrance	1971

9.	Spine of Osiris	1971
10.	Triad	1971
11.	Night-Sky	1971
12.	Cornish Landscape	1971

Gouaches

13.	Oread	1970
14.	Rowan	
15.	Willow	
16.	Vine	
17.	Beech	Dryads 1971
18.	Oak	
19.	Silver Fir	
20.	Altar to Pan	1971
21.	Serapis	1971
22.	Volcano-spirit	1971
23.	Marsh-spirit	1971

Collages

24.	Alchemy up-to-date	1960
25.	Tarzan	1969
26.	Permutation (I)	1969
27.	Permutation (II)	1969
28.	Permutation (III)	1969
29.	Forms	1970
30.	Computer Stains	1970
31.	Hill-Forest	1971
32.	Geometric	1971
33.	Graphomania : red	1971
34.	Graphomania : blue	1971
35.	Graphomania : black	1971
36.	Graphomania : blue-black	1971
37.	Graphomania : green	1971
38.	Graphomania : pencil (I)	1971
39.	Graphomania : pencil (II)	1971
40.	Graphomania : mixed colours	1971

from the *Western Morning News*, May 3, 1971
Vincent Wilson in one-man show
An exhibition of paintings by the Saltash artist, Vincent Wilson, is now being held in the new one-man showroom at the Newlyn Art Gallery until the end of the week.

He is a painter who looks at the granite uplands and moors of Devon and Cornwall for his inspiration, using blocks of colour, and blending his tones and images to convey a very personal impression of what he sees there.

from *The Cornishman*, August 26, 1971
Two-man show at Newlyn
Two well-known painters of the Cornish landscape, Margo Maeckelberghe and Ken Symonds, are now sharing an exhibition in the one-man showroom of the Newlyn Art Gallery...

The Penzance artist, Margo Maeckelberghe, fresh from a successful show of her work at the John Campbell Gallery in London...She offers a number of small gouaches that, in a few sweeping strokes, capture the essential elemental quality of the land forms, wind, sea and sky, of West Penwith...

One has grown to associate the St Erth artist, Ken Symonds, with studies of the relics of Cornwall's industrial past, but in this show he returns to the fundamentals of landscape with a series of carefully controlled and beautifully-observed etchings...A single large canvas 'Porthgwarra Cliff' filled with dark rolling shadows, rock shapes and shifting surfaces is good...

THE ARTS BALL of 1972 to be held on 25 February
Theme: 'HOLLYWOOD'

from *The Western Morning News*, May 5, 1972, by Frank Ruhrmund
PAINTER WITH DISTINCTIVE STYLE

An exhibition of paintings and sculpture by Conor Fallon is now being held in the one-man showroom of the Newlyn Art Gallery.

A painter whose work has impressed in mixed exhibitions in recent years, this is his first individual show there and possibly his last, unfortunately, as he is shortly returning, I understand, to his native Ireland. He will be missed, for he is a painter with a very personal style and vision...He is a painter with ideas and courage; he demonstrates his versatility and puts himself at risk by including four 'Maquettes for Owls', a series of plasters for bronzes; hollow-eyed, white, yellow and orange, they are a delight...

from the Minutes of the NSA Meeting, April 7, 1972
John Miller (Chairman)

...The sculpture forecourt was discussed. This was finally considered to be impracticable in the light of the very real vandalism risk, the litter problem, the high rate of insurance and the limited amount of large sculpture that would probably be available...

...Details were given of the completed arrangements for the Plymouth Museum Exhibition for which 62 works had been sent in. These would go to Plymouth on Monday, 10th April.

from *Leave Tomorrow Behind*, by John Miller
...John and Ella Halkes opened the Orion Gallery in Penzance (1972) after he retired from the Air Force. It was the first gallery to show contemporary paintings since our own [John Miller & Michael Truscott's] at Number 5 Chapel Street in the early sixties...But John and Ella opened the Orion just at the right time. People were beginning to regain an interest in art. Nevertheless, works by the now famous Newlyn School of Painters could still be purchased for a few hundred pounds...

from the Minutes of the NSA Meeting, August 15, 1972
...It was agreed that a Christmas Exhibition should again be held from Saturday, 2 December until the 16th...a private view on Friday, 1 December.

...The Committee expressed regrets at the loss to the Society of Dod Procter, R A, one of the original Members of the Society who contributed considerably to the Arts during her long life.

THE ORION GALLERY -- Christmas 1972

Artists of Cornwall Exhibition at the University of Birmingham

27 November - 22 December, by kind invitation of the Dean of the Faculty of Arts

from the *Introduction*

...The Orion Gallery was established earlier this year in Penzance, now the most important town of the area, with the aim of providing a relaxed and informal location where some of the professional artists could exhibit and sell their work throughout the year.

The project has been extremely successful and the Gallery is pleased to end this eventful year by mounting an exhibition, similar to their own currently showing in Penzance.

136

The artists
Jack Pender
Ithell Colquhoun
Joan Whiteford
Rosemary Ziar
Michael Praed
Bryan Wynter
Robert Brennan
Diane Alexander
Albert Reuss
Dame Barbara Hepworth
Roger Veal
Roger Hilton
Ken Symonds
Joan Gilchrest
Biddy Picard
Tony Giles
Geoff Ogden
Margo Maeckelberghe
Reg Watkiss
Rose Phipps
Ann Nicholls
Robin Hirtenstein
John Miller

The Orion Gallery, Morrab Road, Penzance

from Denys Val Baker, Spring at Land's End

...Although the Penwith [Gallery] is now much the larger and most powerful art gallery, with a substantial London reputation and financial backing on a grand scale from the Arts Council of Great Britain, Jess and I have always found we enjoy ourselves better at the somehow more intimate gatherings at the Newlyn Gallery...At Newlyn we all seemed more cheerful. Perhaps, dare I say it, this was contributed to by the simple fact that at that opening ample supplies of pleasant white and rose wines were provided by the Gallery? At any rate we spent a pleasant couple of hours wandering around looking at works which were perhaps generally a little more traditional than the Penwith, but included many painters whom we all found impressive -- notably Margo Maeckelberghe, with her breathtaking vistas of lonely Cornish landscapes, Jack Pender, of Mousehole, with his instinctively true interpretations, in modern techniques, of local fishing boat scenes, and one or two primitives like Mary Jewels of Newlyn...

from the Minutes of the NSA Meeting, April 13, 1973
...The financial position of the Society was discussed at length in the light of the letters from the Bank Manager asking for guarantees for the loan by overdraft. The Secretary explained that the expense incurred by the Committee in redecorating the gallery had created a seriously overdrawn position. this had not been allowed for in the budgeting for the year...
...The Chairman suggested that an Associates Section might be formed. This should improve the Society's income and encourage interest. In some cases this could lead to full membership...
...The Arts Ball had to be cancelled for 1973 through lack of interest...

from *Night Letters and selected drawings*, Roger Hilton
from the *Introduction* by Michael Canney
By the spring of 1973 Hilton had completed a substantial number of his new gouaches and was anxious to show them, but there seemed to be little interest. He became convinced that he was being neglected, although this was not strictly true, for a London retrospective was already under discussion. However, it was a fact that his work was not selling and that he was financially at a very low ebb. He was therefore much encouraged when in June, the small Orion Gallery in Penzance took the initiative and staged a successful exhibition of his new gouaches. The enthusiasm of visitors and friends raised his morale and the sale of two-thirds of the paintings helped him financially; moreover the new gouaches were seen to represent a significant stage in his development.

from *Western Morning News*, 22 June, 1973

INTERNATIONAL STAR IN ORION CONSTELLATION

by Frank Ruhrmund
The Exhibition of 35 recent gouaches by Roger Hilton, now being held at the Orion Gallery, Morrab Road, Penzance, is an artistic occasion of considerable importance.

Although he has worked in Cornwall for many years it is, I believe, his first one-man show to be presented in the country -- an astonishing fact when one considers his achievements and reputation which are, of course, enormous.

One of Britain's leading modern painters, a first prize-winner in the John Moores Exhibition 1963, he has exhibited at Gimpel Fils, Tooths, and the Waddington Gallery, London; the Tokio Biennale, and the International Biennale, Venice.

His paintings are included in the permanent collections of among others, the Tate Gallery, the Arts Council, the Gulbenkian Foundation, the Victoria & Albert Museum, Edinburgh's Museum of Modern Art, and the National Gallery of Canada.

Despite all this -- or perhaps because of it -- this exhibition is almost certain to create more comment, if not controversy, than any other yet mounted by the adventurous Orion Gallery.

Inevitably it will revive all the arguments prompted by modern art: "Is it art or rubbish?"; "A child of six could do better."

It is, in fact, an exhibition easy to dismiss at a moment's notice. The obscurity of a few is quite baffling, the secret of their intent remains the artist's but the majority are a delight, and if one pauses for a while to really look at them they begin to work.

A rare opportunity to see an artist of national and international repute in a light-hearted, essentially happy, mood, the exhibition is on view until June 29.

THE ORION GALLERY
morrab road, penzance, cornwall
tel. 5648

Roger Hilton
recent paintings

12–29 JUNE 1973
TUESDAY-SATURDAY 10-6

The thirty-five gouaches in this exhibition were painted during the first half of 1973

from *Spring at Land's End,* Denys Val Baker

As it happened only the evening after the Newlyn opening, Ken and Jane and Jess and I found ourselves unexpectedly engulfed in a very jolly occasion...This was a private view of a one-man show of the paintings of Jack Pender at a new gallery recently opened in Penzance, the Orion. I have always felt that anyone enterprising could make really good business out of an art gallery in Penzance, and John Halkes had gone ahead and proved just this, by turning some old shop premises into a very smart modern art gallery...To begin with Jack Pender's paintings are so visually exciting and satisfying that it was sheer pleasure just to stand and savour them. How we wished we could have afforded to buy one of the big semi-abstract views of fishing boats!

All this art gallery-itis must have completely gone to our heads. Almost unbelievably, two nights later, we found ourselves at yet another one-man private view, in yet another small gallery in Penzance, the Framers' -- drinking yet another round of bubbly drinks, this time to the work of John Miller, another of my favourite painters...

from the Minutes of the NSA Meeting, August 31, 1973
Ken Symonds (Chairman)
...The Chairman read to the Committee the letter from the Curator (Alister McLeod) advising the Committee that owing to the financial position of the Society they should dispense with the services of the Curator/Secretary as from the end of October. This course was necessary to avoid an indebtedness in future which the bank would not be prepared to meet...

from the Minutes of the NSA Meeting, September 10, 1973
Ken Symonds (Chairman) John O'Dell (Secretary)
...After the receipt of the Arts Council grant the Society would have a credit balance at the bank sufficient with careful management to carry them through until April 1974 when the new subscriptions and other incomes would come in. The secretary did however explain that in his opinion a much larger revenue was required to maintain the gallery. An increase in members, higher membership fees, increased commission on sales and other positive methods of achieving this would have to be considered in the next few months...

from the Minutes of the NSA Meeting, December 7, 1973
Ken Symonds (Chairman)
...It was suggested that we try to arrange an exhibition of paintings of the Old Newlyn School -- with a future aim of having a permanent exhibition.
...It was suggested that it might be worth experimenting with Sunday opening... .

A note of the meeting between Ken Symonds, John Miller, Peter Bird (ACGB) and Hugh Stoddart, December 14, 1973
The whole function and financial state of the Society was discussed freely and at length. These are the main points to emerge from the discussion.
The Arts Council and SWAA are both prepared to give us financial support on the basis that we in turn:
1 Broaden the concept of the Society
2 Make more use of our main asset -- space, particularly during the winter months.
3 The key figure in whatever we attempt to do will be the curator...we should attract the right sort of person and decide the terms of office.

A STATEMENT OF POLICY BY THE NEWLYN SOCIETY OF ARTISTS

We, the committee on behalf of the members are resolved to broaden the scope and function of the Gallery by promoting more local involvement. By extending our programme of activities throughout the year, we shall be more positively contributing to the furtherance of the Arts in Cornwall.

Projects for the future:

The formation of an Activities Group composed of Members, Fellows and Trustees whose function will be to organise in cooperation with the curator the following:

Music and poetry recitals

"Cornish Evenings" eg 'Potter, Poet and Painter'

Talks and demonstrations by Members

Visiting lecturers

Classes. Tuition by Members in painting, drawing, art history, etc.

Exhibitions: Local childrens work, Arts Council and SWAA, one-man shows, exchanges, film shows, associate members

The setting up of a permanent collection, in particular the old Newlyn school

A members room for informal chat evenings

from the Minutes of a Special Meeting, December 19, 1973

Ken Symonds (Chairman)

...The Chairman read his report of the meeting with Peter Bird and Hugh Stoddart. John Miller pointed out that they were very emphatic that the gallery should be used for other purposes than Art Exhibitions...he again emphasised that at present the gallery is used only half the year...

...The Chairman then gave his ideas about John Halkes' proposed scheme...The committee then left the general discussion until after hearing from John Halkes himself...

New proposals for NSA

John Halkes arrived and put his proposals to the committee, he then answered questions and a full discussion was held. Members felt that it was too important to take a decision immediately and that a further meeting should be held early in the new year to consider the matter further.

from *Leave Tomorrow Behind*, by John Miller

...Then one day Gabriel White retired and the Arts Council had an entirely different attitude towards things. At lunch with the new man, whose name I cannot remember, he explained that we had to become an educational organisation and that no grants would be given to maintain a small local society of artists. This was the end of an era and the beginning of a new one when John Halkes brought his professional expertise and saved the day...

from the Minutes of the Special Meeting of the NSA Committee, January 3, 1974

Ken Symonds (Chairman)

...the sole purpose of the meeting was to discuss the principle of an amalgamation between the NSA and John Halkes of the Orion Gallery.

The proposal is that we unite our interests under the Directorship of John Halkes. That by getting together and becoming a new complete entity this would:

1 Benefit the members of this Society

2 Benefit a much larger group of people becoming involved in such a merger

3 Focus all the art activities in the area under a central body

NEWLYN

140

SOCIETY OF ARTISTS

1895   1973

from the brochure prepared by Alister J McLeod & the Newlyn Society of Artists, 1973, printed by A Chapell, New Street concerning Fellowship of the Society

...In 1968, encouraged by Mr Gabriel White, the then Art Director of the Arts Council plans were put forward for an extensive remodelling of the Gallery interior. The work was started in the winter of that year and completed in the winter of 1969 and by the valuable aid of The Arts Council "Housing the Arts" Fund, The Carnegie Trust, The Museums Association, The Penzance and West Penwith Councils, individual donations from Members, Fellows and Private Companies and a most successful Auction Sale of Paintings, Antiques and Curios given by the Members and Fellows, the whole cost of these improvements were met within a few weeks of their completion. For a small, independent Society far from any large centre of population this was indeed a triumph of organisation and collective effort by the 50 Members and the Fellows who now number over 200...

...There are problems with a Gallery such as this and there are also great possibilities, and the more people who can share both, the greater can be the contribution made to a creative way of life. ...Alister J McLeod

Letter from the Department of the Environment, February 4, 1974
BUILDINGS OF SPECIAL ARCHITECTURAL OR HISTORIC INTEREST
Art Gallery, Fore Street, Newlyn

1 I am writing to you as the owner to let you know that the above-named building has been selected for inclusion in the statutory list of buildings of special architectural or historic interest compiled by the Secretary of State. If you do not own the building I would be grateful if you would, after reading this letter, send it on to the owner for his information.

2 The list is about to be given legal effect, after which copies will be deposited with your local council. Thereafter, any member of the public who wishes to do so may inspect the list at the council offices...

THE NEWLYN ORION GALLERIES

DIRECTOR'S FIRST ANNUAL REPORT 1974/75 (John Halkes)

The Newlyn Orion Galleries (NOG) organisation was formed on the lst November 1974...NOG was formed to make maximum use of the galleries in Penzance/Newlyn. The organisation runs the Newlyn Art Gallery and the Orion Gallery and has applied for registration as an educational charity. The organisation is a new one. It brings together the various components of the visual arts in West Cornwall; the Trustees of the Newlyn Gallery, the NSA and the directors of the Orion Gallery, and these bodies are represented on the Management Committee...

It may seem strange to some people that we attempted to set up a new organisation with such a wide range of activities at a time of national economic recession. However, it was obvious that without some concerted action we could have lost everything. So it was 'the best of times and the worst of times'. We were ready to take advantage of the recent moves to decentralise the Arts from London and by offering a varied programme we were able to gain support from the Arts Council and South West Arts. We were also established at a time when local government had reorganised and was more able to support the cultural commitments of the district. During this period though, the arts were being hit by unprecedented inflation. Over the two year period since our organisation was first mooted we have experienced inflation of 48%. Correspondingly, in the general trading recession the commission from sales, which was needed to complete our budget, fell drastically in 1975.

In April an association of Friends of the Galleries was formed and two existing members of the Management Committee, Peter Ellery and Eileen Hunt, kindly agreed to represent the Friends on that committee. They undertook with exceptional vigour a fund raising campaign to see us through the cash flow problems arising from low sales...

...at the October meeting the Management Committee confronted by the survival nature of the Arts, decided to close the Orion Gallery after Christmas, 1975. this step was taken after lengthy consultations with the ACGB and SWA so that we could ride out the storm at Newlyn, without building up an unmanageable deficit...

The Permanent Collection:

A start was made on the Permanent Collection two months after the Galleries formed. We realised that without any existing material or money we would have to rely largely on the generosity of friends; but since we had such an enthusiastic response from them we were able to go ahead...

The Future:

...We are lucky to have such a fine building and site and we must try to make it fit the needs of the community in 1976. West Cornwall still attracts good artists, who come here to live because of the stimulus of the environment and the historic artistic impetus of the area. They themselves are a resource which we cannot afford to waste. Likewise, the galleries and studios in West Cornwall attract thousands of visitors throughout the year -- every year; for the economic and cultural good of this area we must not waste their potential. Lastly we have a role within our local community. The art of looking and seeing needs practice and encouragement. People often live in the dark -- unable to understand the artist and the visionary; often unable to see the drastic changes to their environment. We ignore the essential education of our senses and the nourishment of our souls at our peril.

Treasurer's Report for the Year 1974/75
Peter Ellery

...whatever the final outcome of the Newlyn Orion organisation may be, the fact remains that the Society, having been relieved of the financial pressures of running the Gallery, has received a breathing space in which to recover its financial position during a particularly depressing economic period.

...It will, in my view, require all the ingenuity imaginable on the part of the Management Committee and others concerned in the producing and the carrying out of a policy for exhibitions and other activities in the Gallery which will not place any undue strain on the resources which will be available. In this respect I am sure the Society and its members will do all in their power to co-operate with the Management Committee and its staff in, what will prove to be, a difficult task.

142

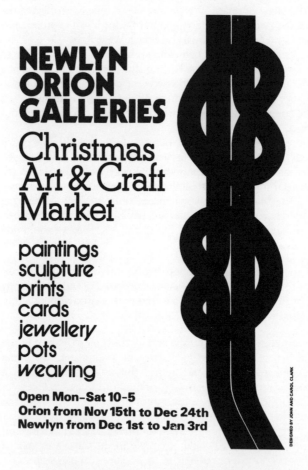

X: 1975-1984

The Newlyn Orion Galleries

The Orion Gallery, Morrab Rd., Penzance, Cornwall. TR18 2QS Tel. Pz. 5648
Newlyn Art Gallery, Newlyn, Penzance, Cornwall. TR18 5PW Tel. Pz. 3715

from THE NEWLYN ORION GALLERIES DIRECTOR'S REPORT for 1975 -- John Halkes
Gallery exhibitions: 24
Outside/touring exhibitions: 6
Loan exhibitions: 1
Performance: 1
Events/lectures/openings: 18
TOTAL EXHIBITIONS AND EVENTS 50

Chairman's Report (Newlyn Society of Artists), November 14, 1975 Ken Symonds (in the Chair)

There is no denying that the year has been disappointing. From the outset the amalgamation was bedevilled by inflation and the artists hit badly. Despite our good intentions and the moral and financial support we have received, the Orion Gallery has been forced to close. This is a sad blow, and I think everyone will regret its passing. Not only as our town shop window: during its existence it created its own very warm and friendly ambience, and was an asset to Penzance and also to the Society.

No one could have forseen that sales would have dropped so disastrously. Inflation is running at 40% a year in the Arts, according to an Arts Council spokesman, and unless a definite government policy is forthcoming in the near future, the Arts council budget will not even cover this rise in costs.

Despite the economic crisis the Newlyn Orion Galleries organisation did go ahead with its programme for the year and put on many varied exhibitions and events. New work was seen, both in one-man shows, group shows and Arts Council touring exhibitions. Inevitably, they have been received with mixed feelings on the part of the artists, members and the general public. I gather that a large number of people have enjoyed the opportunity of seeing work from outside the area (which is a very relevant point - living as we do in the far south west.)

Things are not nearly so gloomy from the Society's standpoint. Our financial position is quite good and we should actually clear our overdraft in the near future.

We have a larger membership which now includes the following members elected during the year: Tony O'Malley, Jane O'Malley, George Dannatt, Charles Howard, Roy Walker, Paul Nicholls, John Maries.

Some former members have been re-invited to join the Society and have accepted. These include: John Wells, Karl Weschke, Denis Mitchell, George Lambourn, Rosemary Tunstall Behrens.

Other artists have been invited to join the Society and accepted: Terry Frost, Francis Hewlett, Bill Marshall, John Barnicoat, Robert Adams.

Again on the positive side, we have formed an associate membership to the Society and this now stands at 75. It is good to know we have a battery of newcomers coming along...

Perhaps one of the most outstanding achievements of the year has been the setting up of the Permanent Collection. This really has been a brilliantly successful operation on the part of the Director and gives immense pleasure to everyone...It is on the strength of an anticipated rightful setting -- the building of an extension -- with the help of interested bodies --and this will properly house the historical paintings by our founder members.

It is with regret that I must mention that three of our members died during the year: Ivy Pearce, one of our older members; Peggy Frank who served as both active painter and committee member; and Bryan Wynter, a most loyal and active supporter of the Society. It is sad when we lose good painters and even sadder when they are nice people as well.

from the Minutes of the NSA Committee Meeting, 30 January 1976
Ken Symonds (Chairman)
...*PROPOSED EXTENSION TO THE GALLERY* John Halkes outlined and explained the proposals for an extension to the Gallery and produced a model and plans for the Committee's consideration. The Committee were informed that the Newlyn Orion Galleries Management Committee and the Trustees had approved the scheme and that the Arts Council's Housing the Arts Committee had indicated that they supported the scheme and would provide £8,500 towards the costs. The Committee unanimously and enthusiastically approved the proposed extension to the Gallery.

from the Newsletter, Spring 1976
27 February - 23rd March: ITHELL COLQUHOUN
One of our first exhibitions at Newlyn in 1976 is about surrealism. We are lucky to have a distinguished surrealist author, poet and painter, Ithell Colquhoun living near Penzance. The Exhibition promises to be very exciting and should give a remarkable insight into a movement which has enormous influence on painting, drama and writing today. This Exhibition is a two year touring project by the Newlyn Orion Galleries and will cover the South of England.

from the Minutes of the AGM of the NSA, October 15, 1976
Ken Symonds (Chairman)
Extension to the Gallery - John Halkes, Director of the Newlyn Orion organisation, at the request of the Chairman, reported that the project had been pursued throughout the year and that all necessary Planning and Building-Bye law approvals had been received and that the English Tourist Board had been approached. However the Arts Council's Housing the Arts grants had been cut by 50% and that there was virtually no building now in the public sector. In the circumstances it would appear that the project would have to be shelved for the time being...However, an improved lighting and heating scheme for the gallery would be pursued as the extension project could not be carried out...

from the Chairman's Report (Ken Symonds) 1976

I think everyone would agree that the range of exhibitions and activities we had this year has been one of the most interesting and exciting we have ever had in the Gallery. Each exhibition came as a surprise. The idea of one-man and group shows, instead of our usual long mixed ones is, although a break from our old tradition, a very worthwhile experiment. I hope it can be sustained in the future. I think it is most rewarding for both artist and public to see a range of work by a given artist and a chance to study in depth and in contrast makes this format very successful.

For instance, the Ithell Colquhoun show was an impressive experience. Ranging over a long span of years it showed the developing stages in her evolution as a painter within the Surrealist movement.

...Not all the state sponsored shows we get are greeted with enthusiasm. The Arts Council shows are more often as not, noted for their lack of content. I believe they think we are deprived if we don't see what's new in the London art frontier. Yes, we do like to see originality but most of it doesn't appear to have much to do with painting, or art for that matter...

...The Francis Hewlett one-man was a real *tour de force*. The ceramics were original and great fun and the small paintings gave out real pleasure in the paint...I was going to say 'let's give him a big hand folks!' But he already has one! Ceramic, of course.

1977 Exhibition Calendar

28 March - 26 April
SPRING EXHIBITION NSA mixed exhibition
MARY JEWELS paintings
2 - 31 May
JOHN HENDERSON 'Rural Realist' paintings
RAY ATKINS paintings & drawings
ROBERT MORLEY paintings & watercolours
1 - 30 June
PATRICK HUGHES paintings & prints
ROSE HILTON recent paintings & drawings
DAVID KEMP paintings & watercolours
26 July - 13 August
RAY AMBROSE
NSA Summer Shows (undated in records)
Autumn/winter shows not recorded

from the Newsletter, 1977
NEWLYN ORION GALLERIES

As we enter our third year as an arts organisation we are pleased to announce the start of a quarterly newsletter. Our audience has doubled in size since we started. Last year we had twenty thousand visitors to the gallery at Newlyn and entertained nearly three thousand people during our Summer Festival...

from the Hon Treasurer's Report (John O'Dell) of the NSA, March 31, 1977

It gives me great pleasure to present this financial report...particularly so as the Society's financial state is very healthy after many years of anxiety as to whether the Society would survive the running of the Gallery...Now that the Society does not have to contend with this and its escalating costs, there is no doubt that its position has been strengthened and it can now pursue other activities should it so desire by virtue of having funds available for this purpose.

145

Certificate of Incorporation
I Hereby certify that

NEWLYN ORION GALLERIES LIMITED

is this day incorporated under the Companies Acts
1948 to 1976 and that the Company is Limited.
Given under my hand at Cardiff the 22nd April 1977
D.A. Pendlebury
Assistant Registrar of Companies

from a Letter from John Halkes to Mary Jewels & Cordelia Dobson
30th June 1977

As you know -- the Ikon Gallery at Birmingham are anxious to have a Mary Jewels in their exhibition of British Primitive and Naive Painting this summer. Now I <u>know</u> you do not like the title but I think the exhibition would be incomplete without one of your paintings, Mary -- you would have to do nothing more than agree (and you could even register your disapproval of the exhibition title while taking part!)...

from the Minutes of the NSA Committee Meeting, September 23, 1977
John Emanuel (Chairman)
...*Exhibition at Pont Aven* Gwen Legrand described how, arising out of remarks at the AGM, she had approached the artists in Pont Aven. There was no Society equivalent to ours but the Secretary of the artists offered the NSA the town hall in Pont Aven for an exhibition. This consists of 3 rooms which are regularly used for exhibitions. [From us] they would like a booklet in French with a brief history of the NSA. Gwen had also checked distances -- it is 80 miles to Plymouth this side of the channel and 80 miles from Roscoff to Pont Aven the other...

from the full report on the Pont Aven trip by Jane Symonds
...The first hint of trouble arrived when there was no one resembling an agent (007 or more mundane) waiting for them at Roscoff, and it took them a little while to find out that the French customs close at 7pm whilst the ferry arrives at 9pm! The result was that Ken and Jane (Symonds) spent the night in the back of the van on Roscoff harbour...The van was unloaded on the Friday evening in Pont Aven and the work spread round the walls. Saturday saw all 13 of the group over for the opening, working like mad to get everything ready for the evening...The Société were very good hosts; the party was greeted with a large sign 'Newlyn Society of Artists' over the door...They

organised the official opening with the mayor in attendance...Everyone was bowled over by the number of people visiting the gallery each day, at least 900 or more...They looked and they bought!

...To sum up briefly: Who would have thought it was so complicated -- let alone expensive -- to transport paintings to and from a fellow Common Market country? We could not have managed without the French agent to deal with the customs over the figures involving VAT. In spite of all the hassle, worries, extra cost and 'human errors' the Society should count the exhibition a success. 18,000-20,000 new people saw the work of the 40 members who took part -- and many paintings sold...

RAY AMBROSE
RAY ATKINS
GILES AUTY
W BARNS GRAHAM
MARY BERESFORD-WILLIAMS
BOB BOURNE
CHARLES BREAKER
BARRIE BRISCOE
ALAN BROUGH
JOHN BUCHANAN
CAROL CLARK
DAVID COLLINGS
ITHELL COLQUHOUN
GEORGE DANNATT
THERESA GILDER
FRANCIS HEWLETT
SHEILA HICKS
ROSE HILTON
DAVID KEMP
DENIS LANE
GWEN LEGRAND
MARGO MAECKELBERGHE
JEANNE DU MAURIER
JUNE MILES
JOHN MILLER
DENIS MITCHELL
SONIA ROBINSON
COLIN SCOTT
PETER SMITH
PAUL NICHOLLS
BIDDY PICARD
MICHAEL PRAED
KEN SYMONDS
WILLIAM TUDOR
ROGER VEAL
JOAN WHITEFORD
BARBARA WILLS
VINCENT WILSON

Poster designed by Mary Beresford Williams

from *A BREATH OF FRESH AIR*

Location: Brittany

Narrative: The origins of this colony [at Newlyn] lay not in Cornwall, but across the sea in Brittany at fishing villages like Pont Aven....Today, in summertime, Pont Aven is an overcrowded tourist trap - put firmly on the map by the reputation of Paul Gaugin who painted here in 1886...Gaugin described Brittany as "that unspoilt land of old world customs, quite different from our atrocious civilised communities." Indeed, artists at that time, from all over Europe, were anxious to escape from their studios in crowded cities like Paris, to come to Pont Aven, Cancale, Quimperle and Concarneau. Here they hoped to study and paint the simple open-air life of Breton peasants and fishermen...

from *The Observer Magazine,* 11 June 1978

FAMILY FEELING by Caryll Faraldi

Norman Garstin's view of Penzance, 'The Rain it Raineth Every Day' was not a success with the local worthies. They wanted people to think the sun always shone there, and kept the painting locked up for many years. Now the works of Garstin and his daughter Alethea can be seen in exhibition...[at St Ives' Penwith Society of Arts]

...In the 1880s a vigorous and versatile Irishman, Norman Garstin joined the Newlyn band. Always a painter but a dilettante one, he ironically turned professional artist after losing an eye in a riding accident...He subsequently studied architecture, dug for diamonds in South Africa and established a reputation as a brilliant journalist in Cape Town...His third child and only daughter, Alethea, born in 1894, painted virtually all her life until her death this year...The show was suggested to Alethea by her neighbour, the artist Patrick Heron, and organised by art historian Michael Canney. It is the first time the works of father and daughter have been shown together for over 50 years...The exhibition evokes her life, travels, personality and ever-observant and humorous eye: tiny shimmering landscapes from France, the unmistakable scenes and landscape of Cornwall, gentle portraits of children, animals affectionately and accurately recorded.

Alethea Garstin at the time of her exhibition with her late father

---

TOP TEN Touring Exhibition of South West Arts Major Award Winners in Fine Art: 1978
South West Arts has been running its Major Award scheme for two years. The scheme was originally devolved from the Arts Council...Tony Foster, Visual Arts Officer (SWA)

Winners associated with Newlyn Art Gallery:
Mary Beresford Williams
Anthony Currell
Francis Hewlett
Philip Hogben
Geoff Ogden
Karl Weschke
Toured to Cirencester, Bath, Dorchester, Exeter, Plymouth, and Penzance [20 October - 17 November] at the Newlyn Art Gallery

from the Minutes of the AGM of the NSA, September 29, 1978
John Emanuel (Chairman)

from the Chairman's Report
...for the first time we have had sufficient funds to pursue and achieve really positive goals. Our membership stands at 82 and our associate membership at 201.

...I must thank our secretary Jane Symonds for her noble work in ALL fields of our activities and our Treasurer John O'Dell for his continued sage counsels.

...also the sub-committee -- particularly Mike Praed and Gwen Legrand -- which organised the Pont Aven exhibition this past summer. It was a great success. Our exhibitors owe a very real debt to Polly Jackson, Liz Ham and Beatrice Kurnow. They did a grand job looking after the show and it would not have worked at all without them...

THE NEWLYN AND PENWITH GALLERIES 2 February 1979
Joint report by the Directors to the two committees
[John Halkes and Hugh Scrutton]
Following the wishes of the two committees we have met three times in 1978 to discuss the work of the two galleries and consider how our two organisations might usefully co-operate.

We began by looking at a few facts. The total membership of Newlyn Orion is 354. this includes 81 full members of the NSA and 177 associate members of the society. The Penwith Society of Arts has 43 full members and 250 associate members. There is probably nowhere in the country, outside of London, with anything like so many resident artists. All, of course, want to exhibit -- and most want to sell work. Apart from our two Galleries, Cornwall is very badly off for art galleries -- public or private. It is therefore not surprising that there is a demand from artists for both our Galleries to continue. What may surprise outsiders -- and perhaps some insiders too -- is that 25 artists or craftsmen are at present members of <u>both</u> societies -- and they also share 50 associates...

149

from *The Cornishman*, Thursday, May 10, 1979

NOSTALGIC EXHIBITION AT ORION OF EARLY NEWLYN SCHOOL

In 1884 a report in "The Cornishman" stated that there were no less than twenty-seven artists then residing in Newlyn and Stanhope Forbes, who was to become the doyen of the Newlyn School of Artists wrote, "They are flocking in here each day". An exhibition of paintings by sixteen of the best-known of those artists is now being held at the Newlyn Art Gallery. It closes on June 9.

This is the first major exhibition of its kind for many years and, as such, must be the artistic event of the year in Cornwall.

Organised by a team, working under the aegis of Newlyn Orion, with financial support from the Arts Council of Great Britain, it has received assistance and encouragement from literally hundreds of people...

These painters may have been sentimental, even romantic in their approach to their subject matter - the fishermen and women of Newlyn - but, whatever their faults, no one can deny that they certainly knew their craft.

They knew how to draw, they could handle paint, and in their quest for realism, painting out-of-doors and on the spot "en plein air," and in their search for atmosphere and light, they were successful...Frank Ruhrmund

[Catalogue book. See Bibliography.]

from *The Cornishman*, May 24,1979

TOP CORNISH POET
FOR NEWLYN
D M Thomas, the distinguished Cornish poet returns to his native land tomorrow to give a reading from his work at Newlyn Art Gallery, Penzance.

D M Thomas was born in Redruth in 1935 and received his early education at Redruth Grammar School. After taking a First in English at Oxford he became a teacher and lecturer -- and continued to write poetry. He is currently head of the English Department at Hereford College of Education.

In 1971 D M Thomas toured the USA giving readings with Peter Redgrove, who lectures at Falmouth School of Art. In the winter of 1978 he again toured the USA this time in company with Charles Causley. Both Peter Redgrove and Charles Causley have previously read their work at Newlyn Art Gallery in the series organised by Newlyn Orion.

This reading has a particular relevance as it comes during the showing of the splendid exhibition, "Artists of the Newlyn School".

Letter from John Halkes to Joan Gillchrest
November, 1979
> *...At last night's Council of Management meeting in the Gallery I presented your splendid painting of the 'Newlyn School Exhibition'. The Council members have asked me to write and say how much they appreciate your kind and generous gift, and that it would enter the permanent collection of Newlyn Orion.*
>
> *May I add my personal thanks and just say that it is quite the most witty and observant painting which I am absolutely sure will bring fond memories and much happiness to the viewers.*
>
> *Bless you Joany, lots of love from us all here.*

150

1980 Calendar
April
SPRING EXHIBITION NSA Members & Associates
May
ALBERT REUSS Retrospective
FIRST DAY COVERS
June - July
ALEXANDER MACKENZIE Recent paintings
NIGEL INGLIS Jennings Farm photographs
July - August
SUMMER '80 NSA group exhibition;
One-man shows by Carol Clark, Derek Jenkins, Vincent Wilson, Sheila Stafford, Sue Lewington, David Kemp
September - October
ROGER HILTON Gouaches (National Tour)
SYLVIA PRIESTLAND *West of Hayle River* photographs
COLIN SHEWRING 'To Begin at the Beginning...' paintings
November
CORNWALL COLLECTION Paintings for schools
ROGER MAYNE Landscape photographs
December
CHRISTMAS EXHIBITION NSA mixed show
GAY SAGAR-FENTON Solo

from the programme notes

FIRST DAY COVERS

'One of the headaches of arts organisations in 1980 is fundraising - whether for survival or laying down foundations for future work. On the other hand one of the pleasures is that imaginative and effective fundraising can bring together whole communities, create new friendships and be great fun.

These first day covers are all original works by leading British artists who responded most generously to our request for help. The covers have value as works of art and items of unique philatelic interest...The money we raise will go towards improving and

NEWLYN ART GALLERY – CORNWALL
27 February — 23 March 1976

SURREALISM — ITHELL COLQUHOUN
PAINTINGS DRAWINGS COLLAGES 1936 - 76

FIRST DAY COVERS
CATALOGUE

ART GALLERY
Passmore Edwards Art Gallery,
Newlyn, Penzance, Cornwall.

NEWLYN ART GALLERY

EXHIBITION OF COVERS – 3 MAY – 31 1980
AUCTION OF COVERS IN AID OF GALLERY FUNDS – SATURDAY 31 May at 7.30pm

Photographs
by Sylvia Priestland
WEST OF
HAYLE RIVER

Newlyn Art Gallery 17 Sept.-11 Oct. 80
Mon.-Sat. 10-5   Admission Free

PUBLICATION
West of Hayle River by Gerald & Sylvia Priestland
and is published by Wildwood House

LECTURE
Gerald Priestland
Newlyn Art Gallery, Friday 19 Sept. 8 p.m. £1.00 & 50p

Ian Hunter
Paintings and Drawings

Newlyn Art Gallery, Penzance.
26 April–21 May 1983

Broken Boat Series 27" × 40" Charcoal on paper.

extending the Gallery here at Newlyn which has a very special place in the local community and the wider world of art.

I would like to thank the artists who have taken part so enthusiastically - particularly Mary Beresford-Williams whose idea it was...

1981 Calendar
January - February
OPEN HOUSE 2   NSA Associates show
March
JOHN LOKER Paintings (Arnolfini tour)
GUNILLA TREEN Jewellery (Arnolfini tour)
8 April - 9 May
SPRING EXHIBITION NSA mixed
JUNE MILES solo
May
GEORGE DANNATT   Paintings, Drawings and Constructions
IAN CARRICK   Sculpture
30 June - 13 July
HUNDRED YEARS OF FISHING A visual history of Newlyn & Newlyn Painting
STANHOPE & ELIZABETH FORBES Paintings, Drawings and Etchings
20 June - 13 July
JENNINGS FARM SERIES: Nigel Inglis, photographs.
(Plymouth touring exhibition)
30 July - 5 September
SUMMER EXHIBITION NSA mixed
NINE SOLOS David Collings, Ray Ambrose, Mary Griffen, Gwen Legrand,
Bernard Evans, Michael Forster, Roy Ray, Sheelagh O'Donnell, Jane O'Malley
11 September - 6 October
DAVID MACFARLANE, MARIANNE EDWARDS (Westward Open Award
winner), MAURICE SUMRAY Figurative paintings
12 October - 14 November
MICHAEL PRAED Paintings [then toured to Truro: Royal Institution]
CHRISTMAS EXHIBITION
[1981, occurred over the time of the loss of the Penlee Lifeboat; attendance low.]

26 January 1981
ROGER HILTON: Night Letters and Selected Drawings
Derek Southall, writing in *Artscribe* in August 1980, concluded his long and sensitive review of our recent publication thus:-

Hilton writes with wit. It could hardly be otherwise from a man who could distinguish pictorial wit from whimsy. At other times he appeared to court his death with irritating little jabs, to dare fate to make an end of him while he assisted with drink. He succeeded too well and we lost a painter with many more pictures in him. The words are interlaced with drawings, sometimes separate, sometimes part of the text. The writing incidentally is in his own hand, not tidied up into print, and his eccentric spelling is therefore also present. The drawings alone are worth the price of the book. But Hilton's work can only be reached by feeling. The hints and pointings in these letters are a valuable aid to those who have no other access to him, and they are by turns diverting and saddening to those who have. But they are only an aid. His work is not difficult to reach, except perhaps for those whose training or attitude makes a formal reading the only available one. The expositions of Alan Bowness and others are helpful; but too often his work has been treated as though the formal devices were its *raison-d'etre*. It is a strength in his work, reflected in these writings, that they subvert their own formal means. You either submit to the feeling and are touched by it or you do not. It is because they share a little of this spirit that his letters are worth reading.

[The limited edition was published in March 1980]

Thank you.

And let there be no moaning at the bar, when I set out to sea.

1982 Calendar
January
OPEN HOUSE 3   NSA Associates exhibition
6 February - 6 March
FROM OBJECT TO OBJECT (Arts Council Touring)
FALMOUTH SELECTION: Painting, Sculpture, Print & Photography
by students of Falmouth College of Art
CAROLINE BROADHEAD, Jewellery
18 March - 17 April
SPRING EXHIBITION NSA mixed
23 April - 19 May KEN SPRAGUE: Recent Work
GEORGE LAMBOURN 1900-1977: Paintings and Drawings
26 May - 26 June
CAREL WEIGHT RA (RA/ARTS COUNCIL) Exhibition
9 July - 10 September
SUMMER '82 NSA mixed
SOLOS: Breon O'Casey, Fred Yates, Morwenna Thistlethwaite, Geoff Ogden,
Staff from Penzance School of Art and John Piper
21 September - 13 November
COASTLINE: John Hubbard, Derek Southall, Janet Nathan,
Michael O'Donnell, Richard Wiltshire, Ian Carrick, Hamish Fulton,
James Ravilious, Nigel Inglis. (TSW/SWA touring)
1 December - 5 January
COASTLINE II NSA Christmas Exhibition
SOLOS Gill Watkiss, Barrie Briscoe, Amy Schofield (Jewellery)

from the programme notes, July - September
Group Exhibition by the Staff of Penzance School of Art:
Joan Whiteford (etchings and prints, aquatints), Ruth Tudor (embroidery sculptures, embroidery dolls), William Tudor (drawings, watercolours, and oils), Barbara Tribe (bronze, ash, sandstone sculptures)

The Penzance School of Art, one of the earliest in this country, was originally very much associated with the Newlyn School of Painting (the Forbes School). It later gained a high reputation through its association with other well-known artists, either members of staff or those who had been students at the school.

In more recent times Bernard Leach and his sons Michael and David have taught pottery at the school, John Tunnard, fabric printing, and Bouverie Hoyton was its previous Principal. Many well-known artists including several local ones were students at the school.

At present the school is devoted entirely to the teaching of part-time students of all ages and of various artistic experience. It caters for several crafts along with the traditional Fine Arts. The present staff pride themselves on having a very catholic outlook to their teaching, but are united in regarding good draughtsmanship as an essential basis to all work.

JOAN WHITEFORD NDD, ATD, NS is a printmaker specialising in etching. She is a member of the National Society of Painters, Sculptors & Printmakers, and the NSA.

RUTH TUDOR ATD is an embroideress who is a member of the National Embroiderers Guild and serves on its Executive Council. She is also a member of the Red Rose Guild of Designers & Craftsmen and the Cornwall Craft Association.

WILLIAM TUDOR NDD, ATD, the Principal, on leaving the Royal Navy, became a lecturer at High Wycombe College of Art & Design. He is a member of the NSA and has exhibited at the Royal Academy, the New English Art Club, the Royal Society of British Artists and the Royal Institute of Painters in Watercolour.

BARBARA (SINGLEMAN) TRIBE, ARBS, is in charge of sculpture. She is a member of the Royal Society of British Sculptors, and the NSA. An Australian who studied at the Royal Academy School, she has works in many private and public collections, and had a large one-man show in the City Art Gallery, Stoke on Trent.

Position Paper for Council of Management October 1982
BUILDING PROJECT
Since the demise of the Orion in 1975 we have had plans to enlarge the building here at Newlyn...Briefly the plans suggested a granite faced extension on the south and east sides of the gallery with internal restructuring to give clear floor areas in the main gallery, a larger shop, a permanent collection space and better storage facilities. The 'L' shaped extension was to house extra contemporary exhibition space, workshops, restaurant, library/seminar room and additional office space. The plans were drawn up by Barrie Briscoe, MArch, MA and his drawings were seen as an extension of the present Victorian building. The bill of quantities was prepared and tenders received in 1978.

Future
Before committing considerable effort to relaunching the scheme the Director would like to discuss the whole project [and] proposes that a building sub-committee is formed to assist with the fundraising programme and with the finalising of a new brief for architects.

155

1983 Calendar
14 January - 12 February
PAUL RYAN Prints and Papers
FOUR OF A KIN:Alan Brough, potter; Sheila Brough, Dress Designer;
Adrian Brough, Potter; Bernard Brough, printmaker
PERMANENT COLLECTION
23 February - 16 March
OPEN HOUSE 4 NSA Associates Show
23 March - 16 April
SPRING EXHIBITION NSA mixed
SOLOS Jenny Croxford, Tony Giles
26 April - 21 May
IAN HUNTER Drawings and paintings
CORNWALL: ANDREW LANYON Photographs, Drawings
30 May - 2 July
ROBERT ORGAN paintings
LAURIE ANN FINESTONE drawings and etchings
13 July - 9 September
SUMMER '83 NSA mixed
SOLOS: Anthony Frost, Christa Maria Herrmann, Barbara Wills,
Peter M Smith, John Henderson, Ken Symonds, Marjorie Holland
21 September - 21 October
MAX WALL: Pictures by MAGGI HAMBLING
29 October - 22 November
MICHAEL CANNEY paintings, collages, constructions
BEN HARTLEY watercolours
1 - 23 December & 28 December - 7 January
THE FOUR SEASONS NSA mixed

from *The Western Morning News*, January 15, by Frank Ruhrmund
DISPLAY BY FAMILY FOUR
A whole family of craftsmen and designers must be rare and something special by any standard, and "Four of a Kin" -- an exhibition of work by the Brough family, now being held at Newlyn Art Gallery -- is just that. At the head of this talented family is potter Alan Brough, who worked with Bernard Leach at St Ives for some years when he first came to Cornwall...His wife Sheila, recently a finalist in a national dress design competition, designs and makes clothes of distinction, and writes on fashion...The elder son, Bernard Brough...is a specialist in print-making...The youngest member of the family, Adrian, is like his father a potter...

from the Autumn Newsletter

AUTUMN POETRY It so happens that one of the best publishing houses for contemporary poetry is based at Liskeard in East Cornwall. It is there that Harry Chambers of Peterloo Poets publishes the works of approximately fifty leading British Poets. Newlyn Orion will be mounting readings of the Peterloo Poets in the coming year and the gallery bookshop will be stocking a wide range from the title list. The first two in our series are Ursula Fanthorpe and Sylvia Kantaris, both of whom have strong associations with the South West region and both have recent publications.

from the programme notes, 21 September - 21 October

MAX WALL, Pictures by Maggi Hambling

'...Maggi Hambling was artist in residence at the National Gallery in 1981 when Max Wall was appearing in his one man show "Aspects of Max Wall" at the Garrick Theatre, opposite.

"I find him very moving -- he is like paint that moves, he has that magical quality of making you want to laugh and cry at the same moment"...This exhibition is a celebration of the life of a great performer. It is also a tribute to the remarkable talent of one of our best younger generation figurative artists...'

ALBERT REUSS 1889 - 1975

Newlyn Orion owns over 200 paintings by Albert Reuss, who lived and worked in Cornwall from 1948 - 1975. Following the major exhibition in 1980 we have mounted occasional exhibitions of selected works. This autumn we shall show some previously unseen paintings as well as some of the better known works from our permanent collection...A short illustrated biography is available.

Albert Reuss, from
O'Hana Gallery
Exhibition Programme
1968

AUTUMN LECTURES

This Autumn Newlyn Orion, in association with the Extra Mural Department of Exeter University, is arranging a set of four illustrated lectures by Jonathan Meuli MA (Cantab) BFA (Oxon) on 'The Religious Attitude in 20th Century Art'. Jonathan Meuli is a practising artist and art historian -- his approach is essentially lively and down to earth. 26 September: The Mystics (i) Cezanne, Bonnard, Chagall: debunking the idea of Cezanne as purely formalist; 10 October: The Mystics (ii) Klee and the German tradition: was Klee more an heir to Cezanne than, for example, the Cubists? 14 November: Optimists versus Realists: The Brave New World of Leger versus the cynical realism of Bunuel and Duchamp and 5 December: The Prophets (Expressionism) An intrinsically hopeless attempt to use humanistic language to express religious ideas? Van Gogh, Roualt, Bomberg, etc.

4 October - 29 October

Bridgewater Arts Centre, Somerset, are mounting the exhibition, FIVE NEWLYN ARTISTS. They have selected the artists Anthony Frost, Denis Mitchell, Geoff Ogden, Roy Ray and Ken Symonds for this first exhibition in their new gallery.

29 October - 22 November

MICHAEL CANNEY - Recent Works

This is Michael Canney's first solo exhibition since he retired as head of Fine Art at Bristol Polytechnic. The exhibition reflects his pre-occupation with the work of art as a real object, as opposed to an illusion. The paintings and reliefs have a classical quality which stems from their mathematical purity.

In the *Foreword* to his catalogue, he writes,

'For a number of years now my work has been broadly related to the Constructivist tradition. However, since 1979 it has relied upon a simple principle, in which the work constructs itself from itself. Based upon a systematic re-orientation of parts of the square, this process suggests an infinite range of possibilities...'

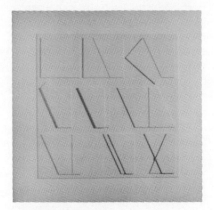

Systemic II (Hinged)
Relief 20 × 20 ins.

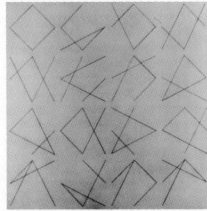

Sgraffito No. 3
Sgraffito on board 14 × 14 ins.

What too could be more appropriate than the fact that this exhibition and this publication are brought first to the public at Newlyn Art Gallery, where Michael Canney was, from 1956 to 1965, a distinguished Curator and Secretary to the Newlyn Society of Artists. In fact, throughout his varied career, Newlyn has been a constant : as a student, curator, broadcaster, exhibitions organiser, teacher, art historian, painter and lastly, of course, as a Cornishman, this area and this gallery in particular, have I suspect, been of lasting importance and inspiration. All I can say in this short foreword and introduction is that he has never given short change for that inspiration. Numerous students are especially grateful to him for introducing them to his own source of joy. And through his many broadcasts, films and exhibitions an appreciative public has come to know and love the work of the famous artists who have lived and worked here in West Cornwall.

Now it is, rightly, Michael Canney's turn to show the results of his quiet determination through the bustling and busy years as a communicator and the resolution of his ideas as an artist.

I should like to use this occasion to express my gratitude to Michael for his friendship and support in the past and for his sheer professionalism in preparing this exhibition.

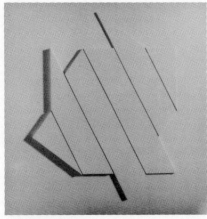

Oblique Two · 1983
Relief 20 × 20 ins.

John Halkes
Director - Newlyn Orion

158

from Newsletter - Winter 1984

Gillian Ayres

Main Gallery: 27 Feb - 27 Mar

'Throughout her career Gillian Ayres (b 1930) has always been considered one of Britain's leading abstract painters. She was associated with the 'tachiste' and Abstract Expressionist movements in the 50s and exhibited with the hard-edge painters of the 'Situation' group in the early 60s. She returned to the medium of oil in 1977 with an expressive language entirely her own and an unrivalled instinct for handling intense colour... The newest works have gem-like areas amidst large snaky lines, wild dots and flowery bursts. The imagery seems to reflect not just a love of abstract painting but also the rural atmosphere of her new home in North Wales...'

RECENT ADDITION TO THE PERMANENT COLLECTION
John Armstrong ARA 1893-1973

Veronica as Harlequin.
Oil on canvas. 30″ × 24″ c1950

This painting, which is a superb example of John Armstrong's later work, has been kindly donated to the Newlyn Orion Permanent Collection by Miss Frankie Freeth of Lamorna.

John Armstrong came to work in Cornwall in 1947 after a period as a most successful theatre and film designer in the thirties and as an official war artist from 1940-45. He lived at Oriental Cottage, Lamorna until the mid-fifties until he moved back to London. He was made ARA in 1966.

John Armstrong ARA 'Veronica as Harlequin' oil on canvas c1950

24 September - 20 October
HAPPY RETURNS to Newlyn Orion Galleries
by Frank Ruhrmund ·

Ten years ago I wrote in these columns of the formation of the Newlyn Orion Galleries, an amalgamation of the Newlyn Art Gallery and the Orion Gallery with John Halkes as its director. The idea came from his wife: "I laughed at the idea, thought she was crazy at the time, and wanted nothing to do with it." Fortunately he changed his mind, the concept became a challenge he couldn't resist, grew increasingly attractive and possible and, after a long year of discussion and debate, became reality.

At the start he outlined his proposals and hopes for the new organisation, most of which have been achieved. Not content to rest on his laurels he is now leading Newlyn Orion Galleries towards even bigger and better things. To follow the highly successful exhibition *Artists of the Newlyn School, 1880-1900* that brought 11,000 people into the gallery in 1979, a major survey exhibition *Painting in Newlyn, 1900-1930,* with complementary television films and a nationwide tour, is planned for early next year and, it is hoped, positive steps will be taken soon towards realising a most exciting and ambitious development, an extension to the building which will provide space for the gallery's permanent collection, seminar and library room, an enlarged shop, a sculpture and activity space, and even a restaurant overlooking Mount's Bay.

There is no doubt that Newlyn Orion Galleries, together with the Newlyn Society of Artists which retains its independence within the organisation and continues to hold three major exhibitions of its own each year, has become an artistic powerhouse; and the dynamo that drives it is John Halkes. A man of enviable energy, enthusiasm, ideas and vision, he is more than the director of a successful gallery, he is a man who believes firmly that people matter. A man very much aware of his dual responsibility to both artists and the public, who believes that he has an obligation to make art available to all. A man who, in ten years since he has been its director, has put Newlyn Orion Galleries on the artistic map and placed it in the forefront, in the first division, of galleries throughout the country gaining both regional and national recognition for the organisation.

To mark its tenth anniversary *Happy Returns* contains work from 50 artists each of whom has held a major solo exhibition here during the last decade. An impressive collection that would grace any gallery, it underlines its strength and shows quite clearly how far the organisation has travelled in its ten short years...

Major Solo Exhibitions 1974-1984

Karl Weschke 1974
Tony O'Malley 1975
Ithell Colquhoun 1976
Francis Hewlett (ceramics) 1976
David Patten 1977
Terry Frost 1977
Ray Atkins 1977
John Henderson 1977
Patrick Hughes 1977
John Tunnard 1977
Ken Symonds 1977
Anthony Currell 1977
Rose Hilton 1977
Paul Mount 1977
Denis Mitchell 1977
Richard Long 1978
John Hubbard 1978
John Miller 1978
Geoff Ogden 1978
Francis Hewlett (paintings) 1978
Ivon Hitchens 1979
David Haughton 1979
Alexander Mackenzie 1980
Albert Reuss 1980
Roger Hilton 1980
Michael o'Donnell 1980
Nigel Inglis 1980
Roger Mayne 1980
Ian Carrick 1981

John Loker 1981
Michael Praed 1981
Marianne Edwards 1981
Maurice Sumray 1981
George Dannatt 1981
David Macfarlane 1981
Carel Weight 1982
Ken Sprague 1982
George Lambourn 1982
Maggie Hambling 1983
Robert Organ 1983
Paul Ryan 1983
Ian Hunter 1983
Ben Hartley 1983
Michael Canney 1983
Laurie Ann Finestone 1983
Andrew Lanyon 1983
Gillian Ayres 1984
Andrzej Jackowski 1984
John Eaves 1984

Small Solo Exhibitions 1974-1984
Albert Reuss 1974
John Maries 1975
Rod Walker 1975
Roy Walker 1975
Anthony Frost 1975
June Miles 1976
Tony Smith 1976
Tina Day 1976
Mary Jewels 1977
David Kemp 1977
Robert Morley 1977
Jeff Instone 1977
Kathryn Morcom 1977
Peter Joseph 1978
David Tremlett 1978
Cyprian Bridge 1978

Richard Rush 1978
Andrew Lanyon 1978
Charles Roff 1978
James Millett 1978
Maggie Saxby 1978
Marjorie Brimacombe 1980
Sylvia Priestland 1980
Colin Shewring 1980
Gay Sagar-Fenton 1980
Gunilla Treen (jewellery) 1982
Caroline Broadhead (jewellery) 1982
Amy Schofield (jewellery) 1982
Albert Reuss 1983
Handel Edwards 1984

Major Thematic and Group Exhibitions 1974-1984
The Square Collection (ACGB) 1974
The Recollection (SWA) 1974
Sculpture of the Penwith I 1975
Three Abstract Painters (Wells, Mackenzie, Dannatt) 1975
An Element of Landscape (ACGB) 1975
Drawings of People (ACGB) 1975
Jigsaw (Cornwall College Design Dept) 1976
Four on Tour (SWA) 1976
Sculpture of the Penwith II 1978
Arts and Crafts: Crafts and Arts 1978
Examine Art (CSE work, West Cornwall) 1978
Neue Sachlichkeit (ACGB) 1979
Artists of the Newlyn School 1880-1900 1979
Top Ten (SWA Award Winners) Westward TV Open 1980
7 & 5 Society 1980
Cornwall Collection 1980
One Hundred Years of Fishing 1981
Stanhope and Elizabeth Forbes 1981
Ten Cornish Artists in Cuxhaven 1981
Bath Contemporary Arts Fair 1981
Falmouth Selection (FSA) 1982
From Object to Object (ACGB) 1982
Coastline (Touring) 1982
Bath Contemporary Arts Fair 1982
Four of a Kin 1983
Cornwall: Andrew Lanyon, Peter Lanyon 1983
Bath Contemporary Art Fair 1983
Five from Newlyn (NOG/Bridgwater Arts Centre) 1983
Dortmund Art Fair 1984
TSWA National Competition 1984
Second Nature 1984

An exhibition of
Happy Returns
At Newlyn Art Gallery

Exhibition Dates
24th September - 20th October 1984

Newlyn Art Gallery
Penzance, Cornwall.
Tel: (0736) 3715

Acknowledgements

Since its inception Newlyn Orion has received out-standing support from the Arts Council of Great Britain, South West Arts and Artists and Public members of the Company. We should like to take this opportunity of recording our warmest appreciation.

from John Miller, *Leave Tomorrow Behind*

Soon after *To the Lighthouse,* Kevin Crooks, the television producer used our house and garden for *A Breath of Fresh Air,* his film about the Newlyn School of painters. Michael Culver played Stanhope Forbes with Nanette Newman as his wife, Elizabeth. I played the part of Frank Bramley. Nanette opened my exhibition at David Messum's the following year and her husband, Bryan Forbes, bought a painting of Venice. Bryan wrote a most generous foreword to the last catalogue...

A BREATH OF FRESH AIR
Stanhope Forbes   Michael Culver
Elizabeth Armstrong Nanette Newman
Frank Bramley   John Miller
Walter Langley   David Shaw
Members of the Shiva Theatre company
Script by   Michael Canney
Additional dialogue John Oakden
Research   Caroline Fox
Musical Director   Ed Welch
Director   Kevin Crooks
TSW - Television South West Ltd 1984

161

Cricket Team photo by Andrew Besley

Photograph by Mary Beresford Williams.

Photograph by Mary Beresford Williams.

Photograph by Mary Beresford Williams.

SECOND NATURE

An exhibition and a book which explores the relationship between the artist and the land. Newlyn Orion are pleased to be mounting the first showing of 'SECOND NATURE' in association with Angela King and Sue Clifford of Common Ground and Jonathan Cape Ltd. who publish the book on the first of November.

"There is hardly any need to elaborate on the fact that, over the last decade, our relationship with the land and with the natural world that depends on it, have become matters of increasing concern. Nor that this is the latest expression of a very much older set of arguments about man's place in the natural scheme of things, about ownership of, and rights over, the land, about the importance of locality to a sense of personal and cultural identity.

What is new is the narrowing of the terms of the argument. Until comparatively recently these issues were central concerns of mainstream English writing and painting. Now they have been largely commandeered by scientists and economists, in whose view the complex emotional and richly symbolic roles which the countryside and nature still hold for us belong in the debased territory of 'sentimentality'.

So, by default, we have seen a series of dis-locations — at one extreme, for example, the rise of the idea that the natural world can be adequately conserved, and experienced, in scientifically defined sites and reservations; at another, the appropriation of a well-meant 'love of country' in the disturbing revival of aggressive patriotism.

The aim of 'SECOND NATURE' is to re-open the traditional *cultural* debate, and to invite a group of writers and artists who have demonstrated their concern about these issues (but who do not necessarily share a single point of view) to explore the idea that our relationship with the land and with other organisms, is a vital part of our imaginative, cultural and social life".

Common Ground 1984

Contributors:

Essays

John Barrell
Michael Berkeley
John Berger
Edward Blishen
Ronald Blythe
Leonie Caldecott
John Fowles
Fraser Harrison
Peter Levi
Richard Mabey
David Measure
Bel Mooney
Norman Nicholson
David Pownall
Kim Taplin
Colin Ward
Fay Weldon
Raymonds Williams

Art

Roger Ackling
Norman Ackroyd
Conrad Atkinson
John Blakemore
Stephen Dalton
Chris Drury
Elizabeth Frink
Hamish Fulton
Gay Godwin
Andy Goldsworthy
Paul Hempton
Paul Hill
John Hilliard
David Hockney
John Hubbard
Sirkka Liisa
  Konttinen
Jorge Lewinski
Richard Long
David Measures
Henry Moore
Alexander
  Mackenzie
Jamie McCullough
David Nash
James Ravilious
Robin Tanner

Henry Moore on site.

XI: 1985 - 1995

14 January - 2 February OPEN HOUSE 6 NSA Associates Show
14 February - 13 April PAINTING IN NEWLYN 1900-1930
14 April - 31 May SPRING EXHIBITION NSA mixed
8 June - 16 July EXCHANGE ART: 8 artists from Cuxhaven & Stade,
MARJORIE MORT: fifty years of painting
25 July - 14 September SUMMER EXHIBITION Part I & II NSA mixed
17/18/19 September WORKING PARTY Event/installation: Peter Smith, John
Clark, Michael Chalwin, Jonathan Meuli
September 26 - October 26, 1985 PATRICK HERON FROM EAGLES NEST :
Paintings and Drawing 1925 - 1985
1 - 27 November LANDMARKS Photographs by Paul Hill DENIS MITCHELL
Recent Sculpture, MISOME PEILE A Tribute

PAINTING IN NEWLYN 1900-1930
The great success of our 1979 touring exhibition 'Artists of the Newlyn School 1880
- 1900' prompted us to follow up with the sequel, 'Painting in Newlyn 1900 - 1930'.
Once again we have aimed to produce a popular exhibition which is both enjoyable and
informative. A full illustrated catalogue and twenty new postcard images are available,
and an interesting list of lectures and seminars has been arranged...The Exhibition has
been generously sponsored by Phillips the Fine Art Auctioneers and Television South
West. David Messum Fine Paintings has kindly sponsored the postcards...the directors
of the Queen's Hotel, Penzance made a large donation towards the costs of the
catalogue...
The Tour
Newlyn Art Gallery -- 14 February - 13 April
Plymouth City Art Gallery -- 20 April - 11 June
Barbican Art Gallery -- 10 July - 8 September
Birmingham City Art Gallery -- 23 September - 9 November*
*At the Barbican Art Gallery the exhibition expands to encompass the period of the
Early Newlyn School 1880-1900. This then tours to Birmingham.
[Catalogue book. See bibliography.]

Full list of contributor-artists: Stanhope Forbes, Walter Langley, Edwin Harris, Ralph
Todd, Leghe Suthers, Henry Scott Tuke, Alexander Chevallier Tayler, Fred Hall, Frank
Bramley, Thomas Cooper Gotch, Elizabeth Stanhope Forbes, William Fortescue, Nor-
man Garstin, Frank Wright Bourdillon, Henry Meynell Rheam, Harold Harvey, Lamor-
na Birch, Alethea Garstin, Frank Dobson, Charles Simpson, Ernest Procter, Dod
Procter, Laura Knight, Harold Knight, Alfred Munnings, Cedric Morris, Stanley
Gardiner, Gertrude Harvey, Frank Heath, Eleanor Hughes, Robert Hughes, Charles
Naper, Ruth Simpson.

from the Newsletter, February 15 1985
Frank Ruhrmund, the Newlyn-born poet will read from his new book *Brother John*. His reputation has steadily increased since the publication of his first volume, *Penwith Poems*. He is a frequent broadcaster and his poems appear in *South West Review* and the *Western Morning News...*

from NEWLYN ORION PRESS RELEASE
British Rail are mounting the 'Art Special' on Saturday 23 March

leaving Penzance at 6 am and returning later that evening...The British Rail sales team at Penzance led by Mr Reg James worked quickly to find a comfortable train for the day for which they are able to offer tickets at only £12 a head from any of the principal stations in Cornwall and including Plymouth...

164

from *The Cornishman*, 21 March 1985
NEWLYN MEETING
Sir, -- Regarding the proposal to take down the bridges at Newlyn to have a roundabout, and cap the Coombe River to widen the road. Penzance has had nearly all its unusual features ironed out and is, only saved from looking like any other town by the Terrace. Surely we are not going to let Newlyn be "ironed out" too?

I understand there is to be a public meeting at Newlyn Art Gallery on March 28 at 7.30 to discuss the proposals and air the problems affecting Newlyn. I do hope all those interested in the future of Newlyn will come so that we may find ways for the port to thrive without losing all the character of the town.

G Sagar-Fenton
Tolcarne Farmhouse
Newlyn

Charles Breaker's sweaters are still to be seen around Penzance

from *The Cornishman* Thursday, July 11, 1985
IT IS impossible to think of the artist Charles Breaker who died last week, without thinking of colour. His paintings, worked in clean clear colour, "a touch of Matisse", his colourful knitwear which he designed and made, his cottage and its garden, "a pretty Burmese jungle", filled with flowers and a riot of colour -- he was a colourful character and the streets of Penzance will seem drab without him... Then, in 1947, attracted by its climate and past artistic activity they [friend, Eric Hiller & CB] came to this corner of Cornwall, living first of all in Mousehole. "I bought Jack Pender his first sketch book." Soon after they found Gernick Field Studio, high on the hill above Newlyn harbour, and it was there, together with Marjorie Mort, that they began the celebrated Newlyn Holiday Sketching Group...A past chairman and life member of Newlyn Society of Artists, his work was a standard part of exhibitions in St Ives and Newlyn for years, and he also exhibited in a number of other centres from Edinburgh to Johannesburg...Charles Breaker was a man who refused to grow old...

[Above is an extract from a fuller personal tribute by Frank Ruhrmund, which was reprinted in the programme notes for A MEMORIAL

EXHIBITION in summer, 1986, of some fifty watercolours and a selection of knitted jackets, mounted at the Newlyn Art Gallery with financial assistance from South West Arts.]

1986

17 January - 8 February OPEN HOUSE 7 NSA Associates Show
20 February - 15 March ANTHONY FROST 'On Colour'
22 March - 16 April SPRING EXHIBITION NSA mixed
26 April - 31 May JONATHAN MEULI, Recent Paintings,
LITZ PISK, Drawings
10 June - 12 July ARTS & CRAFTS IN NEWLYN 1890 - 1930
CHARLES BREAKER (1906 -- 1985) Memorial exhibition
23 July - 13 September SUMMER EXHIBITION Part I & II NSA mixed
20 September - 25 October Tony O'Malley, ISLAND AND OCEAN
Recent Paintings from the Bahamas
1 - 28 November NO PASARAN!
An Arnolfini touring exhibition of photographs and posters of the Spanish Civil War
10 December - 3 January CHRISTMAS EXHIBITION -- SIX SOLOS
Six exhibitions by members of the Newlyn Society of Artists:
Russ Hedges, Leonie Whitton, Clive Blackmore, Robert Jones, Sue Lewington,
Theresa Gilder

from The Director's Report, 1985 - 1986
From April 1985 to March 1986 Newlyn Orion had the busiest year in its history. The exhibitions at Newlyn had record attendances and 'Painting in Newlyn 1900 - 1930' had a rapturous tour to Plymouth, London and Birmingham. Another Newlyn Orion touring exhibition 'Second Nature' was also shown in London.

Policy : In previous years by force of circumstance we had rather a lot of thematic and group exhibitions in our programme...However it has always been Newlyn Orion's policy to engage the public with serious and comprehensive exhibitions showing the development of individual artists. Hence the shift during this year to a series of substantial solo exhibitions...

from the Preface, by John Halkes, to the exhibition book, *Arts & Crafts in Newlyn, 1890 - 1930*, Hazel Berriman (exhibition researcher & author).
Following the success of our two major touring exhibitions in 1979 and 1985, the story of Art in Newlyn is now well known. But restrictions of time and space in those exhibitions prevented us from describing fully the fascinating developments in the Crafts, which came to thrive so strongly between 1890 - 1930 in the warm artistic climate of the place. This book and the exhibition it accompanies tells a remarkable story of how Art stimulated Craft and attracted inspired individuals who achieved work of great quality -- and in the case of the Art Metalwork and 'Cryséde' Silks -- went on to establish major local industries.

This story is not without contemporary relevance. We know that today over two thousand artists and craftworkers are working in Cornwall...

...Newlyn Orion is especially indebted to Polly Walker for her kindness over the years during which we have discussed her father's work, and now for her practical help with the 'Cryséde' story; also to Peter Garnier for the fascinating essay on his parents. Thanks are also due to John Laity and John Foster Tonkin for invaluable help with the story of Newlyn Copper...

1987

18 May - 6 June, -- CELTIC VISION
The Cornish choices are Trewin Copplestone, Jack Pender, Tony O'Malley,
Michael O'Donnell and Virginia Veran...
15 June - 11 July, ROSE HILTON . MICHAEL UPTON
22 July - 12 September SUMMER EXHIBITION Part I & II NSA mixed
21 September-31 October LOOKING WEST
7 November - 3 December
PAUL HEMPTON paintings, watercolours & prints
JEM SOUTHAM, Photographs of Paintings from the West of Cornwall
[in collaboration with Watershed, Bristol]
CHRISTMAS EXHIBITION -- SIX SOLOS 9 December - 8 January
Six exhibitions by members of the Newlyn Society of Artists: George Dannatt,
Carole Page, Bernard Evans, Fred Yates, Gill Watkiss, Barbara Tribe

166

from the Newsletter
EDUCATION
Access & Education -- Newlyn Orion has an active education programme. In the
gallery the work centres on the current exhibitions and schools and groups are encouraged to work in the gallery. Tours, talks and lectures can be arranged to suit the needs
of visiting groups. Outside of the gallery there is a continuing programme of artist
placements in schools and special initiatives in adult education and artists' lectures.
Tutors and group leaders are encouraged to contact Newlyn Orion Organiser, Rachael
Hansen for further details or discussions.

from the programme notes, ROSE HILTON
'...When Rose and her late husband, Roger Hilton, came to Cornwall they settled in
the far west of the Penwith peninsula in the village of Botallack, near St Just...Here the
wind never stops blowing, the light is subtly dramatic. Some people find it unsettling --
but for Rose this has always been a positive and creative place...
MICHAEL UPTON: The paintings of Michael Upton remind us that important work
can still be done on a very small scale; each piece could be seen to relate to another in
quietly deliberate cross-referencing loaded with social, political and personal implications
and intimations...Mel Gooding in *Art Monthly*.

Arts Review, 19 June, 1987
Review by Frank Ruhrmund
I saw Rose Hilton's first solo show when she was signing her work with her maiden name of Rose Phipps. That was fifteen years ago in this very gallery... This major show is long overdue, and with it she bursts on to the scene with the sense of relief and release of a butterfly emerging from its chrysalis and with all of its new-found beauty, life and colour...Carel Weight once described her as one of the best colourists he had ever taught, and it is easy to see why...

...From a full length study of fellow painter Mary Stork to an anonymous Visitor to the Studio, from the dramatic, narrative element in a hotel scene with its echoes of 'Hotel du Lac' and 'Separate Tables' to the mediterranean blue which she lends Mount's Bay -- and anyone familiar with the place will know this is no flight of fancy -- this is an exhibition that may have been a long while in the making but one that proves to be well worth waiting for. ROSE HILTON (Sponsor: Parkin Fine Art), MICHAEL UPTON (Sponsor: Anne Berthoud)

Alexander MacKenzie 'Farm Buildings, Penwith' c.1950

Looking West

Paintings inspired by Cornwall from the 1880s to the present day
[in collaboration with the National Trust, sponsored by Phillips]
'Looking West' is an exhibition to celebrate the spirit of West Cornwall. It contains landscape paintings from the past hundred years by artists who have come here to work, some for a few weeks, some for a lifetime. It includes works by the greatest painters of the period as well as exploring those lesser-known by-ways for which English art is famous. Landscape has been a crucial inspiration since the late 19th century and particularly important as a basis for the development of abstraction. It has also been an evolving intellectual idea, to the plight of humanity or from romanticised country life to a source of pure colour. In this exhibition, painters can be seen extracting from what they saw around them...

...The paintings have been brought together from public and private collections from Aberdeen to Newlyn itself by the organiser Elizabeth Knowles. After the Newlyn showing the exhibition travels to the Royal College of Art in London, from 10 to 27 November.

The project has been a most welcome collaboration between Newlyn Orion and the National Trust as part of the Enterprise Neptune special appeal for the Penwith Coastline...

The Exhibitors:
I
Samuel John 'Lamorna' Birch (1869-1955) Storm over Sheffield, 1910; Tregiffian Cliff, near Lamorna, c 1922
Stanhope Forbes (1857-1947) Fitting Out, Mousehole Harbour, 1919
Norman Garstin (1847-1926) View of Mount's Bay with the North Pier, c 1893
Thomas Cooper Gotch (1854-1931) The Silver Hour, 1902; Cornfields, Newlyn, c 1910-1920
Henry Moore (1831-1895) Off Dodman Head
Julius Olsson (1864-1942) Sunset at Land's End
William Osborn (1868-1906) St Ives Pier, c 1895
Henry Scott Tuke (1858-1929) French Barque in Falmouth Bay, 1902
II
Adrian Allinson (1890-1959) Spring Riot, Cornwall, 1940
Gluck (1895-1978) Cornish Farm House, c 1925
Cedric Morris (1889-1982) Landscape at Newlyn, 1919
Joseph Southall (1861-1944) The Old Seaport (Fowey Bay) 1919
Alec Walker (1889-1964) Road Over the Moors, 1927
Billie Waters (1896-1979) Mousehole Fields
III
David Bomberg (1890-1957) Towards St Ives, 1947; Trendrine in Sun, 1947
Alethea Garstin (1894-1978) Cottages, Penzance; Newbridge Chapel; Post Office; Cornish Farm and Burnt Carn; Thaw at Zennor
Charles Ginner (1878-1952) The Mullion Wireless, 1921; St Just in Penwith, 1923
Allan Gwynne-Jones (1892-1982) Zennor, 1919; Poltesco Farm, Ruan Minor, 1920-21

landscapes of West Cornwall
from the 1880s to the present day

exhibition dates:
Newlyn Art Gallery,
21 September to 31 October 1987

The Royal College of Art,
10 to 27 November 1987

Harold Harvey (1874-1941) Cornish Landscape, 1935

Dod Procter (1892-1972) Early Morning, Newlyn, 1926

Ernest Procter (1886-1935) Penlee Point, c 1926-27

Borlase Smart (1881-1947) Morning Light, St Ives, 1922

Matthew Smith (1879-1959) A winding Road, Cornish Landscape, 1920; Cornish Landscape, 1920; Cornish Landscape, 1920-21

Stanley Spencer (1891-1959) The Harbour, St Ives, 1937

IV

Wilhelmina Barns-Graham (b 1912) Grey Day, St Ives 2, 1942; Three Trees from Goonhilly 2, 1971

Sandra Blow (b 1925) Cornwall, 1958

Terry Frost (b 1915) Brown and Gold, Tregeseal, 1956; Blue Harbour, c 1959; Black, Yellow and Blue, 1959

David Haughton (b 1924) Tregeseal, 1958; Cape Cornwall Road, 1973-78; St Just from Carn Bosavern, 1979

168

Patrick Hayman (b 1915) Events by the Sea, 1970

Barbara Hepworth (1903-1975) Night Sky (Porthmeor) 1964

Patrick Heron (b 1920) Summer Painting, 1956; Cave: September, 1956

Roger Hilton (1911-1975) Rocky Landscape, 1959; Untitled, c 1959; November, 1964

Peter Lanyon (1918-1964) Oarscape, 1962; Green Buoy, c 1959; Harbour, Coast and Open Sea, 1963; Untitled (Autumn) 1964

Denis Mitchell (1912-1992) Gypsy Encampment, Trink, 1946; St Ives from Lelant, 1946; Snow, Trencrom, 1947

Alexander MacKenzie (b 1923) Farm Buildings, Penwith c 1950

Ben Nicholson (1894-1982) 1946 (Towednack); November 11 1947 (Mount's Bay)

Adrian Ryan (b 1920) Mousehole, c 1945; Sennen Church, c 1960

Alfred Wallis (1855-1942) Steamer and Lighthouse; Street of Houses and Trees; Penzance Harbour; St Ives Houses at the Water's Edge

John Wells (b 1907) Cove, c 1930; Dark Hill, 1950; Folded Cliffs, 1954; Journey, 1955

Karl Weschke (b 1925) Gale, 1974

V

Hamish Fulton (b 1945) A Two Day Walk Round the Coastline from Penzance to St Ives, 1980

Richard Long (b 1945) A Sculpture Left by the Tide, 1970

VI

Edward Bawden (b 1903) Palm Trees and Church, St Ewe, c 1980

Bob Bourne (b 1931) The Gymkhana, 1983-87; Working study, c 1983; Working study, c 1983

Michael Chalwin (b 1943) Food for the Redwing, 1986

Richard Cook (b 1947) Newlyn from North Corner, 1986

John Miller (b 1931) Carn Brea, 1984; Farm at Sancreed, 1985; Mount's Bay from Sancreed Beacon, 1987

Fred Yates (b 1922) Priest's Cove, 1986; Cornish Cottage, c 1987

Christopher Wood (1901-1930) The Red Funnel, Mousehole, 1930

Bryan Wynter (1915-1975) Cornish Farm, 1952; Landscape with Stone Hedge, 1952; Cliffscape with Boat, 1952; Impenetrable Country, 1957

from Gerald Priestland, *The Unquiet Suitcase,* November 9, 1987

John Halkes, director of the Newlyn Orion Gallery, has asked me to open an exhibition he's put on at the Royal College of Art: a hundred paintings by various artists of the past century, inspired by the Penwith coastline. The object is to underline the National Trust campaign to save as much of it as possible from the developers. So I tell a few jokes, get a few laughs, and declare it open. As always at NT affairs, the eats and drinks are excellent.

The Trust is moping a bit at the way Land's End has become a rich man's capital gains plaything -- it changed hands a few days ago at almost 7 million -- but then, Land's End is a fairly dreary place anyway; not a patch on Cape Cornwall, which was given to the Trust earlier this year by Heinz the Beans. And they've managed to buy the Foage Valley at Zennor, which will please Patrick Heron. Patrick isn't at the show, but cheerful old Terry Frost is.

1988

15 January - 6 February THE PICTURE SHOW
Open show for Newlyn Orion members
13 February - 12 March PERCEPTIONS
with TAM JOSEPH, BRIAN BUCKLEY & the children of St Gluvias Primary School,
Ponsanooth, & RAGHUBIR SINGH (from the National Museum of photography) --
perceptions of life in three separate communities by artists
23 April - 3 June MICHAEL CHALWIN, Paintings, Prints and Constructions
11 June - 13 July JENNIFER DURRANT New Paintings and Works on paper
Summer of 1988: Opening of Trelissick Gallery in partnership
24 July - 9 October 1988
THE ARTIST AND THE GARDEN
Paintings Drawings Prints Constructions
DENIS MITCHELL Recent sculpture in Bronze and Slate
31 October- 30 November CRAFT WORK

169

from the programme notes, MICHAEL CHALWIN, by Elizabeth Knowles
...Penwith is not a place usually thought of for deep woodlands, but Trevaylor is a
broad-leaf wood with tall beech trees growing in a narrow valley cutting into the Penwith
moors to the north-east of Penzance [the Newmill valley]...Chalwin began to work there
in 1982...Taking another step nearer to a satisfactory formal integrity, Chalwin began
to use the idea of the ground surface as a carpet, making dense and richly textured
paintings with titles such as 'Wounded Earth'...

...Partly from doubts about the 'carpet' works and partly from the exigencies of
working in a small space, Chalwin destroyed a large number of works around 1984. He
began to work on paper, concentrating his image into a smaller area...This condensing
of his means was also influenced by looking at icon paintings: he wanted his work to
move closer to the intensity and independent physical character of an icon...

from *The St Ives Times & Echo*, undated, by Frank Ruhrmund
MARJORIE MORT, A PAINTER OF THE OLD SCHOOL
THE ARTIST Marjorie Mort, who died recently at the age of 83 was a long standing member of the St Ives Society of Artists...She settled
in Cornwall immediately after the end of the
Second World War, and in 1949 joined forces
with artists Charles Breaker and Eric Hiller to
form the well-remembered Newlyn Holiday
Sketching Group...continuing to exhibit regularly with the St Ives and Newlyn Societies of Artists, spending the last 25 years or so of her
artistic career working quietly and patiently in
her tiny studio above Lloyd's Bank deep in the
heart of Newlyn...

Photo: Spectrum

MICHAEL CHALWIN
Biographical Details
Born 1943

1959-63	Oxford School of Art. Painting and Lithography.
1963-67	Part-time tutor, Salesian College, Oxford.
1967-68	Full-time painter.
1968-70	Printmaker, part-time lecturer, Oxford School of Architecture.
1970-72	Mountaineering, Isle of Skye, Scotland.
1972-73	Certificate of Education, Culham College, Oxford.
1973-78	Art Tutor, Fitzharry's School, Abingdon, Oxford.
Since 1978	Full-time painter, Newlyn, Penzance.

from the *Arts Review*, 7 October, by Frank Ruhrmund

Laetitia Yhap . Robert Jones

Robert Jones   Photo: Ashley Peters

While the works of these two artists could hardly be more different, they contain enough common factors -- a constant search for truth, good drawing, a fascination with the sea and the people who work on and by it -- to make their brief marriage within these walls a happy one.

Laetitia Yhap's 30 or so paintings and drawings, 'The Business of the Beach'are the end result of a twelve years old affair with those who work, wait and watch, on and off the beach at Hastings. It is a world without women, she is a fisher of men and boys, their boats and their dogs, and records their regular activities with the eye of an early documentary film maker...

...Robert Jones is a young Cornishman of the sea who actually works as a fisherman off the very cliffs and coast that provide the material for many of the 50 exhibits, gouache and coloured crayon on paper that he presents here...His mackerel or herring, for instance, are more than mere still life studies and emerge from his layers of colours and lines as if surfacing, coming up for air, from a great depth...An artist whose technique is well-nigh faultless, whose lack of pretentiousness is total -- his drawings could not be more direct -- and whose awareness of and sympathy for his native county is absolute, he is definitely one to look out for.

from Minutes of the Council of Management, October 17

Clive Bennetts (Chairman)

...John Halkes reported on the success of the Summer exhibitions. Both Jennifer Durrant and Michael Chalwin had mounted excellent shows. The latter had been very successful with sales and the former had just been announced as the winner of the Athena Art Award, one of the UK's major cash prizes...He went on to praise the current exhibitions of Laetitia Yhap and Robert Jones: these had stimulated a huge number of school visits and workshops, and Robert Jones in particular had enjoyed very successful sales....

CRAFT

WORK

31 October - 30 November '88
Sheelagh O'Donnell, Exhibition Organiser
This show is designed to spotlight the wealth of talented craftsmen living and working in the South West. Anthony Bryant and Norman Stuart Clarke present a careful selection of their most recent work which is shown together with a survey of the top tapestry weavers working in the South West.

Anthony Bryant -- Norman Stuart Clarke -- Stella Benjamin -- Bobbie Cox -- Candace Bahouth -- Pat Cross -- Grace Erikson -- Pat Johns -- Sue Marshall -- Christine Sawyer

1989

14 January - 4 March THE ART OF PHOTOGRAPHY
a three-part exhibition to celebrate 150 years of photography
THE GARDEN fifty photographs by Anne Hammond & Mike Weaver
EDWIN SMITH in Cornwall and the Scillies
CLASSIC IMAGES twenty-five classic photographs selected by Mike Weaver
29 April - 3 June THE TREE OF LIFE
Events: WOODLAND WALK (Trelissick Estate, Feock);
Illustrated lectures; Schools Community Projects.
16 September - 21 October MICHAEL FINN Recent Works
SHANTI PANCHALL, Earthen Shades
28 October - 25 November CHRISTOPHER WOOD - THE LATER WORKS
AUTUMN MISCELLANY A Selection of works by artists working in Cornwall:
ANNA MINSHALL, JENNIFER SEMMENS, DAVID KEMP, SIMON AVERILL
Trelissick Gallery
1 July - 24 September TO THE SEA AGAIN
11 November - 22 December CHRISTMAS ARTISTS' MARKET
& FRANCIS HEWLETT -- Ceramic Sculptures:
THE SECRET VICE OF CERAMIC
6 December - 6 January 1990 WINTER WORK NSA mixed exhibition

Minutes of the Council of Management, February 20
Clive Bennetts (Chairman)
...Restructuring of Newlyn Orion
a) Context: The Director gave a brief survey of the national and regional changes in the funding of the arts. He suggested that there would be a move towards greater decentralisation, from the centre to the regions and subsequently from the regions down to sub-regions, which would probably be at County level. Increasingly the emphasis would be upon self-reliance and partnership funding with business or local authorities. In real terms revenue grant aid would remain on a level or even decline.

b) Options: The various options for Newlyn Orion were now becoming clear...the need to concentrate on the quality of exhibitions and the development of self-generated income through a more dynamic trading option. He explained that a feasibility plan on extending the Shop gallery was under way and that the staffing and cost implications would be considered as part of this...

from *The Cornishman*, March 23, by Frank Ruhrmund

The Newlyn Society of Artists currently has 100 full members and seven elected associate members. To stimulate interest in its spring exhibition, Newlyn Contemporaries, now being held in Newlyn Art Gallery, it invited each of them to submit a single work to be judged by top London art critic, Tim Hilton, who would award three of them prizes. In the event more than 80 accepted the challenge...and the prizes, all of equal value, went to Tony O'Malley for his abstract painting "Atlantic Studio with Mask" (awarded by Poynton Bradbury Associates, St Ives); to Daphne McClure for her semi-abstract impression of Hayle (awarded by Spectrum Design and Print, St Ives) and to Clive Blackmore for his still-life painting (awarded by the NSA themselves).

from the Newsletter, Spring 1989

NEWLYN ORION/ ARTSHARE

The Artshare programme is a service which provides arts opportunities with disabilities and special needs, indeed anyone who needs special provisions to enable them to participate in arts activities and events. The programme provides a wide variety of arts activities and all the work is undertaken by artists who have a special aptitude or experience of working with people with disabilities and special needs. At present several projects are being successfully maintained in the Penwith area, notably at West Cornwall Hospital and Nancealverne School and there are plans for many more. Diana Morris, the Artshare Organiser at Newlyn Orion [since 1987] sees a priority in actually identifying individuals or groups who could benefit from and enjoy art activities...Newlyn Orion is grateful for the sponsorship of Marks & Spencer PLC and W H Lane & Son Fine Art Auctioneers with this important community development.

W BARNS-GRAHAM A RETROSPECTIVE

Newlyn Art Gallery
10 June-7 July

Wilhelmina Barns-Graham was born in Scotland in 1912. She came to St. Ives in 1940 as the town was developing as an important centre for modern British painting. She remained based in St. Ives until 1973 and has been closely involved with artistic developments there, including the founding of the Penwith Society of Artists. Her work stems from the tradition associated with the St. Ives artists of that period, in particular Ben Nicholson and Barbara Hepworth, with its emphasis on translating the form and colour seen in the landscape into abstract works. Taking her inspiration from the landscapes of Cornwall and Scotland, Barns-Graham pares the elements of form, line and colour down to their most basic nature. She delights in drawing and the importance of hard, precise line is very much evident in her work. During the 1950s and 60s her work became more conceptually abstract, but in the 1980s she has returned to the warm, nature-based painting of her youth.

Now in her 70s W. Barns-Graham divides her time between St. Ives and her native Scotland, where she continues to work and contribute to contemporary British painting. This retrospective exhibition celebrates that contribution of nearly fifty years, and includes line drawing, abstract reliefs and paintings.

This is the first showing of Barns-Graham's retrospective, which will tour to venues throughout England and Scotland. The exhibition is selected by Douglas Hall, former Keeper of the Scottish National Gallery of Modern Art, and organised by Edinburgh City Arts Centre with the support of the Scottish Arts Council.

W. Barns-Graham,
White Cottage Cornwall, 1944.

Long overdue tribute

Art

by FRANK RUHRMUND

THE retrospective exhibition by Wilhelmina Barns-Graham, now being held in Newlyn Art Gallery, pays a long overdue tribute to a major artist who came to live and work in St Ives almost half a century ago.

A member of both the Newlyn and St Ives societies of artists as early as 1942, she was also a founder member of the breakaway Penwith Society of Artists in 1949, and was at the epicentre of the creative explosion which rocked the art world in the 40s and 50s.

Reflect

While she has since exhibited extensively throughout this country and abroad — from Manchester to Manhattan — this is her first retrospective exhibition.

An artist with strong Scottish connections, Wilhelmina was born in St Andrew's, studied at Edinburgh College of Art, and for several years, since inheriting a house near her birthplace, has shared her time between Scotland and St Ives.

Although she has not always enjoyed good health, she has surprising stamina and has travelled widely in

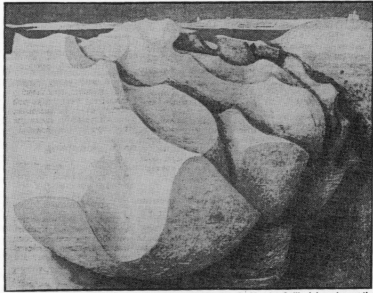

PRECISE WORK: Wilhelmina Barns-Graham's Rocks, St Mary's, Scilly Isles shows the constant precision in her work.

her pursuit of perfection.

Whether looking at the "Sleeping Town" of St Ives, the rocks of St Mary's on the Isles of Scilly, the Grindelwald glacier, a clay working at Chiusure, the coast of Spain or Glasgow airport at night, the sense of precision of her work is constant.

The careful construction and inner geometry of her compositions may reflect the influences of such as Naum Gabe and Robert Adams, but their liveliness and movement, the hard backbone of drawing in them and the way she handles her colour, are absolutely her own work.

One of the surprises of the exhibition is her emergence as a considerable colourist.

From her restricted wartime drawings of St Ives to its famous "Box Factory Fire" just after the war, from her marching squares of the 70s to her most recent and musical abstracts, this show stands as a potted history of art in the town.

Tomorrow in Newlyn Art Gallery (2.30) there is a rare opportunity to join a guided tour of the exhibition led by the artist herself.

THE ARTIST WILL GIVE A GUIDED TALK OF THE EXHIBITION
Wednesday 21 June 2.30pm
admission free

W. Barns-Graham, Antonia Reeve

An opportunity to enjoy a guided tour of the exhibition with Wilhelmina Barns-Graham. This will be an informal afternoon with an opportunity for questions and discussion.

LECTURE
St. Peter's Hall, Newlyn
Monday 12 June 8pm
admission £1.50 conc. £1

The Gallery will be open from 6.30-7.30pm for viewing of the exhibition prior to the lecture.

We are most pleased that Douglas Hall, the exhibition selector, will be coming to Newlyn to give an illustrated lecture on Wilhelmina Barns-Graham's life and work. He will follow the development of her work over the years and consider it in relation to the work of other St. Ives artists of the period.

Exhibitions to celebrate the centenary of Cornwall County Council, 1889 - 1989

(organised by Newlyn Orion on behalf of Cornwall County council and sponsored by Barclays Bank plc)
-- comprises 140 art works executed in Cornwall during the last 100 years
-- works will be on show from the Early Newlyn School through to the present day
-- many of the paintings come from private collections and have not been shown before publicly

A CENTURY OF ART IN CORNWALL 1889-1989
an exhibition to celebrate the Centenary of Cornwall County Council

PART I: AN HISTORICAL PERSPECTIVE

John Armstrong	Roger Hilton	Jack Pender
W. Barns-Graham	Mary Jewels	Dod Procter
Lamorna Birch	Laura Knight	Ernest Procter
Frank Bramley	George Lambourn	Albert Reuss
Charles Breaker	Walter Langley	Henry Rheam
Ithell Colquhoun	Peter Lanyon	J T Richardson
Paul Feiler	Bernard Leach	Charles Simpson
Elizabeth Armstrong Forbes	Alexander Mackenzie	Borlase Smart
Stanhope Forbes	Thomas Maidment	Leghe Suthers
Terry Frost	William Martin	John Guttridge Sykes
Leonard Fuller	John Milne	A Chevalier Tayler
Alethea Garstin	Lionel Miskin	Ralph Todd
Norman Garstin	Denis Mitchell	Barbara Tribe
T C Gotch	Marjorie Mort	Henry Scott Tuke
Louis Grier	Paul Mount	John Tunnard
Harold Harvey	Ben Nicholson	Alfred Wallis
David Haughton	Bernard Ninnis	John Wells
Arthur Hayward	Julius Olsson	Karl Weschke
Frank Gascoigne Heath	Tony O'Malley	Christopher Wood
Barbara Hepworth	William Osborn	Bryan Wynter
Patrick Heron	John Park	
Francis Hewlett	Bryan Pearce	

CONTACT
COUNTY HALL
(0872) 74282

PART II: A CONTEMPORARY VIEW

Ray Atkins	Daphne McClure
Bob Bourne	John Miller
Michael Chalwin	Michael O'Donnell
Joe Coates	Geoff Ogden
Richard Cook	Jane O'Malley
John Emanuel	Carole Page
Michael Finn	Michael Praed
Tony Foster	Peter Smith
Anthony Frost	Peter Macdonald Smith
Russell Hedges	Jem Southam
Rose Hilton	Ken Symonds
Philip Hogben	Andrew Waddington
Ken Howard	Roy Walker
Diane Ibbotson	Gill Watkiss
Robert Jones	David Westby
David Kemp	Jerry White
Stuart Knowles	Leonie Whitton
Andrew Lanyon	Barbara Wills
Jeremy Le Grice	Fred Yates
Mary Mabbutt	
Mary Martin	
Margo Maeckelberghe	

CONTACT
COUNTY MUSEUM
(0872) 72205

WMN 10/10/89

Show by the living, for the living

THE CELEBRATION of Cornish art continues at the County Museum & Art Gallery in Truro with an exhibition called A Contemporary View, which brings us right up-to-date with developments in the Duchy.

John Halkes and his helpers, Ella Halkes and Elizabeth Knowles of Newlyn Orion, have mounted a show by the living for the living.

As they see it, this is art in Cornwall now!

Links remain with the painting and sculpture at County Hall and the continuing influence of Newlyn and St Ives is clear, but there is a particularly strong contribution from those working at, or closely connected with, Falmouth

School of Art and, up-county, Mary Martin represents the borderlands of the Tamar Valley.

St Ives painter Jane O'Malley tells of the importance of the coastline to Cornish art and her Sea Window and Mussel Shell — with a glimpse of Porthmeor and the Atlantic beyond — sets the scene at Penwyth, and Roy Walker reminds us that we live in the Twentieth Century and that this is the age of the machine.

Not all artists rely on the natural splendours of the region for their inspiration.

Two young painters — Michael Chalwin and Richard Cook — have close connections with Newlyn Orion but both are broadening their horizons and Chalwin in

particular is a subtle and delicate image-maker.

Compare Cook's Newlyn From North Corner, painted in 1987, with Norman Garstin's The Rain It Raineth Every Day, painted in 1889, and you instantly recognise that, in the intervening years, art has changed — as it must — but that the urge to put brush to canvas has not.

Falmouth has a fine art tradition and the outstanding painting, as one might expect, is by Mary Mabbutt.

Self-portrait with Martha is both domestic in its subject and fraught with the tension that we know to be the reality of motherhood.

She will surely be seen in the coming Tate Gallery of the West

in St Ives.

Leonie Whitten too is a powerful picture-maker and sculptor.

Michael O'Donnell's Sky Drawing lies quietly — flat on the floor

Forty-one artists contribute to the exhibition, and its success lies in the fact that Gill Watkiss, with a typically well-observed St Just CP School — Home-time and Michael Finn, with a pure abstract Blackhorse 11, can be seen to hang happily together in one room.

It is the sheer variety that excites the organisers and those with the responsibility of fostering the arts in Cornwall can take heart from what they see.

— *John Furse*

Thursday, July 6, 1989

To: *Council of Management, Staff, Consultants*
<u>Tate of the West/Newlyn Orion</u>

You will be aware from my briefing that there is now a stronger thrust within the County Council to make the 'Tate of the West' project in St Ives a reality. Newlyn Orion has welcomed such a project for the general benefits it would bring to cultural tourism and international appeal of Cornwall. However the emergence of such a gallery with its capital and revenue needs has implications for Newlyn Orion, currently the largest visual arts organisation west of Bristol.

Martin Rewcastle, the Director of South West Arts, has been instrumental in steering and encouraging the Tate project. He is also mindful of the future needs of Newlyn Orion. On this date Martin will meet the Council of Management, staff and consultants, to outline his vision of the visual arts in the Penwith...

from the Programme Notes, by John Halkes

Michael Finn: (Upper Gallery)

...In 1958 Finn was appointed to the post of Principal of Falmouth School of Art and over the next fourteen years he became the main architect of its success. building upon the advantages of the beautiful site and the strong tradition of painting and sculpture in Cornwall, he worked with a gifted staff, the support of local artists and the Education Authority to put Falmouth firmly on the national map as a leading centre of learning and practice in the visual arts. Its tenaciously held primacy today is rooted in those years of sensitive liberality and intellectual stimulation.

In 1972 Michael Finn moved with his family to Bath to become Principal of the prestigious Bath Academy of Art at Corsham...on retirement from Bath Academy, he moved with his wife Cely to St Just in Penwith, near Land's End, and began the hard task of working his way into full-time painting...

...whether by painting or construction, the full expressive potential of abstract painting was unlocked. He had in more than one sense 'come home'.

Shanti Panchall: (Lower Galleries)

...Today he is one of the most successful artists from the Indian sub-continent resident in Britain. His striking figurative watercolours reflect his reverential view of people and nature which stems from his Hindu background.

Black Crucifix 1989
48 x 37 in

Michael Finn, St. Just,
Cornwall, 1989.

1990

17 January - 10 February THE NEW GENERATION
17 February - 24 March
TONY FOSTER EXPLORING THE GRAND CANYON
Watercolour Diaries, 1988- 1989
LANDSCAPE DRAWINGS
JOHN EAVES: charcoal drawings of the Inner Circle of Stonehenge
RON BOYD: drawings based on the Forest of Dean in Gloucestershire
HUW MORGAN: graphite & ink drawings on Pembrokeshire and Devon
3 - 28 April NEWLYN CONTEMPORARIES NSA spring exhibition
Critic's Choice Award for paintings awarded to Philip Hogben, Daphne McClure,
and Alexander MacKenzie by the art critic, Peter Fuller.
5 - 31 May IMAGES OF THE TEES
Drawings by Len Tabner and Photographs by Ian MacDonald
25 - 28 May FIFTY FIVE YEARS OF THE SWALLOW &
THE BUTTERFLY
A swimming pool performance by Lumiere & Son. Jubilee Pool, Penzance
5 May - 24 June STILL LIFE STILL LIVES
A contemporary expression of a traditional obsession (Trelissick)
25 June - 23 September 1990 COASTLINE
An exhibition to celebrate 25 years of the National Trust Enterprise Neptune
7 June - 7 July DOD PROCTER, RA (1892 - 1972)
15 September - 13 October GILL WATKISS A Retrospective
20 October to 24 November GEOFFREY OLSEN
Recent Paintings & Works on Paper, including Places of Burial series, &
DAPHNE MCCLURE: ASPECTS OF HAYLE
10 November - 23 December INSIDE OUT
Looking out and outside looking in (Trelissick)
Oils, watercolours, drawings and prints produced by invited artists.
5 December - 5 January ROOM FOR THE NEW:
[In upper galleries, new & mainly younger artists; In lower galleries, a selection of
other works by NSA members.]

from the programme notes, THE NEW GENERATION
Exhibition of work by third year fine art students at Falmouth School of Art and
Design has been selected to show the diversity of contemporary and traditional concerns
which characterise the BA (Hons) Fine Art Course. Emma Grover, Helen Claire
Manmon, Jim Noble, Phil Hughes, Graham Martin, Camilla Peters, Judy Buxton,
Christina Lamb, Owen Thomas, Cheslaw Prygodzicz, Michael Chaikin, Simon Smith,
Ruth Catlow, Cathryn Davidson, Robert Bransley, Andrew Rollo, Andrew Gadd. OPEN
HOUSE Professionals or semi-professionals who have recently come to live and work
here, talented amateurs...

Minutes of the Council of Management, February 14, 1990
Mike Conboye (Chairman)
...Diana Morris (Education & Access Organiser) joined the meeting and gave a short
briefing on the impact of the Education Reform Act on education work in the arts. It
was noted that the days of grant aid were receding and that the education sector was
moving towards the buying in of services. There would be a new tier of decision makers
in the newly constituted school governors...The company had to be well equipped to
enter this market and to some extend had to be ahead of the game. Diana introduced
the idea of the Education/Access Marketing Pack which was currently being worked on
by the staff and for which sponsorship was being sought...

from *Daily Telegraph*, April 3 by Frank Ruhrmund

Elizabeth Lamorna Kerr, the painter, who has died aged 85 was the uncrowned queen of Lamorna, the remarkable artists' colony in Cornwall, founded by her father S J "Lamorna" Birch...As a child "Mornie" was a particularly popular model and sat for John, Laura Knight, T C Gotch and Algernon Newton...Influenced by her father alongside whom she exhibited at the Royal Academy, she painted in a manner freer than his: more Post-Impressionist than Impressionist. Her subjects were most commonly still-life and landscape -- frequently the sweeping views of Lamorna Cove. She did much to keep interest in her father's work alive until the spectacular revival in enthusiasm for the Newlyn School of recent years...

DOD PROCTER, RA (1892–1972)

7 JUNE – 7 JULY

One of the highlights of Newlyn Orion's 1985 Summer exhibition 'Painting In Newlyn 1900 – 1930' was the wall of paintings by Dod Procter, Newlyn's last full Royal Academician ,who died in 1972. Naturally the eight paintings on show were to some extent dominated by the centre piece 'Morning ', the painting which became acclaimed nationally when it was shown at the RA in 1927. But the other works were equally compelling and we put a marker down to exhibit Dod Procter in a more extensive retrospective exhibition when the opportunity arose. We were grateful, therefore, to discover recently that the Laing Art Gallery at Newcastle had similar plans and that we would be able to work together to present this 1990 exhibition.

The exhibition reflects Dod Procter's single-mindedness as an artist . This is not to say that she became stylistically rigid for, indeed, her work went through several identifiable phases during a long painting career: it is rather a description of someone who lived through her visual perception. It influenced everything she did, from arranging flowers, posing a model or gardening. She became one of the leading female artists of her day and certainly one of the most interesting of the group who continued the tradition of painting in Newlyn after the turn of this century.

Dod Procter came to study with Stanhope Forbes and Elizabeth Forbes at their school of painting in 1907 at the age of 15. As the illustration "Steps at Oakhill Cottage" shows, by 1910 she was a most accomplished painter of exceptional maturity. During this period she developed a special friendship with Ernest Procter and met

Alfred Munnings and Laura Knight who described her as 'a charming young thing, with a brilliant complexion, enormous dark eyes and long slender legs – swift and active as a gazelle'.

It was after the first world war that Dod Procter's career developed. A large commission in Burma with her husband, Ernest, was followed by a most successful series of portraits, mostly of women. These showed the absorption of modern influences and have a sculptural quality and a haunting beauty.

In the early 1930s, Dod Procter's style changed. The paint thinned and the hard edges became soft. The colour took on a translucent quality and the now famous still-life pictures and the portraits of children she loved to paint on her extensive travels have an extraordinary lightness and harmony. In 1942 she was elected a full member

of the Royal Academy. Ernest Procter, himself a distinguished artist and teacher, died in 1935. Dod continued to live and work from her North Corner base in Newlyn until her death. She took an active part in the artistic life of Cornwall and was a regular exhibitor at Newlyn Art Gallery.

LECTURE PROGRAMME

There will be a full programme of talks and lectures during the Exhibition. If you are not a member of Newlyn Orion and wish to be mailed – please send a s.a.e . to Diana Morris at Newlyn Art Gallery.

ILLUSTRATED CATALOGUE: DOD PROCTER, RA

Through the generosity of a number of private patrons, a well illustrated catalogue with an essay by Elizabeth Knowles will be available.

Concession price during the exhibition – £4.95.

For mail order, contact Janet Bennette at Newlyn Art Gallery. Allow £1. p & p.

The Artist's Son 1919   Private Collection
Photo – Bob Berry

Steps at Oakhill Cottage, Lamorna 1910
Private Collection   Photo – Bob Berry

from *The Times*, Friday, August 3, 1990, by John Russell Taylor

There is no doubt that both Dod Procter and Frances Hodgkins have been shamefully neglected in the last few years. Feminists have a reason ready: Procter and Hodgkins were, after all, both women, and therefore subject to the malign workings of the great masculine conspiracy. At least the appearance of significant retrospectives devoted to their work now offers the chance to see whether that was the central issue.

Dod Procter is a peculiarly complicated case. She was long-lived (1892-1972) and in normal terms successful: she even ended up -- what many comparable women artists did not -- an RA. Her husband Ernest Procter was much shorter-lived (1886-1935) and made it only to ARA. The show which is now at the Laing Art Gallery, Newcastle, has already been seen in Liverpool and Penzance, where it was devoted completely to Dod; in Newcastle it has an annexe given over to Ernest...

Frances Hodgkins is odd-person-out for very different reasons. Many of them were of her own making. She was, in a sense, a late developer and was embarrassed about how late...[for the remainder of this review, see Chapter IV, placed against the background of of Frances Hodgkins' visits to West Cornwall.]

Minutes of the Council of Management
September 5 (Terry Newman, Acting Chairman)
...Education and Access: The summer had been extremely interesting and vibrant from the point of view of Newlyn Orion's community arts programme. The Autumn was to be a time of consolidation with much of the education work being done in gallery before the launch of the major cross-county interdisciplinary project for 1991: 'Belonging to Be', Myths and Legends of Cornwall. The Gallery would not be mounting an exhibition on that theme in-house but would be pursuing the development of the project in other locations throughout the county.

from the programme notes, GILL WATKISS, A Retrospective, by Ella Martin Halkes
...A painting by Gill Watkiss has a haunting quality. Part-remembered places, people and activities tug at the strings of our memory and also tug at our emotions. The most poignant and lonely works have a reassuring familiarity about them; 'time present is time past' and yet there is a certainty that the people who populate the images will have 'time future'. Gill Watkiss sensitively records in paint the wondrous contact that human beings have with one another and the world. The fire of feeling and the rose of recognition become one.

from the Minutes of the Council of Management
October 15 (Peter Smith, Vice-Chairman)
...John Halkes suggested that now that the Royal Cornwall Museum and Penlee House Museum had excellent facilities for showing historical works, that the Newlyn Orion collection should be lent out for the public benefit...

from the Minutes of the Council of Management October 30
(Peter Smith, Chairman)

...John Halkes advised the COM that after lengthy consideration he had decided to leave his post early in 1991...after 16 years of leading the company and building it up, that an injection of fresh expertise and enthusiasm would benefit Newlyn Orion...it was time both for him and the company to make the change...

from Priestlands' Cornwall

Alas, the pilchards scarcely outlasted the nineteenth century and the same was true of the tin. But before that happened a small trickle of artists, inspired by the open-air activities of their French colleagues and given greater freedom to roam by the railways, discovered St Ives on the north coast and Newlyn on the south. A certain rivalry still continues between the Newlyn Orion Gallery and the Penwith Gallery in St Ives; for although the Penwith traditionally can claim the great names - the Hepworths and the Herons - it cannot be denied that from the 1970s the Newlyn had the outreach and publicity, thanks to the flair of its curator John Halkes. It does not matter a great deal to the public, for the two towns are now so close together by car, and there is in effect a unified West Penwith community of artists which you can view in both places. But who knows, the balance may be swinging back to St. Ives: the spring of 1990 brought the announcement that not only was the Tate Gallery prepared to lodge its collection of Cornish paintings in St. Ives, but something like two million pounds was to be spent on building a gallery for them on the splendid site of the old gas works, overlooking the beach at Porthmeor, and thanks to a combination of local government, European Community and foundation finance, the money was largely assured.

179

John Halkes

from The Western Morning News, November 13, by Frank Ruhrmund

CHANGE OF DIRECTION

...[In sixteen years] John has mounted some 300 exhibitions, among them such important solo shows as that of Carel Weight and Christopher Wood, Terry Frost and Michael Finn. Perhaps the most significant and certainly the most popular exhibitions were the 1979 "Newlyn School of Artists" and the 1985 survey "Painting in Newlyn 1880-1930."

Three years ago he added another dimension to Newlyn Orion when, in conjunction with the National Trust and Cornwall Crafts Association, he opened the gallery at Trelissick.

The education and access programme run by Newlyn Orion has become widely respected. It is likely that last year's "Tree of Life" project for schools, and the current, "Belonging to Be" exploring Cornish myths, legends and customs, will be regarded as milestones in art education.

[John said} "after 16 years of directing an immensely busy arts charity, for much of that period against the tide of our prevailing culture and coupled with new issues of funding, presentation and so on, I feel it is time for a change...

1991

12 - 26 January 1991 OPEN HOUSE 90
a show about enjoyment and dialogue with the surrounding community.
4 - 16 February METAMORPHOSIS &
SUSAN KINLEY: RECENT WORKS
Metamorphosis: Falmouth School of Art and Design installation -- each day the
gallery will witness the evolution of an original installation sculpture.
25 February - 20 March A SECRET BURNING THREAD,
Paintings by Michael Higgins, 1939 - 1988 A Retrospective On tour from
Oriel Mostyn, Llandudno.
PAUL STRAND, photographs (On loan from the Victoria and Albert Museum)
A GARDEN WALK
John Daniel Centre An Exhibition of Photography, Pottery, Sculpture, Printing
and Painting from students at the Centre.
1 March - 28 April ARTISTS & GARDENS (Trelissick)
The opening exhibition will feature over 25 artists, including John Miller, Francis
Hewlett, Charles Howard, Robert Jones, Phil Hogben, and Carole Page.
27 April - 1 June STUART KNOWLES Recent Works
Lower Galleries: JASON WASON (Ceramics), JO WASON (Sculptures), and
BARBARA WILLS, AUDREY EVANS, JENNIFER CRACKNELL (painting with
gouache -- landscapes and harbours)
3 May - 29 September SUMMER SHOW Part I & II NSA mixed exhibition
14 September - 19 October HERITAGE: IMAGE AND HISTORY
Photographs and works on paper by a dozen commissioned artists looking at 'cultural tourism', theme parks and the fashion for nostalgia
-- from steam-railways to granary bread.
MYTHS & REALITIES, An alternative view of West Cornwall
Photographs by Trevor Burston, Ashley Peters, Annette Robinson
and Paintings by Nicola Bealing
26 October - 27 November GARRY FABIAN MILLER: THE GATHERER
9 November - 22 December CHILDREN'S WORLD
7 December - 18 January 1992 NEWLYN CONTEMPORARIES 4

from the Minutes of the Council of Management, February 26
Peter Smith (Chairman)
...*Tate of the West* The Chairman had met STAG in St Ives...[and been] shown the
gallery site and plans, and advised him of the current state of progress. It was agreed that
when the gallery was built there should be co-operation in areas such as advertising and
education. As far as the exhibition side was concerned, the two galleries would have
different roles and it was difficult at this time to see how they will fit. The Chairman gave
an assurance that Newlyn Orion will co-operate fully with STAG and suggested that
Newlyn Gallery be made available for any fund raising projects that they may wish to
make.
...*Trelissick Gallery* The Chairman produced a graph comparing sales by Orion and
Cornwall Crafts since the Trelissick Gallery's inception (1988), and a table of sales made
in 1990 by each artist shown by Orion at Trelissick...The stated problems with Trelissick
as he saw them [were] insufficient sales, a remote site from management perspective,
and lack of artistic coherence with the programme at Newlyn. It was decided to leave
a decision until...after the Chairman had his meeting with the National Trust...[The

Company ceased its involvement with the National Trust at Trelissick at the end of September 1991, as the deep recession of the 1990s began to bite.]

from the Minutes of the Council of Management, May 14
    Peter Smith (Chairman)
    ...NSA The Spring Exhibition of the Newlyn Society of Artists was fairly successful. Frank Ruhrmund had said that it "was a show not to be missed". Patrick Hughes came to talk about his work and choose the prize winners who were Anthony Frost, Andrew Lanyon and Geoff Ogden.

from the Minutes of the Council of Management, June 18
    Peter Smith (Chairman)
    ...*Loan of Paintings to Penzance Town Council* A timescale of five years has been agreed for the loan of [Newlyn School] paintings from the Permanent Collection, for exhibition at Penlee House. When the anticipated expansion of the gallery has taken place, they would be part of a permanent exhibition there.

1992

6 February - 7 March
FISH OUT OF WATER, a tape slide installation by Thomas Lisle
THE PETER GRIMES SERIES, A suite of 22 etchings by Anthony Davies
FISH SEEKERS: NEWLYN '91 Photographs by Francesca Ausenda
and Steve Tanner
Spring -- JOURNEYS -- FROM START TO FINISH
Diana Morris's third major education project in 15 Cornish primary schools.
12 March -- PETERLOO POETS : Michael Laskey & Maureen Wilkinson
18 March - 25 April PRIVATE VIEWS
The Working Process: Work by 8 members of the NSA Bob Bourne, Bernard Evans, Jeremy Le Grice, Carole Page, Cecil Riley, Tim Shaw, Peter Webster, David Westby
27 March - 20 April NEWLYN CONTEMPORARIES
Exhibition by members of the NSA
2 May - 6 June BT NEW CONTEMPORARIES EXHIBITION
20 June - 18 July MAURICE COCKRILL The Four Seasons
by courtesy of the Bernard Jacobson Gallery
SUMMER '92 28 July - 19 September EXHIBITIONS OF THE NSA, Part I & II
7 November - 5 December SUSANNA HERON, new work, sculpture.
Gallery talk by the artist, 7 November.
CHRISTMAS '92 Exhibition of Drawings by Members of the NSA. GUEST
ARTIST: EILEEN COOPER

from *The Cornishman*, March 19

Newlyn Art Gallery has this week received two grants from national trusts and foundations to enable us to make good the building in time for summer. The first, of £2000 from the Moorgate Trust, has enabled us to remove the 20 year old light screen and to restore window lights beneath the roof of the building...The second grant of £500 from Guardian Royal Exchange, will enable Newlyn to carpet the downstairs rooms... In the same week we have learnt of a major bequest from the late Miss Gertrude Norette Reed, a life-long friend of the Cornish-based artist, Albert Reuss. The gallery will be showing a small display of his paintings until April 25.

1993

23 January 20 February   KEITH ARNATT
'One foot has not yet reached the next street', Large Scale Photographs 1989 - 1992
8 March - 2 April ALISON WILDING: Bare Sculpture 1982-1993
6 - 24 April DEMARCO'S CHOICE
NSA Easter Exhibition selected by Richard Demarco
1 May - 12 June PETER LANYON: AIR, LAND AND SEA
A National touring Exhibition organised by the South Bank Centre for the Arts
Council of Great Britain
19 June - 17 July SWEET HOME
An exhibition of sculpture and installations by Anya Gallacio, Pat Kaufman,
Cornelia Parker and Pat Thornton.
SUMMER EXHIBITIONS OF THE NSA
28 July - 20 August Part 1: CONCRETE
25 August - 18 September Part 2: CHIMERA
29 September - 30 October DEAD SEXY: DEREK JARMAN
Paintings, and Installation by Benjamin Gay, Danielle Hart, David Miles, Pippa
Oldfield, Carol Ann Pegg, Ben Rivers, Becky Troth
6 November - 4 December SECOND SIGHT
Sculpture by Camiel Van Breedam, Andy Hazell, Lucy Casson, Romuald Hazoume,
Andrew Holmes, David Kemp, William Longden, David Mayne, Wilhelm Mundt,
Cleo Mussi, Ron O'Donnell, Ivan Smith, Art Junkies, Nek Chand & Bill Woodrow.
19 February - 26 March Ms.(cellaneous)
Kate Davis, Carole McDowall, Anne Seagrave, Rose Frain, Tracy MacKenna,
Moira McIver, at NEWLYN 2, Market Jew Street.
16 May - 25 June DAVID MACH: Likeness Guaranteed. Artist's talk.
9 - 16 July A BEACH STORY Photographs of Porthcurno by Charles Roff
& SUMMER SURPRISES John Daniel Education Centre show
12 September - 8 October JUDITH GODDARD: Reservoir,
& ALASTAIR MACLENNAN Installation and Performance Art.
Artist's talk & All-day Performance.
14 October - 5 November VIEWFINDINGS
Photography of Landscape & Environment, part of the International Women's
Photography Festival,
Artist's talk: Valerie Reardon
11 November - 7 December GERRY GLEASON The Ulster Saga.
12 - 31 December NSA CHRISTMAS EXHIBITION
Painting, printmaking, sculpture, ceramics and a Performance by Ken Turner, entitled
Doubtless in partnership with students from Dartington College of Visual Performance.
Text: Maggie O'Sullivan

☐ THE new team at the Orion. Back row, from left: Blair Todd, Jane Colliver,
Bob Berry, Nick Sharp, Sandra Leah. Front row: Cairney Down, Emily Ash,
Partou Zia.

from *The Peninsula Voice,* June 1, by Jeremy Le Grice

The exhibition of Peter Lanyon's work at Newlyn until June 12th is a major event in the context of art in Cornwall. Lanyon was a seminal personality, an inventive, reckless, anarchist who led English landscape-painting forward from his stronghold in West Penwith so that it became, for a decade, a major force in European culture, blending with a simultaneous and parallel excursion into the unknown that issued forth from America during the 1950's...Force of colour, substance of paint, the realistic scale of his world of landscape, the vigour and rhythms -- above all, the verve, conviction and creativity, sing from almost every work here...I doubt whether the gallery has seen a more invigorating show in its century of promoting Cornish art. It is proper that this Arts Council national tour ends at Newlyn; Lanyon made this gallery his bolt-hole after splitting from the Penwith and remained an articulate promoter for it even when he had received very wide acclaim...Each of these paintings recalls his delight and experience of gliding but, beyond that, they amount to statements of a knowledge, confidence, scale and bravado that is exceptional in British art since the days of Turner...

5 May 93   Porthgwarra

Pencil drawing by Alexander Mackenzie

from the *Leader,* October 16, 1993

EC GRANT AIDS MAJOR ORION PROJECT

A NEW era has been heralded at Newlyn Art Gallery with the announcement of an award of a major grant of 87,000. This represents some 50 per cent of the total project costs of an ambitious scheme for upgrading and modernising the gallery, now approaching its centennial year. The grant comes from the European commission through the Regional Development Fund. At an open meeting architect Robert Evans showed revised plans for the gallery, this time retaining the existing front door and granite steps, changes to which in a previous design had caused such an outcry...

from *The Guardian,* October 12, 1993 by Rachel Barnes

A DIFFERENT WAR

...In Derek Jarman's journal, *Modern Nature,* he quotes from Huxley's *Doors of Perception.* The words came into his mind as he walked down to the bleak coast from his cottage at Dungeness in the March of 1989. He had been diagnosed as HIV positive two years previously...

If the viewer were inclined to separate Jarman's life from these paintings, the titles would instantly disabuse. Blind Maniac, Scream, Dead Sexy and Sightless executed in the last few months all confront the issues surrounding his illness head on...

...I do not know if Jarman's recent paintings will stand the test of time, nor do I wish to debate their intrinsic aesthetic merit. This is art which communicates deep feeling and deliberately draws attention to an issue which urgently needs compassion and understanding. "All art is concerned with death," Jarman says.

[Ed note: Derek Jarman died in 1994.]

from *The Cornishman*, February 3, 1994

TEMPORARY ART GALLERY IS A GREAT DRAW

PENZANCE'S newest art gallery is proving a great success.

On the first day of opening, the "Newlyn Art Gallery 2"[too] in Market Jew Street, attracted as many visitors as the Newlyn Orion sees during any one day at the height of the summer season.

"There is a lot of interest in the new gallery," said Blair Todd, who is in charge of the main street premises. "Passers-by and shoppers have been calling in, and everybody has said that they hope we will keep the gallery open indefinitely.

But the gallery, with its shop and cafe has been opened as temporary premises while major rebuilding and development work takes place at the Newlyn Art Gallery.

184

from *The Cornishman*, March 10, 1994

LOVEJOY would have been proud of his side-kick, "Tinker", if he had been at the Newlyn Art Gallery's "Attic Sale" last week. For Dudley Sutton (above) not only officially opened the sale but also made a number of bids during the evening's auction. The popular actor of the BBC series "Lovejoy" about the goings-on in the world of antique dealing, has a home in Mousehole and flew down from London specially to help at the auction held at the Acorn Theatre. Penzance auctioneer David Lay lent his professionalism to the evening...the money raised will help towards the cost of renting the temporary art gallery in Market Jew Street...

Dudley Sutton

Tinker's little earner

from *The Western Morning News*, April 27, by Douglas Williams

FAMOUS GALLERY IS TRANSFORMED FOR A NEW AGE

THE most important redevelopment of the Newlyn Art Gallery since it was built a century ago is almost complete. A project costing around 165,000 pounds has brought a brand new look to a building always associated with the Newlyn School of painting...

...Director Emily Ash said the gallery will reopen to the public on May 16.

Renowned British sculptor David Mach has been commissioned to create new large-scale sculptures for the occasion. He will layer 10 tons of newspaper into a sea and boats scene to transform the upper gallery. On the lower gallery he will make an 8 ft 6in high torso entirely of welded metal coathangers.

The gallery has been improved, said Miss Ash, so that it could show the very best of contemporary art, local, national and international. "Newlyn has always been a contemporary gallery showing the art of its day..."

...The funding has come from the Euro RDF, Foundation for Sports and Arts, Penwith District Council, the Rural Development Commission, Henry Moore Foundation, Penzance Town Council and Lloyds Bank.

185

Sea and boats
David Mach, 1994
Photo by Bob Berry

The headlines from *The Peninsula Voice* about the Mach Exhibition, June/July issue,

MACH 1 'The art of engagement' by Mike Venning

The concern with the art of engagement is also apparent in his attitude to the end-product. Once the work is completed it becomes someone else's responsibility. Mach states that he does not see his work as ephemeral; any piece could stay in situ for ever as far as he is concerned. It's up to whoever manages the site to decide on the lifetime of the finished work. Of his site-specific works, one is still in place in Belgium after several years of existence, the rest were dismantled after a matter of months. (Newlyn Gallery's "Likeness Guaranteed" will disappear when the exhibition ends on June 25.

MACH 2 'What to do with your spare coat-hangers' by Martin Green

...He [Mach] will be best remembered, perhaps, for his arrangement on London's South Bank of used car tyres in the shape of a submarine. Farmers all over the country have been slow to follow his example and simply pile theirs in rotund heaps on top of their sileage...The claim for the 'improved' upper gallery (that "it is now a pure, unbroken space") is questionable. When walking into any gallery, a room with only one entrance gives the viewer a feeling of claustrophobia; when he or she can walk through it, the work is not so daunting, is actually enhanced...

MACH 3 'Newlyn Gallery is S-TATE of the Modern Art' by Des Hannigan

...For the official opening, David Mach's great card-splay of layered newspapers filled the key corner; thousands of redundant tabloids in a swooping sea of waves. Never has *The Sun* been more stylishly set. Never has Page Three seen such billows. Passmore Edwards, the old journalist that he was, would have relished the irony...

186

from *Country Living,* November

WOMEN PHOTOGRAPHERS

explore their reactions to the great outdoors in Viewfindings at Newlyn Art Gallery, Penzance. As part of the International Women's Photography Festival, the works challenge romantic notions of the countryside as a perpetual rural idyll. Ingrid Pollard's thought-provoking and poetic shots of black women in the British landscape are some of the highlights...Victoria Millar

from *The Cornishman,* 20 October

WESTCOUNTRY SPONSOR GALLERY

It has been agreed by Westcountry Television to contribute in sponsorship £2,000 to the year-long programme of regular education events at the Newlyn Art Gallery.

Mark Clare, head of Press and Publicity at Westcountry, said that this figure represents one of the largest awards Westcountry Television has given to an individual organisation. Cairney Down, development officer at Newlyn Art Gallery, added. 'We are delighted with this award. It will enable the gallery to market and resource the Education Programme more effectively...As an educational charity, such education work is an integral part of the gallery's activity and is closely linked to the exhibition programme'...

from the Minutes of the Council of Management, 27 October

Peter Ellery (Chairman)

...A written report with garden mapping, was submitted for landscaping the sur-rounds of Newlyn Orion Gallery from Peter Blake, Horticultural Consultant. Generous offers have come from the experimental gardening specialists at Probus, and from Mrs Elizabeth Bolitho of Trengwainton to provide the planting expertise and the plants, respectively.

Cleaning of copper plaques for centennial year: it was suggested that these had been checked approximately two years previously. Charles Thomas commented that the pollution of this century would probably make cleaning completely un-viable.

Bernard Evans told the Council that the NSA has now given Honorary Life Membership to John Wells...

from *The Cornishman*, 8 December, by Frank Ruhrmund

...GERRY GLEASON appears to have done so [making sense of such seemingly senseless struggling and suffering] by developing a voca-bulary which speaks in equal measure of sorrow and hope. He uses social and political visual metaphors in order "to look at life behind the mask" while, at the same time, presenting ques-tions and posing problems that go far beyond the border of Northern Ireland to the world at large...

from the Minutes of the Extraordinary General Meeting, December 13

Melissa Hardie (in the Chair) with Katherine Wallace (Company Secretary)

A quorum was established, and a brief explanation given of the purposes of the proposed name change: to avoid confusion and project a simple and single corporate identity.

The resolution was duly approved:

"It is proposed that the customary, legal and company name of the Newlyn Orion Galleries Ltd, from this time forward be designated as the Newlyn Art Gallery Ltd, retaining as before the guaranteed recognition of John Passmore Edwards as the founder patron."

from *The Western Morning News* by Douglas Williams, December 9

Top artists' work at Christmas show

The Newlyn Society of Artists, one of the oldest artists' associations in Britain, has its Christmas exhibition opening on Monday and continuing to the end of the year.

Founded in 1895 -- the centenary is not far away -- it has a long shared history with Newlyn Art Gallery.

It presents some of the very best artists working in the South West, and this latest show will embrace the work of the broadest spectrum of members. It will include painting and print-making through to sculpture and ceramics.

Ken Turner, the first performance art mem-ber of the Society, has been invited to take part. "He will perform his latest work 'Doubtless' at the gallery in advance of the opening of the main exhibition," said a gallery spokesperson. 'Doubt-less' combines performance, poetry, dance, painting, music and sculpture...

1995 THE CENTENNIAL YEAR

7 - 28 January THE ARTS COUNCIL COLLECTION
New Painting (selection from 27 contemporary artists)
3 February - 11 March
MILES PETER RICHMOND Painting: The Continuity of Practice 1947-1994.
A Middlesborough Art Gallery Touring Exhibition. Artist's Talk, with poetry of Rilke
read by Michael Bird.
17 - 25 March ARTiculate Now: EXHIBITION OF EDUCATION WORK
Easter Show -- NSA mixed exhibition
29 April - 3 June TERRY FROST -- NEW WORK AT EIGHTY
10 June - 5 August
NEWLYN ART GALLERY: 100 YEARS Context and Continuity
15 June
100 YEARS AT NEWLYN, Diary of a Gallery -- Book Launch
12 August - 23 September
NSA 100
The Newlyn Society of Artists Centennial Show
4 October - 4 November ELEMENTAL
Graham Gussin, Tania Kovats, Philip Napier and Craig Wood
10 November - December 16
CONTEMPORANEOU.S. NEW WORK FROM NEW YORK

from the Exhibition Catalogue
Miles Peter Richmond: 'My work has always been rooted in the notion of the 'locus'.
The physical environment from London as a child to Rounton as an old man, the sense
of place has always been manifest. Painting can deal, in a unique way with the physical
sense of being in the world and for me, the actual 'locus' is important.'

from the Newsletter, Spring 1995
Terry Frost celebrates his 80th birthday in 1995 as Newlyn Art Gallery celebrates
its centenary. In this birthday show, he is exhibiting his newest paintings, created for the
occasion. As one of the most prominent and respected artists in the development of
British Modernism, Terry Frost played an important role in the St Ives School and in
the exploration of the abstract form. Most widely associated with St Ives, Terry Frost
has been living and working in Newlyn since 1974. He is a member of the Newlyn Society
of Artists.

100 YEARS AT NEWLYN... CONTEXT & CONTINUITY
The objective of this exhibition is to represent as broadly as possible the creative force
which has uniquely characterised Newlyn Art Gallery from 1895 to 1995 and projects
forward. The idea has been to explore through an exhibition of paintings, sculpture,
ceramics, copperware, artefacts, photographs, and supporting documentation, the
unique identity and character of Newlyn Art Gallery as it has developed, and the
climactic changes for the Arts. Simultaneous publication by the Patten Press, of the
book, *100 YEARS IN NEWLYN, Diary of a Gallery*.
THE EXHIBITIONS
Part one: (1895 - 1939) NEWLYN SCHOOL
Part two: THE MIDDLE PERIOD
Part three: CONTINUITY

XII: A Century of Honoured Friends

The purpose of this volume of memories is to act as a birthday book, a type of scrapbook to cover a century. What it cannot do is to ensure that every person connected in any way to the Gallery receives his or her full recognition. Nor can every exhibition mounted in the Gallery receive pictorial coverage. In the archives we have little visual record of the first half-century other than many reprints of paintings. Photographs that we do have, have been employed frequently in several art histories about the early Newlyn colony and are therefore a familiar part of public record. The current editor has attempted to employ visual material which may only have been seen by newspaper readers contemporary to the event, or to relatives and artists with a private photographic collection . In many cases, old and new visual images as well as newspaper reports have been available to us in photocopied form. This will explain, if not excuse, the relatively poor quality of some of our reproductions.

189

Since the nineteen-fifties and especially since the change in exhibition policy after 1974, the reverse holds sway: there is a plethora of printed material to select from, much of it in full colour, making the selecting process invidious and the potential reproduction in a new publication exceedingly expensive. Nonetheless, there is still a lack of personal photographic record, as opposed to that which show the works of art. The lack of a complete collection of exhibition programmes has excluded the possibility of listing individually the artists and craftsmen exhibiting at the Gallery, with their exhibits. Such a list would include hundreds of names, known and unknown to posterity, but it would be a valuable resource to the many family and academic researchers who come to discover what part this or that particular artist took in the artistic community here. As mentioned in Chapter I, this is now a planned archival project, and the contributions of biographies, photographs, and personal records of individual artists willing to share this information will be warmly welcomed.

We have relied wholly on printed sources, with all the attendant difficulties of obscurity and mis-information that this implies. Frequently today's newspaper reports get details and names twisted and wrong; so it has always been! Sometimes there is no definitive way -- except by consulting birth records or personal correspondence, neither of which occur with any frequency in Gallery archives -- to confirm the spelling of a person's name, as it can be found regularly in several different forms. Minutes of meetings show that disgruntled letters have been directed to the Press since the nineteen-twenties asking that news editors try to set the record straight. Even curators/secretaries/Directors make curious errors in their reports; undoubtedly, so has this Editor. To those who may not find their names where they expect to, sincere apologies are offered.

In Chapter XII, the purpose is to provide an organised list of those artists and others who engaged themselves to furthering the artistic purposes of the Gallery over the past century. List-reading may in itself be a boring occupation, but such a mass of information provides a summary index of data contained in the archives, and as such will aid future researchers. Many of the subscribers to this volume have personal connections to individuals and groups in the following lists; some of the subscribers are, of course, principals themselves in the story of the Newlyn Art Gallery. It is with certain pride and gratitude that our 'honoured friends' are named. In summary, their names appear under five general headings: The Committees, The Newlyn Society of Artists, The Permanent Collection, The Trustees, and the subscribers to this volume.

The Committees/Council of Management of the Passmore Edwards Art Gallery

The following lists name only those artists and others, appearing in the archival records as having served on The Committee, the hanging committees, or other activity sub-committees. The dates of taking up appointment and of resignation or death were not recorded with regularity, and are therefore not included.

Artists often exhibited in the Newlyn Art Gallery both before and after their years of active service on the Committees, and their works were shown after their deaths. (Trustee) indicated are those Trustees <u>or</u> their appointed agents which took active part in the Committee's activities by attending its meetings on an irregular basis. ** Indicates individuals made Honorary Life Members of the Newlyn Society of Artists or the Gallery for their services to the activities of the Gallery.

Secretary/Curators/Directors
[Acting both for the Passmore Edwards Art Gallery & the Newlyn Society of Artists]

1895	Percy Craft, Hon Sec pro tem
1896	T Robins Foster, Asst Secretary to Craft
1897	H M Rheam, Hon Sec
1920	Reginald Dick, Acting Sec, Hon Sec
1921	Miss Churchill Tayler, Asst Hon Sec & Miss Hall, Custodian
1934	Mrs Wallace Nicholls, Secretary/Curator, & Wallace Nicholls, custodian
1952	Wallace Nicholls, pro tem
1952	Eileen Hunt
1956	Michael Canney
1964	David Coad
1965	David Smith
1967	Alister J McLeod ('Mac')
1973	Without curator in winter months
1974	John O'Dell, pro tem
1974	John Halkes, Director, John O'Dell, Administrator
1990	Janet Bennette, Acting Administrator
1991	Gerald Deslandes, Director, Newlyn Orion
1992	Janet Bennette & Elizabeth Knowles, Acting Administrators
1993	Emily Ash, Director, Newlyn Orion

Caretakers (early support staff)

1896	Mr and Mrs Deacon
1911	Mr and Mrs Vincent
1920	C Richards
1924	Miss M A Hall, asst with Miss Churchill Tayler
1934	Curator/custodian combined, with additional cleaning help.

191

192

II From 1974-95
The Newlyn Orion Galleries: the new company at the PEAG

First meeting of the Management Committee: 12 July 1974
Founding members of the Management Committee: J Barnicoat, T Craske-Rising, Peter Ellery (Treasurer), Ella Halkes, John Halkes, Eileen Hunt, Denis Mitchell, John O'Dell (Secretary, PEAG,NSA), Jack Pender (Chairman), Ken Symonds (Vice-Chairman), Professor Charles Thomas, Bill Tudor. Observers from the Penwith District Council: Councillor C Ash, Mr Shorten (Treasurer's Department)

First elected Council of Management 1977: Clive Bennetts, Peter Ellery, Denis Mitchell, Dr Patricia Moyer, W Thornley, Jack Pender, Ken Rumsey, Gay Sagar-Fenton, Ken Symonds.

[Note: When an abbreviation follows the name, this denotes representing this organisation on the Management Committee of the Gallery. Abbreviations: ACGB: Arts Council of Great Britain; CCC: Cornwall County Council; Co-opt: initially, a co-opted member; FSA: Falmouth School of Art & Design, now FCA: Falmouth College of Arts; ICS: Institute of Cornish Studies; NSA: Newlyn Society of Artists; Obs: Observer; PDC: Penwith District Council; SWA: South West Arts]

193

**Newlyn Orion Galleries Ltd.
Staff employed in administering the Gallery since 1974**

Janet Bennette
Bob Berry
Lesley Burton
Michael Chalwin
Lilias Chapman (Trelissick)
Sue Clarke
Jill Clements
Jane Colliver
Cairney Down
Ben Gay
Ella Halkes
Judith Hancock (Trelissick)
Rachael Hansen
Liz Hewlett (Trelissick)
Lynne King (Trelissick)
Elizabeth Knowles
Mr Lake
Sandra Leah
Isabell Livingston (Trelissick)
Linda Martin Morley
Elsa Morley
Diana Morris
John O'Dell
Nick Sharp
Shelagh Shore
Jane Symonds
Blair Todd
Elsa Wainwright
Paul Wainwright
Caroline White
Jean White
Polly Wilkins
Suzanne Woodward (Trelissick)
Partou Zia

Auditors/Accountants:
Previous: Whitaker & Redfearn, Chown & Robins, Accts Anthony Williams & Co, Whitaker & Redfearn, 1983- present.

194

*1995 Honorary Life Members
of Newlyn Art Gallery*
(formerly Newlyn Orion)
Presented with this honour due to their outstanding service.

Joyce Blakey
Mr & Mrs T Craske Rising
Graham Dark
Terry Frost
Ella & John Halkes
Mrs Margaret Halls
Eileen Hunt
Lisette Keeble (Sussex)
Mrs Sheila Lanyon
Ms Elma Mitchell & Ms J Taylor
Terry Newman
Jack Pender
Mrs Phoebe Procter
Shelagh Shore
Leonora Simpson
Mrs Mary Smith
Denys Stephens
Dorcie Sykes
Margaret Symons
Polly Walker
John Wells

The Newlyn Society of Artists

The Constitution of The Newlyn Society of Artists was set out in 1895, in Articles 1 - 11, specifying the name, the purpose, the geographical focus, the consent and reversionary clauses related to Trustees of the Passmore Edwards Art Gallery, and the rules of submission of works for the Society's Exhibitions. Article 2, stating the purpose of the Society, reads: 'The Society is established solely for the purpose of promoting Graphic Art or the art of Sculpture, or both such Arts and Arts Craftsmanship, and is not conducted for profit.'

It was suggested in 1960 at the AGM by Michael Canney 'that various amendments had been made to the Constitution and had never been issued in printed form as a completely up-to-date Constitution, and that some of the original clauses in the printed copy that he possessed now no longer applied.' He suggested re-writing it, but it was held over until a further meeting of the Executive, and not pursued. The Original form of Constitution was amended and clarified on the 2nd day of June 1970 by the addition of 21 Clauses, and as set out in the Minutes of the Annual General Meeting of that date.

The 21 Clauses modifying the original Constitution were then revoked on the 27th day of September 1974, 27 Clauses being put in their place. In September 1980 further amendments to the 27 Clauses concerning membership, annual subscription, the executive committee, the hanging committee, hanging rules, and frequency of general meetings were effected. The original Constitution of the Society did not specify an upper or lower limit of Society members. In March of 1974, the NSA Committee proposed to the Membership (AGM) that the then limit of 50 members, as specified in the Clause 19 of the 1970 Constitution, be removed. Membership limits would in future be decided from year to year. This Clause was re-confirmed as Clause 2 in the 1980 revision.

There is no extant list of the original members of the Newlyn Society of Artists, nor a complete register of members over the century. In 1921, in his appeal for support to resurrect the Gallery after the Great War, Norman Garstin indicated that in 1895 there had been 'about a dozen Trustees, about twenty-six artists, and about seventy associates' (public subscribers, non-artists) who had made possible the initial foundation. Many of the artists names can be gathered from the records, but these 'chop and change' rapidly, with artists coming and going, paying their subscription one year, and then not the next. Except for the opening exhibition in 1895, where it was stipulated that the artists showing their work should have connections with Cornwall, it has not been the policy of the Gallery to display only the arts of NSA members. The following list recognises the members in good standing of the NSA in 1995.

The Chairmen are listed from 1952, as this is the date from which elections first appear in the Minutes. These 'officials', as explained in Chapter I, held the joint responsibility of Chairmen of The Committee of the Gallery itself and the Society until the re-organisation of 1974. The organisational and supporting office of Honorary Secretary up to and including 1974, was carried by the salaried Curator-Secretary of the Gallery, and the Honorary Treasurer's duties were usually undertaken by local bank managers. The names of these important people in the life of the Gallery are listed in the previous section about those serving the Committees of the Gallery. After 1974, the Council of Management and the Committee of the NSA separated into two, some, such as Ken Symonds (Chairman, NSA; Chairman: 1973 Working Party; Vice Chair, Council of Management, 1974), continuing to serve on both.

Chairmen of the Newlyn Society of Artists

1952-53 E Bouverie Hoyton
1953-56 Elizabeth Lamorna Kerr
1956-57 Denys Law
1957-58 Charles Breaker
1958-59 Jack Pender
1959-60 Peter Lanyon
1960-64 Charles Breaker
1964-66 John Miller
1966-67 Jack Pender
1967-72 John Miller
1972-76 Ken Symonds
1976-78 John Emanuel
1978-80 Michael Praed
1980-81 Theresa Gilder
1981-82 John Piper
1982-84 Bernard Evans
1984-87 Peter Smith
1987-89 Mike Chalwin
1989-91 Robert Jones
1991-92 Leonie Whitton
1992-93 Shared by executive
1993-95 Bernard Evans

Members & Associate Members 1995

[*Abbreviations are for the following exhibitions: Painters,* selected for 'Painters in Cornwall, 1960', for the City Art Gallery, Plymouth; *Art Share,* a contributing artist to the important Charity Art Auction of 1988, held by W H Lane in aid of the Newlyn Art Gallery; *Century,* selected for 'A Century of Art in Cornwall, 1889-1989' organised by Newlyn Orion to celebrate the Centenary of Cornwall County Council; *Top Ten,* selected by South West Arts as Major Award Winner in Fine Art, 1978, & exhibited at Newlyn Art Gallery, 20 October - 17 November. All of the following artists enter their paintings for the thrice-yearly exhibitions of the NSA.]

Note: In 1995, in recognition of a time-honoured tradition of association with the Royal Academy of Arts by some of our prominent Newlyn artists, a 'joint' submission to the RA Summer Show will occur. NSA members who will be 'sending-in' via the Newlyn van are marked with an asterisk. *

Members

Jeremy Annear
*Ray Atkins, Solo Exhib 1977, *Century, Sun Moon & Stars* 1989
Simon Averill, *Autumn Miscellany,* 1989
Wilhelmina Barns-Graham, *Painters 1960, Looking West,* 1987, *Century, Retrospective,* 1989
Nicola Bealing, *Myths & Realities,* 1991
Mary Beresford Williams, *Top Ten,* 1978, Art Share 1988
Clive Blackmore, 1 of 'Six Solos' 1986, Art Share 1988, Critics Choice, 1989
*Sandra Blow, RA
Philip M Booth
*Bob Bourne, *Looking West,* 1987, *Century, Private Views,* 1992
Angus Brent, *Painters,* 1960
Jennifer Brown
Anthony Bryant, Art Share 1988, *Craft Work,* 1988
Molly Bullock, Art Share 1988
Judy Buxton
Zoe Cameron
Michael Chalwin, *Working Party,* 1985, Solo 1988, *Looking West,* 1987, *Century*
David Collings, Art Share 1988
Richard Cook, *Looking West* 1987, Art Share 1988, *Century*
Bob Crossley
George Dannatt, Solo 1981, 1 of "Six Solos" 1987, Art Share 1988
Phil Darby, Art Share 1988,
Steve Dove, Art Share 1988,
Julian Dyson
Marianne Edwards, Solo 1981,
John Emanuel, Art Share 1988, *Century*
Audrey Evans, Art Share 1988, Small group 1991
*Bernard Evans, 1 of "Six Solos" 1987, *Private Views,* 1992
Ray Exworth
Michael Finn, *Painters 1960,* Art Share 1988, Solo Exh, 1989, *Century*

Laurie Ann Finestone, Solo 1983
Peter Fox
Ralph Freeman
Anthony Frost, Solo 1975, 1986; Art Share 1988, *Century*, Critics Choice 1991
*Terry Frost RA, *Painters* 1960, Solo 1977, *Looking West*, 1987, Art Share 1988, *Sun Moon & Stars* 1989, *Century*, Solo 1995
Joan Gillchrest, Art Share 1988
Nic Harrison, Art Share 1988,
Christa M Herrmann, Art Share 1988,
Francis Hewlett, *Painters* 1960, Solo Ceramics 1976, Solo Paintings, 1978, *Top Ten*, 1978, Art Share 1988, Solo Ceramics 1989 (Trelissick), *Century*
*Rose Hilton, Solo 1977, 1987, Art Share 1988, *Century*
Phil Hogben, *Top Ten*, 1978, Art Share 1988,
William Ashley Hold
Derek Holland, Art Share 1988,
Marjorie Holland
*Ken Howard RA, Art Share 1988, *Century*
Kurt Jackson
Derek Jenkins
Robert Jones, 1 of 'Six Solos' 1986; Solo 1988, Art Share 1988, *Century*
Susan Kinley, Solo 1991
Andrew Lanyon, Solo 1978, 1983, Art Share 1988,*Century*, Critics Choice 1991
Gwen LeGrand
Jeremy Le Grice, *Celtic Vision* 1988, *Century*, *Private Views* 1992
Amanda Lorens
Louise McClary
Carole A McDowall
Margo Maeckelberghe, *Painters* 1960, *Century*
Frances May
June Miles, *Painters* 1960, Solo 1976, Art Share 1988
*John Miller, Solo 1978, *Looking West*, Art Share 1988, *Century*
Moreen Moss

Daphne McClure, Art Share 1988, *Century*, *Sun Moon & Stars* 1989, Critics Choice 1989 & 1990, Solo 1990
Alexander MacKenzie,*Painters* 1960, Solo 1980, *Looking West* 1987, Art Share 1988, *Century*, Critics Choice 1990
Philip Naylor
Paul Nicholls
Breon O'Casey
Sheelagh O'Donnell
Jane O'Malley, Art Share 1988, *Century*
Tony O'Malley, Solo 1975, 1986; *Celtic Vision* 1987 & 1988, Art Share 1988, Critics Choice 1989, *Century*
Geoff Ogden, Solo 1978, *Top Ten*, 1978, Critics Choice 1991, *Century*
Matt Osmond
Carole Page, 1 of "Six Solos" 1987, Art Share 1988, *Century*, *Private Views*, 1992
Bryan Pearce, Art Share 1988, *Century*
Jack Pender, *Painters* 1960, *Celtic Vision* 1987, Art Share 1988, *Century*
Stuart Peters
Biddy Picard, Art Share 1988,
John Piper, Art Share 1988
Michael Praed, Solo 1981,Art Share 1988, *Celtic Vision*, 1988 *Century*
Roy Ray, Art Share 1988
Cecil Riley, Art Share 1988, *Private Views* 1992
Joan Riley, Art Share 1988,
Sonia Robinson
Dorothy Searle
Jennifer Semmens, Art Share 1988, *Celtic Vision* 1988, *Autumn Miscellany*, 1989
Stephen T Shaw, *Private Views*, 1992
Peter Smith, *Working Party* 1985, *Century*
Peter MacDonald Smith, Art Share 1988, *Century*
Andrew Stonyer
Mary Stork
Maurice Sumray, Solo 1981

David Symonds
Ken Symonds, Solo Exhib, 1960, 1977, Art Share 1988, *Century*
Morwenna Thistlethwaite
Roger Towndrow
Barbara Tribe, 1 of "Six Solos" 1987, Art Share 1988, *Century*
Michael Truscott
***Rosemary Tunstall-Behrens,** Art Share 1988,
Rod Walker, Solo 1975
Roy Walker, Solo 1975, *Century*
***Gill Watkiss,** Solo 1979, 1 of "Six Solos" 1987, Art Share 1988, Retrospective 1990, *Century*
Charles Watts
Peter Webster, *Private Views* 1992
John Wells, *Looking West* 1987, Art Share 1988, *Century*
David Westby, *Private Views* 1992, *Century*
Jerry White, *Century*
Leonie Whitton, 1 of 'Six Solos', 1986, Art Share 1988, *Century*
Barbara Wills, Art Share 1988, *Century, Sun Moon & Stars* 1989, Small group 1991
Vincent Wilson, Art Share 1988
Tamsin Woodford
Fred Yates, 1 of "Six Solos" 1987, Art Share 1988, *Looking West* 1987, *Century*

Associates in 1995
Simon Allen
Catharine Armitage
Gerry Blaxall
Sandra Boreham
Jerry Browning
Jessica Buckley
Clare Burke
Rudolf Calonder
Jenny Cook
Tony Eastman
Peter Hayes
Bo Hilton
Elizabeth Hunter
Graham Jobbins
Alan Lake
Rachel Levine
Padraig MacMiadhachain

Richard Nott
*Sheila Oliner, Art Share 1988,
David Pearce
Julia Platt
Lara Reveley
Stephen Ridgeway
Stuart Ross
Dorothy Searle
Tony Shields
Paul Thompson
Ken Turner
Angela Weyersberg
Ineke van der Wal
Partou Zia

Volunteers
Volunteers have served in the Newlyn Art Gallery as invigilators, office assistants, and technical assistants, and often the Gallery heavily depends upon them for remaining open and effective. Many artists not listed here, both within and without the Newlyn Society of Artists, have given generously of their time in the maintenance, exhibition hanging, and decoration of the Gallery.

[There is no complete list extant]
Kate Ackerley
Amy Ashley
Joyce Blakey
Jess Buckley
Matthew Ellis
Ben Gay
Con Humphris
Eileen Hunt
Sax Impey
Alix Kalma
Rachel Kantaris
Barbara Karn
Renate Lawes
Ann LeGrice
Joan Lewis
Rhoda Little
Natasha O'Brien
Eleanor Phethean
Mrs Phoebe Procter
Jeremy Rice
Stephen Ridgeway
Gay Sagar-Fenton
Winifred Simmons
Margaret Symons
Sheila Thornley

Recent friends of our time
Clockwise from Top (L):
Ithell Colquhoun (1906-1988)
 by Margo Maeckelberghe
Denis Mitchell (1912-1993)
Marjorie Mort (1906-1988)
Ray Ambrose (1927-1989)
William 'Bill' Tudor (Died, 1990)

199

The Permanent Collection

from a Lecture given by Stanhope Forbes, January 24, 1935 at the Penzance Library, Morrab Gardens
'Some Story Pictures'

...So year after year right up to the present day both from Newlyn and the neighbouring Art Colony of St Ives work has emanated which has won honours and distinctions for the Artists of the West Country. Is it not very regrettable that so little of this large output of art work has remained in Cornwall, and especially that here in Penzance you have no Museum or Art Gallery, not even a room, in which work of local interest can be preserved and shown? It is true we have in Newlyn the little Gallery which we owe to the generosity of Mr Passmore Edwards, and which we artists with the warm support of many art lovers in this district have managed to maintain successfully for many years past; and that also in St Ives our comrades there have recently founded the excellent Gallery which you doubtless know.

But these cannot supply the need of a permanent collection and it is only in the Cathedral town of Truro that we find an adequate Gallery in which works of art can be seen...

200

The idea of building a Permanent Collection of paintings, sculptures and other art objects was brought up by the artist-chairman, Charles Breaker, in Committee in 1961, and reiterated by the artist, Peter Lanyon. Previous discussion or comment is not recorded, except in the 'formal' context of Stanhope Forbes' lecture at the venerable and historic Penzance Library, as above. Again in 1968 it was raised as a subject for thorough discussion and approved, but with no issue.

It should be remembered that the original conception of Passmore Edwards and the founding artists was to provide exhibition and selling space for contemporary paintings and works of sculpture. Other arts and crafts of a wide variety were not introduced in exhibition until 1924. The building was not envisaged as a museum, and it has not been considered large enough to house a standing collection of representative art, while carrying out its principal function of providing showing spaces for contemporary artists. The subsidiary purposes of providing a meeting room and living accommodation for a custodian or curator, or alternatively a small Gallery and a sometime studio for a working artist, more than stretched the capacities of what was conceived even at first as a 'small gallery'.

With the advent of the Newlyn Orion Galleries in 1974, and subsequent plans to expand the physical plant, the idea of a Permanent Collection became a realisable objective. The Council of Management and the Arts Council considered that this was an appropriate feature of a prestige gallery and one which could attract donors both locally and nationally. John Halkes gave great impetus to the campaign and was largely responsible for the interest and enthusiasm generated. The collection grew.

Unfortunately, the economic climate of the nineteen-eighties did not allow the hoped-for development to take place, and therefore the gathering works of art have resided in the storerooms of the Gallery. In the early nineteen-nineties, the paintings especially relevant to the early Newlyn School have been placed on loan to the Penzance & District Museum at Penlee House, Penzance. A residue is stored currently in the freshly-renovated storeroom at Newlyn.

Subscribers

Joan & Tom Arkell
Paul F Allen
Brian Sterry Ashby
Ted & Barbara Atter
Owen Baker
Barclays Bank PLC
Councillor Shirley A T Beck
Hugh Bedford
Ann Bellingham
Robert Benjafield
Harry Benbow Birch
Bookmark of Falmouth
Sir Alan Bowness, C B E
A R Bolitho
Mrs Simon Bolitho
Angus Brent*
[*tribute to Michael Canney]
Hilda and Howard Budden
Philip Budden
Mr and Mrs J C Burr
Clive Blackmore
Molly Bullock
Michael & Madeleine
    Canney
Sir Richard Carew-Pole
Dell Casdagli
Margaret Chinn
Mr & Mrs A Chisholm
Kathleen Chisholm
Clare, Mike & Jowanna
    Conboye
Judith Cook & Martin Green
Jessica Cooper
Creative Arts Courses,
    Camelford
Jean Crosfill
Mr & Mrs M H Dale
Allegra Eve Dalton
Jane & Peter Dalwood
Ann Dannatt
George Dannatt
Molly & Graham Dark
Peter W Davies
Robin Davis
Vera and Louis Diaz
Dr John R Doheny
Adrian C Edwards
Marianne Edwards
Mary & Peter Ellery
Helen & Bruce Entwisle
Cindy Eppard & Roger Frakes
Bernard Evans
Robert Evans Architects
P B Evans
Falmouth College of Arts
Laurie Ann Finestone
John Fitch
Keith Gardiner
Patricia & Peter Garnier
Dr James Gibson

Joan Godfrey
Mrs E M M Goriely
Ann Haggerty
Margaret R Halls
Jessica Hamilton
Judith & Charles Hancock
Miles Hardie
Mr & Mrs Brian Harvey
Mr & Mrs A G Harvey
Professor J R Heckenlively
Professor August & Elma
    Heidemann
Frank D Heneghan
Francis Hewlett
June Hicks
Jane Hill
Philip Hogben
Sir Geoffrey & Lady Holland
Marjorie & Derek Holland
Mrs E Margaret Hughes
Eileen Hunt
Ann Trevenen Jenkin
J Hilary Jones
Nina Kallis
Carolyn & David Keep
Babe Kennedy
Heather Kent
Judith & Adam Kerr
Peter Keverne
Lynne King
Mrs George Lambourn
Shirley Lane (Books)
Mrs S M Lanyon
Peter Laws
Lyn & Jeremy Le Grice
Robin Lenman &
    Anita Ballin
Mervyn Levy
Mr & Mrs C J Lewers
Sylvia Llewelyn
Elizabeth Machell
Margo & Willi
    Maeckelberghe
Carol Manheim
Christopher R Maple
Rachel Maund
Daphne & George McClure
Susan McCutcheon
Ann McQueen
John Miller
Fay & Peter Mogridge
Peter G Nicholls
Carole Page
Peggy Pentreath-Watson
Penwith District Council
Penzance (Subscription)
    Library, Morrab Gardens
Dr Ronald Perry
Biddy & Bill Picard
Pat Pickles

Michael J Praed
Inga C Priestman-Miller
Phoebe Procter
Eric Quayle
Quill Books, Burford, Oxford
E O R
Roy Ray
Felicity K C Richards
Julie Richardson
Mr & Mrs Frank Ruhrmund
Lord & Lady St Levan
Bernard & Jennifer du Sautoy
Cecil J Savoy
Colin Scott-Sutherland
Hilary Shrapnel
Mr & Mrs Godfrey B
    Simmons
Leonora A Simpson
David Baird Smith*
*[in memory of Alice
    May Ellis,
    pupil of N Garstin, 1912]
Mary E G Smith
Barbara Spring
Esme Stanford
Michael & Mary Stone
Andrew A Stonyer
Mary Stork
Ken Symonds
Dr Katherine Tait
Anthony Taylor
John & Lucy Taylor
P A Theelke
Gwen Thom
Prof A C Thomas
Vaughan L Tregenza
Mr & Mrs A B Trevillion
Barbara Tribe
Michael Truscott
Doreen Varcoe
Diana Wake
Paul & Elsa Wainwright
Katherine Wallace
Polly Walker
Mrs J A Warren
Barbara Webb
The West Family
Marion & Terry Whybrow
P A Wilkins & Co,
    Estate Agents
Tina & David Wilkinson
Vincent Wilson
Professor James W Woelfel
    & Sarah Trulove
Austin Wormleighton
Fred Yates
Partou Zia
& other anonymous
    well-wishers.

202

Bibliography

The Editor & the Newlyn Art Gallery Council of Management would like to thank the following authors and publishers for permission to quote from their works which relate closely to archival material in the possession of the Gallery. Special acknowledgement is made of the courteous permissions granted by the Sir Alfred J Munnings Art Museum, Dedham, Essex to reprint previously unpublished correspondence, to the University of Auckland Press and Editor, Linda Gill for the letters of Frances Hodgkins, to Mrs Sheila Lanyon and Andrew Lanyon for the use of letters, both published and unpublished, of the late Peter Lanyon. Both the County Records Office, Truro, and the Cornish Studies Library, Redruth have provided additional pictoral information.

Berriman, Hazel, *Arts and Crafts in Newlyn, 1890 - 1930,* Newlyn Orion Gallery, Penzance, 1986

Berriman, Hazel, *Crysede, the unique textile designs of Alec Walker,* The Royal Institution of Cornwall, Truro, 1993.

Betjeman, John, *Cornwall,* A Shell Guide, 1964.

Best, R S, *The Life & Good Works of John Passmore Edwards,* Dyllansow Truran, Redruth, 1981

Birch, Mrs Lionel, *Stanhope A. Forbes and Elizabeth Forbes,* London, 1906

Canney, Michael L, 'The Newlyn Notebook, 1956-65', Archives, Newlyn Art Gallery (unpublished)

Colenbrander, Joanna, *A Portrait of Fryn, A Biography of F Tennyson Jesse,* Andre Deutsch, 1984

Cook, Judith, (in press) *Elizabeth Adela Armstrong Forbes,* the life and work of an Artist, Patten Press, 1995

Craft, H B, 'The Percy Craft Scrapbook' [1856-1934] (collated by his son), Archives, Newlyn Art Gallery

Edwards, J. Passmore, *A Few Footprints,* Watts & Co., London, 1906

Folliott-Stokes, A G, *The Cornish Coast and Moors,* Stanley Paul & Co, Ltd, London, (no date).

Forbes, Stanhope & Elizabeth, Cuttings Book, Archives, Newlyn Art Gallery

Fox, Caroline and Francis Greenacre, *Artists of the Newlyn School,* 1880-1900 (Exhibition Catalogue), Newlyn Orion 1979

Fox, Caroline *Painting in Newlyn 1900 - 1930,* (Exhibition Catalogue), Newlyn Orion, 1985

Gill, Linda (ed.) *The Letters of Frances Hodgkins,* Auckland University Press, 1993

Hall, Fred, Archive Scrapbook, Newlyn Art Gallery, 'Cartoons' from *Pall Mall Budget* and *The Sketch,* 1890-95

Holmes, Jonathan, (ed) *An Artistic Tradition,* Two Centuries of Painting and Craft in West Cornwall, 1750-1950, (Exhibition Catalogue), Penzance & District Museum, Penlee House, 1993

Kerr, E Lamorna, *In Time and Place, Lamorna* ed by Melissa Hardie, Patten Press, 1990

Knight, Laura (1936) *Oilpaint and Greasepaint,* Ivor Nicholson & Watson

Laity, John Curnow, *Newlyn Copper,* Newlyn Copper Exhibition, Penwith Town Council, 1986

Lanyon, Andrew, *Peter Lanyon 1918 - 1964,* (1990), *Portreath* (1993), *Wartime Extracts* (in press, 1996)

MacDonald, J J, *Passmore Edwards Institutions,* London, 1900

Magazines & Journals consulted:
  The Art Annual, 1911 Volume
  The Cornish Review, ed. Denys Val Baker
  The Paper Chase, Newlyn, March 1908, Summer 1909
  The Parish Magazine, St Peter's Church, Newlyn 1894-6
  Journal of the Women Artists Slide Library
  The Year's Art, series volumes 1894 - 1917

Miller, John, *Leave Tomorrow Behind,* Studio Fine Arts Publications, London, 1989

Newspaper archives consulted:
  The Cornishman
  The Cornish Post
  Cornish Telegraph
  The Daily Telegraph
  St Ives Times & Echo
  The [London] Times
  The West Briton
  Western Daily Mercury
  Western Morning News

O'Donnell, Sheelagh, 'The Four Copper Plaques', unpublished paper prepared for the Falmouth College of Art, 1995.

Pentreath, Dolly, *In a Cornish Township with Old Vogue Folk*, illustrated by Percy R Craft, T Fisher Unwin, 1893.

Robertson/Russell/Snowdon, *Private View*, Thos Nelson & Sons, 1965

Royal West of England Academy, *Artists from Cornwall*, Exhibition catalogue, 1992

Stevens, Mary Anne (ed.), *The Edwardians and After*, The Royal Academy, 1900-1950, RA & Weidenfeld & Nicolson, 1988

Tate Gallery, *St Ives 1939-64*, Twenty Five Years of Painting, Sculpture and Pottery, (Exhibition Catalogue) 1985

Val Baker, Denys *Spring at Land's End*, Wm Kimber & Co, 1974

  Britain's Art Colony by the Sea, George Ronald, 1959

Visitors Books, Newlyn Art Gallery Archives

  1 Visits of Donors and Fellows from May 27th, 1897 to 31 January, 1900
  2 Visitors Book, September 1908 - October 1917 [Note at end of 1917 indicating that no entries were then recorded for 50 years.]
  3 Visitors Book, Orion Gallery, Penzance, 1972-1975
  4 Visitors Book, March 1974 - 1975
  5 Visitors Book, August 1980 - December 1982
  6 Visitors Book, January 1983 - September 1985
  7 Photographic Visitors Book, Renovations, 1969

Vulliamy, C E, FRGS, *Unknown Cornwall*, with Illustrations in colour and Black and White by Charles Simpson, RI, ROI, John Lane The Bodley Head Limited, London, 1925

Waterfield, Giles (editor) *Art for the People*, Culture in the Slums of Late Victorian Britain, Dulwich Picture Gallery, 1994

Whybrow, Marion, *St Ives, Portrait of an Art Colony, 1883-1993*, Antique Collectors Club, 1994

Wormleighton, Austin, (in press, 1995) *Lamorna Birch, a painter laureate* (a painter and his colony), Redcliffe Press, Bristol.

INDEX OF NAMES

PEOPLE 'PICTURED' & THEIR ARTS

[Numbers indicate the page numbers, where photographs appear which illustrate a person or his/her work. Where one artist has 'pictured' another, both receive notice. (A) indicates an attributed illustration within the first section of grouped plates; (B) indicates an attributed illustration in the second section of grouped plates. Most of the visual material in the archives, unless it appeared in catalogues or newsletters, was not dated. For this reason, biographical dates for artists & their work are given following their name, if known.]